P9-DUF-421

THE COMMON
INTEREST

THE COMMON INTEREST

How Our Social-Welfare Policies Don't Work,
and What We Can Do About Them

LESLIE W. DUNBAR

WITH PRINCIPAL ASSISTANCE FROM
ALEX POINSETT AND FRED POWLEDGE

FOREWORD BY
CHARLES V. HAMILTON

PANTHEON BOOKS / NEW YORK

Copyright © 1988 by Leslie W. Dunbar

All rights reserved under International and Pan-American Copyright Conventions. Published in the United States by Pantheon Books, a division of Random House, Inc., New York, and simultaneously in Canada by Random House of Canada Limited, Toronto.

Library of Congress Cataloging-in-Publication Data
Dunbar, Leslie.
   The common interest : how our social-welfare policies don't work and what we can do about them / Leslie Dunbar ; with a foreword by Charles Hamilton.
      p.   cm.
1. Public welfare—United States.   2. Social security—United
States.   3. Welfare recipients—United States.   I. Title.
HV91.D79 1988
361.6'0973—dc19   88-5911
ISBN 0-394-56558-4
ISBN 0-679-73965-3 (pbk.)

Manufactured in the United States of America

Interior by Robert Bull Design

First Edition

For Linda,
daughter and friend

"The good in the sphere of politics is justice; and justice consists in what tends to promote the common interest."

—Aristotle, *Politics*

CONTENTS

ACKNOWLEDGMENTS

The vignettes that form the bulk of this book, and certainly its most interesting pages, are the work of Anthony Borden, Calvin George, Charolett Baker Goodwin, Alex Poinsett, Fred Powledge, and Wallace Terry. Initials following each vignette indicate who did the interview, as well as the introduction to it. I did one, and my initials follow it.

The greatest number were done by Poinsett and Powledge. Beside their reportorial talents, both men imparted their infectious concerns and enthusiasms, and I am especially in their debt.

But the largest debt by far is to the thirty or so good people who talked to us and so graciously permitted themselves to be recorded. In respect for their forthrightness, all but a few of the interviewees' names have been changed. Pseudonyms are noted on first occurrence with an asterisk.

Michael Musuraca helped with the underlying data. Wendy Wolf, of Pantheon Books, has ushered the book from concept to print with great skill and great commitment to its themes. Hazel Sills not only typed the manuscript with extraordinary care, but kept up the contributors' morale with her own deep interest in what they were trying to do. So, at an earlier stage, did Agnes Asciolla.

The work was carried out with support from the Ford Foundation's Project on Social Welfare Policy and the American Future, of which Charles V. Hamilton, who has contributed a perfectly attuned foreword, is the director. I was senior project associate. None of the views herein has been approved or even reviewed by the foundation.

L.W.D.
Durham, North Carolina

FOREWORD

JUST TWELVE YEARS short of the twenty-first century, the meaning of "full citizenship" in the United States should not be a matter of protracted debate. During the civil-rights struggles of the sixties, which culminated in a series of laudable, if limited, victories, the country grew used to talk of "first-class" and "second-class" citizenship. People who were denied the right to vote because of race were second-class citizens. People who were kept segregated and who suffered discrimination because of their race were second-class citizens. They were less than whole; they were held in lower esteem by others (and sometimes even by themselves).

This condition went by several names, but surely Gunnar Myrdal's phrase "the American Dilemma" captured the case as well as any. The country embarked on a long, arduous road to correct certain wrongs associated with second-class citizenship. Most Americans took that struggle seriously as the dilemma became increasingly clear: segregation was obviously incompatible with the strongly held tenets of American democracy. Myrdal called it the American creed.

People should not be subjugated because of their race, creed, or color. People should have access to a "free ballot." These remain basic values of the country. To define the United States

in any other terms would be to *re*define the nation in a way
unacceptable to most people. These values describe what we
hope to be, what we strive to be, as a national, sovereign entity.
They give us guides to how we understand citizenship in our
society and in these times. Anyone seeking to characterize
American citizenship without including these fundamental
tenets would be out of the norm, out of the mainstream.

Yet, as we approach the last decade of the twentieth century,
there remains much to do in this matter of American citizenship. This book addresses the perennial problems of the poor
and economically vulnerable in our society. And it puts considerable emphasis on jobs and income.

The proposition is not complicated: A major requirement
for full citizenship is "free labor." People must have the capacity to exchange their labor, services, or goods for fair compensation without being hampered by extraneous conditions.
One worker cannot be allowed to prosper at the expense of
others through racial or gender discrimination. Neither should
free labor be a hostage of private decisions made primarily to
maximize profit at the expense of other people's ability to earn
a living. Even more, it must not be based on a market economy
structured so as to relegate vast numbers of people to the permanent category of "unskilled," and thus "redundant."

In the common phrase, people "work for a living." When we
ask, "What do you do?" we mean, "How do you support yourself and your dependents?" Invariably, the answers come in
similar terms: "I'm a barber," say, or a truckdriver, a word
processor, a doctor, or a teacher. We do not reply, "I go to ball
games," when we mean, "I'm a hot-dog vendor" or "I'm a sports
writer." We understand the question in terms of activity aimed
at earning a living. And we expect most people to provide an
answer along those lines. Either one works for wages, salaries,
or commissions, or one is self-employed. The "full" citizen
works, or offers a socially acceptable reason for not doing so.
The unemployed are presumed to be in a temporary and undesirable state. If a person "does nothing," we don't automatically condemn him, but we wonder, "How does he get along?"

Throughout this book the emphasis is on people without

free labor. These of course include the sick, the elderly, and parents with newborn infants, but the primary focus is those who have no such personal impediments and who, indeed, are looking for work. Many people choose not to work, and no one should suggest that they are less than full citizens. But anyone who makes such a choice should not end up dependent on society, but should make use of other resources (investments, family, friends) for support. Most American adults, though, do not have this option. They seek and should be able to find a legitimate means of self-support by freely exchanging their labor for a fair, negotiated income. This is an explicit aspect of the American quest for full citizenship. Anything less renders one "second-class" in this society.

The experience of black Americans in this context is most instructive. This is not surprising in light of the historical role of race in the dilemma of second-class citizenship. After all, blacks, unlike other Americans, were first *constitutionally* excluded from the free labor market. Subsequently, they were legally prohibited from freely exchanging their labor for fair compensation. To be sure, other ethnic groups have experienced labor-market constraints ("No Irish need apply"), but by no means in the explicit way posed by slavery and segregation.

Other Americans have always been drilled in the relationship between work and citizenship. They were taught that *full* citizens—and those who aspired to be full citizens—worked, even if under the most despicable and unfair conditions—imported Chinese railway workers, sweatshop seamstresses in the garment industry, exploited child laborers, abused maidservants from the United Kingdom.

But blacks, the first involuntary immigrants, have a particular historical connection to the American work ethic. They were required to work, but not as free laborers. Unlike the European immigrants, blacks were denied even exploitative wages: they were owned. Thus, while others came to this country seeking to gain property (even under the most devastating conditions), blacks came *as* property—to be bought and sold. Thus, if free labor and full citizenship are to be explained in any context, surely they can best be understood in the worst-case paradigm of black Americans. (As the thrust of this entire book should make clear, however, there is no intention of arguing that the case for work and citizenship can or should be made by or on behalf of black Americans only. The proposition extends to all who would be made whole citizens in this society. Again, anything less would require an insupportable redefinition of American society.)

The black American struggle has always emphasized free labor. We see this in the Reconstruction years following the Civil War ("Forty acres and a mule"); in Booker T. Washington's Tuskegee Experiment at the turn of the century ("Glorify work"); in black demands during the New Deal ("Jobs, not alms"); in the northern boycotts of the 1930s ("Don't buy where you can't work"); in A. Philip Randolph's planned 1941 march on Washington for jobs (Fair Employment Practices); in the 1963 March on Washington for Jobs and Freedom; and in the 1970s political battles for the Humphrey-Hawkins Employment Bill.

Free labor has a very special meaning to black Americans. Always, there has been the quest, the demand for the ability to work for a living. What others could assume as a given, blacks had to struggle to establish. The right to work as a *free* citizen, therefore, became a major criterion for becoming a *full* citizen. Even if many jobs would not pay enough to overcome poverty, they were seen as the basis for establishing a solid foothold in the economic mainstream of society. Jobs are the way people "get started," not how they end up. Jobs do not guarantee economic viability, but such viability can hardly be imagined without them. (An apt analogy can be drawn with voting: The right to vote does not guarantee political power, but political power cannot be imagined without it.)

Thus, while most proposals to create work are appealing, those that do not guarantee an adequate income have a suspicious ring. So do schemes that guarantee an income (at subsistence level) without providing any viable means of work or training.

Likewise, one must be leery of analyses that stress the "redundancy" of the labor force; what this really means is that, by the measure of economic efficiency (profit and loss), such labor is not needed. This is of course too limited an analysis. Full citizenship must be defined in terms of human dignity, not of profit and loss. "Redundant?" one must ask—"In what way? By what or whose measure?" To the end of minimizing cost and maximizing profit? That is unacceptable. Would we think of saying, "We'll grant you the right to vote, as long as not too many of you take advantage of it and crowd the decision-making process." (Some have in fact made this argument in rationalizing low voter turnout.) The concept of redundancy normally has economic connotations that are ultimately irrelevant to our understanding of what makes for a viable political society. Idle people anxious to find work but unable to find adequate jobs are not good for the health of the body politic.

It is the responsibility of the society, therefore, in its own interest, to ensure that people have a means to earn their own living.

This relationshp between the economic and the social demands of first-class citizenship is particularly strong in a market-oriented, or capitalist, economy. No one seriously doubts that the society's constitution must guarantee the removal of negative factors, such as obstacles to free labor. But it must also be called upon to act positively to ensure that citizens are able to participate fully in an economic sense. Where an imperfect private sector is unable to provide such conditions, the state must assume the responsibility: it should do whatever is necessary to guarantee full economic, as well as political, rights. In this sense, the state and individuals join together for the overall societal good.

When free labor is understood as an attribute of full citizenship, it is not necessary or even relevant to ask the economic question—namely, Can society afford the cost? We accept certain values as irrefutable, and must shoulder the costs in whatever way possible. But the first principle cannot be questioned or bargained away.

Clearly this proposition is not limited to any particular race. Black Americans simply provide the clearest historical example

of a group of people denied access to the free labor market. In
stating the case for blacks, we state the case for all Americans.
In an interesting way, this is similar to the perennial struggle
for racial justice in this country. It has always been understood,
or should have been, that first-class citizenship for blacks
would not require diminishing the political rights of others.
But this has been difficult to comprehend in the realm of social
policy and economics, precisely because we have viewed such
policies in the narrow context of fiscal cost, economic budgets,
and market competition. Too narrow, precisely because our
focus should be on economic as well as political *rights*. That
is the essence of full citizenship in a truly free society.

CHARLES V. HAMILTON

THE COMMON
INTEREST

CHAPTER ONE

Observations and Values

SOCIAL-WELFARE policies are about human beings. They are about the national interest also, if anyone can distinguish between the two. But first of all, about people's lives. They are about children, and their chances to grow and find some joy and fulfillment in life; and about grownups, and their opportunities to get fair shares and, as a result, participate in the public life of this democracy. Unless the social-welfare system is permeated by a concern for humanity, its "efficiency" is hardly of much importance.

Whether society can get by on the cheap is no more relevant to these policies than it is to defense expenditures. It would make little sense for Congress to reduce the military budget simply to save dollars; if the guns and all that go with them are needed, they're needed. The current debate about the huge defense budget should focus on the root of the problem: Why do we need such an arsenal? The quarrel should be with the definition of need and the goals to be served. The same goes for social policy, whether concerning economic supports or health care, in the effort to ensure full citizenship for everyone. First define the goal, and next the requisites for achieving it. Then figure out how to pay for them.

Before lawgivers consider a vast reform of our welfare system, however, they must ask themselves why so many people are poor. How has the economy failed so badly, thus creating this problem? In asking that question, one must inevitably face the fact that, historically, the economic, political, and social order in America has never thought of the poor as deserving respect—self-gratifying charity, perhaps, but not respect. The most common reaction to poverty is that the poor must somehow deserve it. And the long American tradition has accorded particularly little respect to poor people of color.

America's poor are seen to be dispensable. If welfare recipients and nonworkers suddenly vanished overnight, society would be rid of a burden, the productive work of the economy would go on about the same, and the rest of us might quite likely be "better off." Gone would be the unsightly ghettos and the crimes they breed. Some crushing, heartrending realization of their dispensability must bear down, constantly, upon the poor. Surely that in itself is enough to infuriate a person, to frustrate and kill the spirit of a young black man of a city ghetto, for example, or to turn his normal human drives to socially destructive pursuits. If we are serious about reclaiming the poor, serious about opening up opportunities for humane living, we must open up socially useful roles for them. In the United States, these roles have ordinarily been based on jobs.

It is a commonplace to point out that the American poor of the 1980s largely consist of the victims, or the descendants of the victims, of systematic oppression by the institutions of American life. Obviously that is true for blacks. It is true also of Appalachian whites, who have been victimized by this country's demand for fuel and lumber and by the rapacious methods by which we mine the coal and fell the timber. It is true of the Mexican-Americans in the Southwest, who in many instances were defrauded of their land and made inferior subjects by conquerors. True as well of our Puerto Rican citizens, whose island of origin was first conquered by arms and then exploited by mainland corporations. It is abundantly true of the American Indians. Of course, history can hardly be repealed—but it can, and must, be remembered. And in remembering, we may note that most of the people devising social-welfare policy today are none of the above.

The long tradition of American social-welfare policies has depended on a belief that the poor must get by on something less than what all the rest of us acknowledge to be the minimum required for a decent existence. Coupled with our charity has been our rebuke, and our way of rebuking has been to give in short supply. Today there is much talk of "new policies," resting on an alleged "new consensus." But there will be nothing new at all unless we first adopt the principle of adequacy: the principle that all citizens are entitled to at least a decent, minimum standard of living.

The poor are those who don't have enough money. A truth as transparent as that challenges some analysts to probe behind it; they will attempt to "disaggregate" the poor, devising specific remedies for various groups. Generally speaking, these divisions depend on the analysts' judgment as to how able or willing people are to take care of themselves. So it has long been. For a great stretch of time, we who talk and write about the poor have accepted distinctions like "deserving" and "nondeserving" or "truly dependent" and "indolent." These terms and distinctions serve to justify different attitudes and policies.

The poor, like the rest of us, are not a homogeneous population, of course. All of them can be called poor because they don't have enough money to satisfy their needs, though the causes of that lack are many and varied. But those causes should be defined, so far as policy-making is concerned, solely in objective terms—never in such subjective, judgmental terms as "deserving" and "nondeserving."

The poor are jobless, or underpaid by their work, or too old or sick to work, or too young. Neither carrots nor sticks nor a combination of the two should be embodied in the public policies that apply to any of those groupings. On the contrary, policies should be built on the assumption that motivation exists, and that all subjects of these policies are worthy of full citizenship. Our schools may reasonably be charged with the responsibility of helping to make good citizens; it is neither reasonable nor realistic to call on our income-assistance policies to do so.

WHAT DOES a 14 percent poverty rate mean? It means more than thirty-two million Americans—including one of every five children—living below the poverty "line," which in 1988 was a mere $11,650 for a family of four.

What does 6 percent unemployment mean, a level of joblessness that many, and not only Republicans, regard as a sign of sound economic policies? It means more than seven million Americans looking for employment, not working at all for wages, plus another million or more no longer even looking.

After Paul Volcker resigned as head of the Federal Reserve Board in June 1987, the noted economist Herbert Stein wrote that from now on, every successor ought to be held—by an oath of office, perhaps—to the proposition that no objective, and specifically not the reduction of unemployment, may be placed on a par with the suppression of inflation.[1] Probably most officials in Washington, and their advisers, agree. What then is to be done for, and with, the unemployed?

There are really only five ways for public policy to respond:

- Do nothing. Let the problems sort themselves out as the poor struggle against each other.
- Define the problems away. Assign the residue as the responsibility of the "private sector." (This is the shady variant of the response above, which is at least honest.)
- Attribute most of the problems to the poor themselves (genetic and environmental explanations equally useful). Argue that the poor need behavior adjustment. Apply token remedies to that end.
- Legislate some form of guaranteed income for all (a serious response, though hard to achieve).
- Create decently paying jobs (another serious response, also very difficult to achieve).

1. *New York Times*, June 7, 1987.

Those are the alternatives: battle, casuistry, manipulation (generally preferred), guaranteed income, and available jobs.

There is nothing essentially new in the nature of contemporary poverty, though today's debaters, who equate patching up welfare administration with "breaking the poverty cycle," seem to think so. The issues have not changed much, so what was said years ago may still be on the mark, as is demonstrated by the observation in 1971, during an earlier period of "reform," by Herbert Gans:

> That problem [welfare] is really in the heart of the American economy, which simply does not need all the unemployed looking for work at a living wage and which cannot provide for all the working poor who require higher wages to support their families. Ultimately, therefore, an end to the welfare problem requires either remaking the economy so that it produces full employment at a living wage, or altering public beliefs about welfare so that the Government will provide the unneeded and underpaid with a decent income.[2]

In 1937 George Orwell published a remarkably fine book, *The Road to Wigan Pier*. The first half expressed his outrage at an economic system that kept masses of citizens unemployed and "on the dole"; the later chapters, his outrage and foreboding (later to be made famous in his postwar novels *Animal Farm* and *1984*) over political ideologies that trample on people's liberties and individualities. The two outrages belong together. He wrote, half a century ago, "We may as well face the fact that several million men in England will—unless another war breaks out—never have a real job this side of the grave."[3] Does America now have to make a similar judgment?

Those prewar years, when Western industrial states were groping their way out of the Depression, were not only worried and anxious but impressively inventive as well. Even the young among us are more or less familiar with the measures collec-

2. "Three Ways to Solve the Welfare Problem," *The New York Times Magazine*, March 7, 1971.
3. George Orwell, *The Road to Wigan Pier* (Harcourt, 1958), p. 84.

tively called the New Deal, and with the social wrongs they were meant to combat. They have given shape to our social order ever since.

In England, even while the war was going on, that same concern and inventiveness gave impulse to a report by William Beveridge, on the new problems and conditions that could be expected after the war's end. Many of the report's recommendations would in fact be enacted by the Labor government soon after the war. Early in the report, Beveridge stated:

> Of all the want shown by the surveys, from three-quarters to five-sixths, according to the precise standard chosen for want, was due to interruption or loss of earning power.[4]

At about the same time, here in the United States, another ambitious social-policy report was completed; unlike Beveridge's, it was destined for neglect. The National Resources Planning Board presented its study, *Security, Work, and Relief Policies*, to President Franklin Roosevelt three days before Pearl Harbor. It remains a brilliant book.[5] If the government truly wanted to illuminate the problems of the poor, it would reissue it, instead of publishing such new frivolities as the Reagan administration's 1986 report, *Up from Dependency*. Contemporary readers would find the board's report abreast of all the issues discussed by a Charles Murray or the latest headliner of that sort, or the deeper scholarship of Frances Fox Piven and Richard Cloward, or of Sar Levitan. All of today's debates are there: dependency and self-sufficiency, incentives and disincentives, mutual obligations of society and individual, workfare, and the causes and effects of unemployment.

That contemporaneity reveals a fundamental truth that must be the starting point of any useful analysis: *the causes*

---

4. Sir William Beveridge, *Social Insurance and Allied Services* (Macmillan, 1942), p. 7. The report noted that "practically the whole" of the remainder was due to "overlarge" families.
5. Based on the work of the NRBP's Committee on Long-Range Work and Relief Policies, which was chaired by William Haber, the 618-page report was submitted on December 4, 1941.

and conditions of American poverty have hardly changed.
There is nothing new about poverty, and little new in the ways
it is thought about, though from time to time the discussion
becomes more or less rational, and more or less mindful of
social duties.

What the 1941 report called its "four main points" are vital
still:

> First, that our economy must provide work for all who are able
> and willing to work. Included in this is a special responsibility
> for an *adequate* youth program, which should be an integral part
> of any governmental undertaking to establish security. . . .
>
> Second, that for great numbers whose work is interrupted,
> the social insurances must carry much of the load of providing
> *adequate* income.
>
> Third, that where the insurances or work policies fail to take
> care of an interruption in income, *adequate* guarantees of min-
> imum aid and assistance must be given both to individuals and
> to families through a general public assistance program.
>
> Fourth, that where *adequate* services essential to the health,
> education, and welfare of the population are not available, public
> provision should be made for the development of such services.[6]

At a later point the board raised questions that, with one
large exception, still frame today's debate:

> The continued dependence of so large a proportion of the pop-
> ulation on socially provided income cannot fail to raise the ques-
> tion whether this is due to a temporary or even permanent failure
> of our economic system to provide adequate opportunities for
> the individual to secure a livelihood by participation in the nor-
> mal processes of production. Or is it possible that during the
> last ten years [contemporary readers might want instead to read
> "twenty years," back to the War on Poverty], measures have
> been adopted which make it all too easy for those in whom the
> spirit of independence is weak, to live at the public expense? Or

---

6. Ibid., p. 1. The emphasis is added, to draw attention to a conviction that
will be apparent throughout this book, that perhaps the principal defect
of social-welfare measures in the United States has always been their
inadequacy, never generous enough to achieve their announced purposes.

does the change mean that the Nation is at last tackling more
adequately a problem which existed prior to 1930 [read "1964"]
but was then ignored? Are there, and were there even in the
days of so-called prosperity, large sections of the population who,
because of low earnings, uncertainty of employment, or physical
disability, live at a level far below what we like to think of as
the American standard?[7]

The one exception, the item left out of today's debate, is the
very first question. Not often today do "experts" on social
welfare raise the possibility that our economic system may be
at fault, with the notable exception of the U.S. Catholic bishops' pastoral letter *Economic Justic for All*. Throughout the
Nixon, Carter, and Reagan years, the assumption of the essential soundness and, above all, the legitimacy of what is perceived as free-market capitalism has been a virtual given in our
political debate, and most intellectuals have been its servants.

The political climate is not the only factor that has limited
the debate; there is also the stupefying complexity of the American social-welfare system, with its mixture of insurance
schemes, means-tested income-transfer schemes, subsidies to
business and agricultural interests, retirement and health care
for military personnel, veterans' benefits, employer-provided
health and retirement schemes (subsidized through tax breaks),
individual retirement and health insurance (also governmentally encouraged), and private charity. It is almost impossible
to think of a single one of us who does not benefit from one
or more of these arrangements. We are all in it, threads of varied
kinds in its fabric. Thus to question the economic order that
has over the past fifty years woven that fabric, with no over-
arching design or plan, would be to risk unraveling the social-
welfare fabric itself—crazy quilt that it is—perhaps even
threatening one's own comfortable corner of it.[8]

---

7. Ibid., p. 11.
8. Nor is this a totally twentieth-century phenomenon. An estimated half
   of all native-born white men of the North were by 1900 receiving Civil
   War pensions for some cause or another, costing about a fourth of the
   federal budget. See Hugh Heclo, *The Welfare State in Hard Times* (American Political Science Association, May 1985).

But lately there has been a stream of reports reflecting concern with that part of the system that specifically assists the poor.[9] It is interesting to ask why that should be. (Indeed, why are we doing this book?) There has been little pressure from the poor themselves, who as a matter of fact have been strangely subdued in the 1980s despite their stagnant or worsening conditions. Certainly there has been nothing comparable to the welfare-rights movement and the poor-people's campaigns of the late sixties and early seventies. Nor have there been any conspicuous scandals in welfare administration to trigger demands for reform. Nor are the problems inherent in the American-style welfare state particularly acute.

Perhaps the interest is always there, and only its nature and focus vary. At periods of resignation or frustration we do not seek changes in policy. In times of quickened compassion, or (as now) of impatience and blame-casting, new policies will likely be proposed. Unlike the sixties and seventies, a few state governments are now very active in welfare. This may be because of the Reagan administration's determination to place more responsibility on the states. But that also is no novelty; states and localities dominated social welfare until the 1930s. And, then as now, they had plenty to do.

Charleston, South Carolina, would not ordinarily be thought of as exemplifying either the depths of southern rural misery or the ruthlessness of nineteenth-century industrialism. Yet from a total 1896 population of about 50,000, Charleston maintained an orphanage for 250 boys and girls, a free health-care clinic, a city hospital that treated 319 white and 758 colored

9. In addition to the bishops' letter, which is the glory of the lot, see *One Child in Four*, from the American Public Welfare Association and the National Council of State Human Service Administrators; *Ladders out of Poverty*, from the Project on Welfare Families (the Babbitt report); *A New Social Contract*, from the New York State Task Force on Poverty (the Cuomo report, much evident in Senate bill 1511, the Moynihan bill); *To Form a More Perfect Union*, from the Committee on Federalism and National Purpose (the Evans-Robb report); *A Community of Self-Reliance*, from the Working Seminar on the Family and American Welfare Policy, a group of noted social scientists (the Novak report, the nadir of the lot); *Up from Dependency*, a report to President Reagan from his Domestic Policy Council (the White House report).

indigents without charge, an almshouse with 76 inmates and 285 "outdoor" recipients of meals, and a home for elderly blacks. Scores of private agencies were also operating. Nor was Charleston acting in isolation: it had leaned heavily for advice and methods on New York, Boston, Baltimore, and Philadelphia, and was itself to be "model and midwife" to undertakings in Cincinnati and Columbus, Ohio, and Augusta, Georgia.[10]

What accounts for the recent surge of interest in reforming welfare? From the day Reagan entered his presidency, he and his administration have attacked the benefits of the poor, with the result that they are lower today than they were before 1981, and poverty rates have returned to pre-1970 levels. Congress halted these reversals after 1984, though conservatives want to carry the attack yet further. The "reforms" being pushed by liberals would merely make that halt secure, while experimenting with superficial revisions aimed at gaining more public support for the programs. That's about the sum of it.

A dominating fact of our time is this: The Reagan administration's military spending and the resulting deficits, created with congressional acquiescence, will essentially determine the domestic policies well into the 1990s, unless political wit and courage are rediscovered.

Lacking both wit and courage, we suffer under a national indisposition to confront the question of how much military spending is enough. This reluctance, in the face of our staggering public debt, leads us to look elsewhere for economies, and social welfare is a large and easy target. Hence reports and reforms.

Another cause for the present ferment is the disappointment felt because the truly immense public expenditures since President Johnson declared war on poverty have not done the job. Not all of the social-welfare programs of the sixties and seventies were well designed, and mistakes were made in implementing them. As a result, these programs have become easy to criticize. The true lesson, however, is that the task was more

---

10. Laylon Wayne Jordan, " 'The Method of Modern Charity': The Associated Charities Society of Charleston, 1888–1900," *South Carolina Historical Magazine*, January 1987, pp. 36–37.

immense than anyone realized. More experimentation was and is needed. Rather than curtailing the effort, a mature Congress and president would press onward until refined policies attained the goal of ending poverty.

Yet another cause is that large-scale academic research on poverty and welfare begun over the past two decades is now bearing fruit, so that now a lot of scholars have things to say. Indeed, most of the recent studies cited above were written by social scientists, and undoubtedly they will keep on speaking out on these issues. This may be the best assurance that this time the issues will not fade away from public view.

Finally, there is the drive during the eighties to reduce the privileges and income of the working class (an apt and necessary term, though few like to use it anymore). Wages have been held down or even reduced in real terms. Moreover, income has been changed structurally. New hires have been brought in on lower wage tracks, and bonuses have been substituted for increases in base wages. These measures weaken unions and reduce workers' control. Benefits and regulations about work conditions and workers' health and safety have been adjusted in management's favor, resistance to unions has grown and become governmentally sanctioned, and manufacturing jobs have been lost on a wide scale through production cutbacks and plant relocations. The tightening of the terms on which social welfare is extended must be seen as a way of driving the work force downward even more. The first Reagan administration induced unemployment in order to scale down inflation. It also championed workfare, requiring people to work for welfare, which restrains the wage rates of low-income workers; now welfare revisionists are disposed to achieve growth by depressing the wage structure that had once made America so proud.

PERHAPS A CLEARER sign of the times is that liberals as well as conservatives can write about social welfare and scarcely mention any role for labor unions. That categorical omission means, of course, that no thought is given toward encouraging the poor to organize in their own interest, whether in labor unions or other forms, thereby finding their own voices and making their own impress upon policies.

If neglect of labor unions suggests one sort of political viewpoint, the neglect of rural concerns suggests another: the poverty problem that worries policy-makers is the one that forces itself on their eyes. Rousseau long ago observed that compassion extends only to the suffering one cannot avoid. Others have pointed out how modern forces have extended the range of our emotional involvement. Electronic communication makes us pay a price in moral discomfort for watching the evening news. The ease of travel is sometimes disturbed by the uneasy visions of poverty evident beyond the world's posher watering holes. It was in both these ways, for example, that Americans learned two decades ago about hunger in the Deep South.

But in the absence of a large social movement, books are about the best way to influence domestic policy. And by and large, books are written by people who live in cities, and it's the poverty these authors can't turn from that challenges their minds—the condition of big-city, ghettoized, ill-mannered, often criminal poor people. Besides their obvious political potential, as shown by the election of black mayors in many major cities, these people gain attention just by their presence, drawing from us powerful emotional response—now and then of compassion, more often of anger, oftener still of disdain. To the rural poor, our class can most of the time be indifferent, satisfied by occasionally boycotting grapes with Cesar Chavez or marching against a ragtag band of Klansmen in a Georgia hamlet—or, more likely, yawning over the call to do either.

Basic to all these reform bills and studies (always excepting the bishops' letter) is the notion that poverty can be overcome or largely reduced through welfare reform. To its credit, the Cuomo report acknowledged that unless the economy generates enough jobs, many people will be trapped in poverty. Having said so, though, it called upon the federal government to promote economic growth through fiscal and monetary policies, and then took up its own real interest, welfare reform. Growth was the report's only "proposal" for ending unemployment.

In short, no one seems to believe that poverty is caused by the malfunctioning of the economy. Poverty is blamed on the inadequacies of the poor, perhaps abetted by marginal education, insufficient upbringing, and ill-designed government programs. Never on the economy, except as it may now and again be sluggish, never on governmental allocations of national resources, never on the investment decisions of private businesses, which, along with federal priorities, determine whom this economy serves and for what purposes.

This is, of course, but logical. If the major premise is that the economy is basically sound, and the minor premise is that poverty nevertheless exists, the conclusion pretty well has to be either that the economy needs some minor, as yet undiscovered adjustment, or that the poor need a major one. Or perhaps both. The basic health of the economy remains unchallenged, and no large adjustments are asked of it. Indeed, the reports from the Reagan White House and from Michael Novak's social scientists, with their low appraisal of the poor, call for scarcely any adjustment of the economy at all. At bottom, the values that analysts (including myself) bring to their studies derive from their views of human nature. The harsh attitude toward the poor that has dominated American social life is based on the decision to regard the poor as unlike the rest of us by nature; they are redeemable perhaps, but not socially fit now, or soon, and therefore they require special discipline and control. For a long time, that view, within accepted mores, was explicitly linked to race. While it is no longer acceptable to talk that way, a shady concept called *underclass* has taken its place.

Thus, all of the reformers are committed to the incentives-disincentives theory, in which the balance of an unpredictable lot of pushes and pulls determines whether the poor take care of themselves or dwell in sloth. Inevitably, the reformers lapse into heavy moralizing, the Novak report being the champion at that, hands down. At one point it even cautions all givers of aid to be on guard against the "counterstrategies" of the poor in avoiding our "incentives and sanctions."[11] This verbally gooey, tiresomely repetitious document reveals how close social science sometimes gets to fantasy, for it shows little or no evidence of contact with real people and actual circumstances in the United States.

Yet its fantasies will all too likely join the similar fantasies that sustain political fortunes today. It brings the reassurance that the economy is sound, that opportunities abound, and that Americans—other than the culpable underclass, of course—are good people, a "community of a special sort." It is, we read, "less plausible today than it was a generation ago to assert that poverty is especially connected with race," but no one not willfully blind can read this report or the others without recognizing that *underclass* has become the code word for lower-income blacks and Puerto Ricans. It conjures up related terms, such as *aristocracy* and *elite*, which, once used, signify agreement that such clear categories exist, always have, and always will. Nor do these reports begin to consider how this country's "underclass" might be connected to the still more impoverished legions of dark-skinned brothers and sisters to be found around the globe. We shall therefore employ the word most cautiously.[12]

A FEW OF THOSE poor people, as well as some who are by no means "underclass," speak in the pages that follow. Most of this book consists of abridged recorded interviews—vignettes, we call them—of persons who illustrate certain applications of social-welfare policy in this country. They span several social classes. The White House report lists more than a hundred "assistance programs," fifty-nine of which it

---

11. The quotations here and in the next paragraph are from pp. 162, 170, and 151–52 of the Novak report.
12. Most recent discussions of the assumed underclass are decked out in polemic. One that is not, and is all the better for that, is in Forrest Chisman and Alan Pifer, *Government for the People* (Norton, 1987), pp. 201–7. Although some of its conclusions are unsatisfying, it is likely the best one-volume review and explanation of the problems with current social-welfare policies.

terms "major." The Congressional Research Service lists twenty-one income-tested "billion-dollar" programs in fiscal year 1985.[13] Our inteviewees show how these programs may work, for each person benefits (though often that hardly seems the right word) from one or more of them. We don't claim that our interviewees are "typical." Who is? But they do illustrate how the policies and programs work, how they translate into people's life experiences. We met the interviewees in different parts of the country. They are recognizably American, and so are their problems and responses.

Their stories reveal a lot about how people manage their difficulties, and as they do, how they are directed by their values and attitudes—generally highly individualistic and generally optimistic. The stories also give very acceptable descriptions of the programs, saving us the trouble and sparing the reader much tedious and abstract exposition.

People think. The vignettes in the next chapter of Vincent Matthews* and Harold Rubenstein* canvass just about every point anyone, including scholar and politician, is making in today's reconsideration of Social Security. Later in the book, two Job Corps veterans say about all anyone needs to about special training for young people. And two Oregonians portray as well as any journalist or social scientist could the experience of a production cutback.

"WHAT TO DO about the poor" is a subject of enduring interest to economists and sociologists. It is hard to see that the poor have ever benefited from that interest, with the all-important exception of those few studies, like those of New Deal days, that led to money being put in their hands. Today's scholars are not primarily interested in doing that, and so one has to doubt that their work will be much help to the

---

13. *Up from Dependency*, pp. 16–21, and Congressional Research Service, *Cash and Non-Cash Benefits*, report #86-161 EPW, Sept. 30, 1986, pp. 3–4.
* Here, and throughout the book, an asterisk indicates that a fictional name is being used.

poor, freighted as it is with "multivariate models" and "regression analysis" and more of the same. Part of this book is in conscious protest against a social science that treats the poor like a foreign nation or refashions them into objects unlike us, against a discipline that speaks mainly for the approval of other social scientists and of legislators, and seldom consults the poor themselves.[14]

Social-welfare policy has from ancient times been afflicted by techniques that parade as values. It is so today. We are deluged by data, and are conditioned to feel that answers for all problems must be quantitative in order to be respectable. There is also a deluge of "new ideas"—for paternal child support or basic skills or community organization or community development and so on. There is nothing wrong with any of those mentioned. But they are techniques, at best means toward goals. And it is the goals that need to be thought out carefully, and with a very lively awareness that the situation of the poor and dependent has long been an issue in the United States. Someone has rightly said that poverty pursues American progress like a shadow pursues a runner.

If the conditions today differ much from those of a hundred, or fifty, or even thirty years ago, it is only in this: that whereas in those earlier years the nation's eyes were nearly shut toward blacks and Hispanics, seeing them if at all as special and peripheral, today they are at the center of the discussion and the agitation, to such an extent that commonly they are perceived to be a larger portion of the poor and dependent than in fact they are. Long out of the "mainstream" even of the poor, today they are sometimes portrayed as the whole of that current.

So the reformers set to work on the behavior of the poor, at changing it rather than the institutions and practices of the larger society. The latter, so they conceive, were well enough worked over by the civil-rights laws of the sixties and seventies.

---

14. Of course, such consultation does not necessarily lead to views similar to those in this book. Lawrence M. Mead's *Beyond Entitlement* (Free Press, 1986) shows some personal familiarity with the poor. It is the most informed as well as extreme representative of its genre, namely books preaching a sink-or-swim policy for the poor.

The problem now, they say, is no longer society's behavior but poor people's.

The poor who speak in this book do not all reveal themselves as model citizens. And we have over a good many years seen enough of the poor, both white and nonwhite, to be neither infatuated with nor awed by them—nor shocked. Worried, yes, and deeply so. What becomes most evident is that the larger struggle by the civil-rights movement for integration still goes on. The challenge of the movement was not satisfied by the rights gained back then. When the goal of integration was announced, it was a warning that the social order would have to make far greater accommodations than those legal rights then gained. Room had to be made in the entire order; the privileges and immunities of citizenship had to be clarified and made firm.

The time to focus on behavior will come after that moment when all citizens have a realistic opportunity within the nation's institutional life for growth and self-fulfillment, not before. Therefore, this book endeavors to suggest, not ways to make people "better," but ways to improve society, to make it more responsible for the general welfare.

It proposes directions to take, not specific measures, while working within the given of the federal structure. That system has much room for improvement, and also much potential. With the proper nudging, it can be made to serve the cause of strengthened social welfare.

The plan of this book derives from a basic outlook. Social-welfare policies need to respond to the differing needs of people as they move through their lives. There are three large age periods—childhood, working age, and old age—but society gradually changes its age definitions for those groups. Childhood lasts longer today than it used to, and old age begins later. Therefore, age categories are not the most useful. So far as social-welfare policies go, the basic division is between those the economy expects to be productive and those it doesn't.

The nonproducing divide into those too young to work and those set aside by the job market because of age or physical handicap. Among those expected to be productive, there are two distinguishable but overlapping sets of people: those not ready for the job market, for whatever reason, and those trying to stay in, enter, or reenter it. These, then, are the subjects of the four main sections of the book: childhood, the two working-age groups, and those withdrawn from the job market because of age or physical handicap.[15] Each group suggests a different policy approach.

In each case, the policy proposals will reflect not only an understanding of political and economic factors but also social ethics. That is, I shall try to argue within what I perceive to be widely if not unanimously accepted ethical views of our society. None of those necessarily holds constant from one generation to another, but they do change slowly enough so that our national practice and sense of what is "right" have their own character, distinguishable from those of other nations.

Underlying all is a conviction that citizens are entitled to opportunities for getting fair shares in this society. *Entitlement* is a word that has fallen into disrepute. It should not have. There is none better for signifying what each should be able to expect by virtue of being part of this political and social order— better said, this constitutional order, this agreement among ourselves to be one nation, where the wellbeing of each is part of the "general welfare," part of the "common interest." A youngster is entitled to public education; an aged person is entitled, we now feel, to cash assistance and medical care. The United States has not understood either of these benefits to be constitutional rights. They have become firmly embedded nevertheless in public practice and values, and the only modifications either will likely sustain are liberalizing and widening ones (though as with the rights guaranteed by the first eight amendments, there are always those among us who would narrow them).

Those advances have come about as the public has realized certain facts: that the definition of "fair shares" has changed;

---

15. A significant number of older persons own capital or rental property, and thus technically are economically "productive." This book is not about them.

so have the requirements that enable people to realize them; and that it is in the public interest to help people meet those changes.

This book's argument rests on additional beliefs as well. It is time to recognize ungrudgingly in principle what has in more or less present form been a fact for half a century—that income and other assistance to those left aside by the economy is an entitlement of citizenship. It is time to acknowledge honestly what has been clear for an even longer time, that the economy unaided by governmental supports does not employ everyone, and therefore those it doesn't are entitled to opportunities to work and a fair return for doing so. And finally, such further enlargement of the entitlements of American citizenship is fully within the Constitution's great vision of a "more perfect union."

CHAPTER TWO

To Receive in Dignity:

THE ILL
AND THE AGED

ALL POLICY IS a matter of choice, even when it is forced into place by circumstances. Social-welfare policy is choice from start to finish—a nation could, after all, simply shrug its shoulders and turn away, but even that would be a choice. The choices arise from several basic factors. Some have to do with goals: What do we want to happen? Some have to do with economic theories: How best can people obtain their shares within the national economy? And some have to do with process: Where—within the social mix of individuals and families, the private sector of business, charities, and services, and the several levels of our very complex government—does responsibility lie?

Such questions admit of more or less clear answers, even if the facts and interpretations are debatable. There is, however, another question always present. It is that of equity—What's fair?—and it cannot be answered in the same terms as the others. No issue more pervades every problem than this one of fairness. In the interviews that make up the bulk of this book, fairness will come up time after time, and always with the particular and often unexpected twists that individuals give to it. Thus, the "experts" of the previous chapter are not the only ones who "moralize"; so do individuals. The important difference is that individuals tend to do so from the particularity of their situations, or those of others whom they can observe. They compare those actual situations with values they believe all others share, as if those values were the known principles of the "American creed."

Probably we all have somewhat differing angles of vision on fairness—not so greatly differing as to close off communication, but distinct enough to give us deep rewards from listening to each other. In the vignettes of this section, the issue of fairness is never out of sight.

Sometimes, as we will see in the diverging views of Harold Rubenstein and Vincent Matthews about Social Security entitlements, values clash in almost stereotypical debate. Yet both of these men hold quite individualized opinions, expressed in their own considered terms, and thus neither man is an uninteresting or uninstructive "type." The subject of fair treatment comes to the fore also in the good-natured contrasting of views about bill-collection by the administrators of Sapphire Valley health facilities.

"The Best Way Possible"

Often views move far from any type. Mary Graham,* for instance, is the mother of four, wife of a professor at one of our less-well-heeled public universities. These parents, with the help of a scholarship here and there, have nevertheless made themselves nearly penniless and destroyed their health in order to put each of their four talented children through very expensive private universities, one right after another.

If we had lived somewhere else, there might have been a cheaper way to educate our kids. Some states have good state universities. Washington, D.C., is not one of them. We once thought of moving to Virginia. But Will would have had to commute. And we do have a right to live in the District of Columbia. And we should have a right to educate our children in the best way possible, wherever that is.

Sending them to Will's school would not have been as cheap as it seems. They would have received half-tuition off. But why shouldn't they go as far as their talents and skills can carry them?

If they are smart enough, you want to see your children in the Ivy League. You know that's where the best minds come from, where the best faculty goes, where the research grants are to attract the Nobel winners. Getting educated in that environment should mean that the graduate will contribute to society in an even greater way. Any civilized society should want the very best educated adults. That's why you need private education. That's why you send young people to the best colleges and universities. We are investing in the future of this country by providing four people who are going to make thousands more in taxable dollars than if they went to public school. Two, three hundred thousand more. And we took some burden off public education by sending them to private school.

But it is so terribly unfair that there is no relief for doing that. The government does not care about us. They are making it ever harder for middle-class families to get guaranteed student loans. Loans! The best possible relief for people like us is to make payments for higher education tax-deductible. Even if it is adjusted to income level, do *something*. After all, the society benefits by having well-educated citizens.

And the qualifications for financial aid should be such that you don't have to sell your home and use up all your capital first to qualify. We should be able to own a modest house, have some savings for *ourselves*.

(W.T.—1987)

There may not be another family in the whole country in exactly that situation, though there are plenty who have sacrificed heavily to support their children through years of college and even beyond. And if this is a rare case, it points up issues all the more clearly. One somewhat impatient response might be that the United States, having invested enormous sums in public higher education, cannot be expected to do more in order to satisfy high-flying demands. But the statement is challenging at some very key points. Americans do approve of parents doing the very best for their children. The country does depend on the flourishing of individual talents. The Ivy League schools are better than most public colleges and universities. Even if they are not actually so, they are perceived to be so, and a diploma from one of them does have a higher cash value. (It also adds to the inequality within our social order.) Moreover, shouldn't people have truly free choice between public or private schooling for their children, and doesn't that require some financial help?

All of the vignettes of this book similarly suggest the complexity of people's lives. Consequently, good policies must not be tight-fitting. On the other hand, there are enough common threads to make social planning possible: all people, if they are lucky, grow old; if they are normal, they all will get sick; and in many other ways they will have similar needs and desires throughout their lives.

This book starts, therefore, where patricians and plebs alike end up if they live long enough, that is at the end of life's work span. The aged and the handicapped are outside the job market; in fact, they are not wanted by the economy as anything other than consumers. What the society does for them is entirely an outcome of society's will, and with the aged if not the handicapped, even full-pocketed policy-makers can, as the word has it, identify.

THE VERY SICK

The needs of the aged and handicapped require money, and will be met in proportion to how much money society decides to spend. Those judgments are both moral and political, and some are intensely difficult, as in the matter of so-called catastrophic illness. There are particular technical problems that have to be solved—actuarial tables and other demographic compilations, and a thousand and one administrative tasks—but underlying all is the simple question of how much money. The slogan-makers may be right that we can't solve the problems of working-class unemployment or of poverty by "throwing money at them." But the nation *can* solve those of the elderly and the handicapped by that method, if it wants to. More money, more solution. Less money, less solution.

From the vignettes that follow, the attentive reader can learn much about the working facts of the social-welfare system; much, too—and this more important—about the situations Americans find themselves in, and the spirit with which they go on about their lives. We begin with examples of the problems called "catastrophic."

"We Don't Have Nothing"

Hank and Betty Rowan* lived a few dozen miles inland from Lake Huron, in a stone house in rural Michigan. They had been married twenty-five years. Before he became ill, Hank was a tool-and-die-maker in one of Detroit's satellite cities. Betty had worked in hospitals and nursing homes. The Rowans moved north to get away from the big city and to provide a better environment for raising their children and coping with illness.

Betty told the family's story, breaking down frequently into sobs. She sat in the kitchen, which was decorated with saffron-colored curtains, a sign that said "Have a Happy Day," and numerous Christmas decorations. It was late summer, but Betty explained that she believed "in the Christmas spirit, *every* day." Then she started to catalogue her sixty-four-year-old husband's profusion of ailments.

It is an extreme case, but not unique. Nor are the Rowans' stamina and their yearning to be independent rare among the country's disadvantaged.

He's got chronic congestive heart failure, he's got an ulcerated esophagus, he has bleeding ulcers which are peptic ulcers, he has the leaking artery going into the brain. He *had* Parkinson's disease for a while, from the medication. I couldn't even begin to tell you all that's wrong with him. He had spinal surgery. He had nine pieces of bone removed from his back and a ruptured disk. If they hadn't been, he would have been paralyzed and died.

He's been on disability since 1968. He had TB of the bone when he was seven; he had twenty-six operations on that. He has no hip. There is a plate in place of the hip down to the knee on the left side. I guess if you would figure the way I figure, there have been many times when I think it would be easier to have a bullet in your head.

What I would like to do is be able to help ourselves. We try. We can't even afford to eat most of the time. We can't pay our medical bills. We can't do our repairs. When you can't exist anymore, why keep trying? Mentally, physically, emotionally, it tears you apart.

We had never even drawn welfare, nothing in our whole life, until Hank got sick. Then we asked for Medicaid and got some food stamps. We want to work, to do things, to be able to pay our own way. We don't want any help. There's plenty of people that are worse off than we are. But when it gets to the point where you can't afford food, you can't afford heat, you can't afford pills—what are you going to do?

The family is falling apart. We have eleven children. Hank had three, and I had three, and we've had five together. Our youngest is fourteen. We used to go to church, used to take the kids places, do things with them. We can't afford to even buy our kids school clothes or necessities. We used to do things as a *family*. Our twenty-one-year-old daughter left home because of her dad's illness. She couldn't handle it. And it is hard on the kids. Little Nellie, her dad's been sick since she's been five. She doesn't *know* any other life. I can't take her anywhere. The kids have no friends over; how *can* they?

Of course, we're lucky. There's never none of them been in jail, or on drugs, or on alcohol. They're a bunch of good kids. The older ones, when they've got the money for gas, they go to church. We've got one left to be confirmed.

We came up here because we wanted a life for the kids and something for Hank to do. We didn't want our kids in the city. We wanted them to learn how to plant a garden, to learn how to *do* things, instead of getting into trouble like most kids.

I don't think things could get any lower. The federal government, sure they pay. But you know, I have suitcases and suitcases full of medical bills I'll never pay. No human being, I don't think, could. That bothers me. Hank and I have always paid, and now we can't.

And the drugstore. He's been good. We owe $170 now, and he won't give us any more credit. So I buy Hank's pills two and three at a time. Some of them are ninety-five cents apiece. I've got two prescriptions sitting at the drugstore now. I haven't got any money. When I dig some up, I'll go get them.

The kids and I have gone over to the neighbors' a few years ago and we have shoveled manure. I bet you there was twenty-five manure wagons we shoveled. And the heat—some days it was almost a hundred degrees. And the man would give us a small cow or some packages of meat. We've done all kinds of stupid jobs. I didn't mind, because it was a way of making ends meet. We could survive. We used to pick up things at the dump. I would pick up things we needed—doors to put on the house, shingles for the roof. Anything we could use: clothes, blankets, anything. If you want to see anything more humiliating than going in a dump, a garbage dump, and sorting through tons of garbage to find things you can use . . . We used to pick up copper and brass and aluminum. You got pennies for it. But it was a way to make money. It would *buy* a few pills, it would *buy* a few things we had to have.

[Betty was asked for her idea of a better system for dealing with the misfortunes of families such as hers.]

Most people don't want to accept help. They don't want charity. But there's got to be *something*. There's got to be ways that they can help themselves. When you start *giving* somebody something, you're taking away everything. You're taking their pride, everything that makes them themselves. We still have to be human beings. We want to be human, just like the next guy. This strips you. It strips you of everything. I mean, I don't want to live like the Joneses. I never did. My kids on the school bus, they got teased. They got teased that we were junk-pickers. We don't have nothing. I haven't been Christmas shopping in fourteen years. I can't buy birthday presents. I can't buy nothing.

[Did she blame any person or agency for their situation?]

No. It's just that our system doesn't have a way yet for people like us. It's just one of those things that happened. Nobody is to blame. Maybe we are. Maybe when we were younger we should have saved more, invested more—I don't know.

[Betty got a spiral notebook from a shelf in the kitchen and calculated her family's income.]

We get $1,185 a month. That's from everything. From Social Security disability. What eats us up is our utilities, our heat, our electric. The house insurance is $80 every three months. The utilities average about $115 a month just for electric. That's every month. It's anywhere from $2,700 to $3,500 a year for oil heat. [This seems high, even for upper Michigan, but the figures are accepted by the Rowans' social worker. The house is drafty and poorly insulated.] The gas is for cooking and hot water and emergency heat for when our power goes off here. We were paying $200 a month for the gas last year. That's year round. We burn a lot in the winter. And this stone house, you've got to heat year round or you'll freeze.

[Betty said she sometimes wondered if things would get better if the family moved back to the city.]

There's more opportunities downstate. I'd go back and get another job in the hospital, like at night. I don't get any sleep anyway. Hank doesn't sleep at night. I'm up half the night waiting on him and running errands. Sometimes he's sick, sometimes he's scared. He can't see, and even if he could see, his fingers lately have been cramping up. He drops everything, or he can't let go. He's got cataracts on his eyes, too.

He's got a hearing aid that's absolutely useless. The batteries last seventy-two hours. And who can afford to buy a battery every seventy-two hours? We haven't bought one yet; we can't afford it. The cataracts they'll remove when they have to. He's got three hernias, and they're not going to touch them until they get bad enough. So many things just keep going wrong that I can't remember them all if I tried.

All I know is that most of the time, he's in a lot of pain.

In the fall, Hank Rowan died. Some of the people familiar with him couldn't even remember which of his many ailments was officially blamed for his death.

Betty wrote a long, moving letter to some of the social workers, thanking them for their help and apologizing for the times when she and Hank had been irritable, when they snapped at the people who were helping them. She herself had had severe medical problems after Hank's death, she wrote, but when she got better she planned to go to work. She wanted, she said, to use her nursing experience to help people who found themselves in similar situations. It would be, she said, "a memorial to Hank."

(F.P.—1986)

"They Gave Me a Runaround"

In the patchwork quilt that is the social-welfare system, some specific ills have their own programs. Kidney dialysis is one; black lung is another. "Black lung," said John M. Rosenberg, the director of the Appalachian Research and Defense Fund of Kentucky, "cannot get better." He spoke a truth that is painfully known by an estimated 10 percent of Appalachia's active coalminers and 20 percent of those who have retired.

Black lung, or pneumoconiosis, comes from inhaling coal dust over a long period of time. The disease makes breathing difficult and it shortens life. It once went by the name "miner's asthma," and the men often refer to their most dramatic symptom, a severe shortness of breath, as "smothering."

Federal law since 1969 provides monthly payments to miners found to be totally disabled by pneumoconiosis. The tax-free benefits, 37.5 percent of the relatively low GS-2 federal salary, are increased for miners with dependents. Payments are also made to widows and surviving children of disabled miners. The awards are reduced by the amount received from state unemployment insurance, workers's compensation, or disability under the federal Supplemental Security Income (SSI) program.

The black-lung program has been administered by two federal agencies—early claims by Health and Human Services, post-1973 claims by Labor. That division, along with the several changes made in the relevant law, has contributed heavily to confusion and to the delays, often stretching over several years, that miners have experienced in getting their claims approved. Some private lawyers have profited extravagantly from this. In many cases, federal authorities have sought to reduce black-lung payments to miners who also receive Social Security disability benefits, or even to demand that they return "overpayments." This action has been challenged by miners' advocates, but it's still commonplace for two similarly afflicted coworkers to receive totally different treatment, even for one of them to be denied payments altogether. American welfare programs are typically choked by administrative overlap and bureaucratic discretion—both usually imposed by Congress—but in this respect, the black-lung program outdoes them all.

Another complaint is that administrative-law judges, who conduct disability hearings, often render arbitrary decisions that seem designed to dissuade disabled miners from seeking the assistance to which they are entitled. The complaint is buttressed by a 1986 General Accounting Office finding that one agency of government, the Social Security Administration, may have wasted from $27 million to $69 million a year between 1981 and 1984 on unnecessary medical examinations and tests in an attempt to remove half a million people from disability rolls. One doctor hired to conduct exams was paid about $3 million for his work.

"A huge administrative mechanism exists virtually for the sole purpose of denying claims," said Rosenberg. The Appalachian Research and Defense Fund, in Prestonsburg, Kentucky, maintains a large docket of black-lung cases. Rosenberg, whose agency is funded by the federal Legal Services Corporation, said that more confusion had been added by 1978 revisions in the law that make the mining companies responsible for payments, thus giving the companies incentive to challenge claims. Where it is not possible to fix responsibility on one operator, benefits come from a trust fund financed by an excise tax on mining companies' tonnage. The resulting system, said Rosenberg, "is insane."

When we think of federal medical programs, it's generally the vast enterprises of Medicare and Medicaid that come to mind. But there are others, smaller ones that give direct care. One small island of good health services in the Appalachian coalfields is Mud Creek Health Services, of Grethel, Kentucky, a federally funded clinic that bloomed from grass-roots action during the War on Poverty. Mud Creek brings basic care to a population that is geographically isolated, in many cases poor, and—as company benefits expire—increasingly without health insurance. Eula Hall, the director, has achieved widespread recognition for her practical, determined approach in bringing the science of medicine to the narrow valley of the aptly named Mud Creek and the hollows that radiate from it.

During a typical day at the office, Hall sees several miners with black lung, or as some of them call it, "rock dust." She invited a resident of the valley to describe his situation. William Davies* is forty-eight years old, stands six feet, four inches tall, makes generous use of an enormous smile, and speaks with a deep, resonant voice that suits his other profession, that of Baptist minister. He no longer makes a living from coal; after fourteen years in the mine, black lung has put an end to that. Davies had to retire when he was only thirty-four.

When I first started in the mines in 1958, we used the shovel to load coal with. After that, we used the machines. All this time I was breathing in the dust. But I thought it couldn't happen to me. My dad come out of the mines with it. He suffered for eighteen years before he died with black lung.

I found out about it in nineteen sixty-nine. I was sick and I went to the doctor, and he told me I had it. I was surprised. The doctors tried to get me to quit work, but I didn't quit until seventy-two. I thought it might take a while to really come down with it. I hated to give up the work I'd worked at ever since I was young.

What it means is, you have to give up a lot of things that you always liked to do. I love to hunt, and now my hunting's cut to a minimum. I can't hunt around here because it's too far to climb the hills. I get too short of breath. If I do hunt, I have to go down the country somewhere where it's level, where I can just about hunt out of the truck.

Getting out walking, that's cut to a minimum, too. I haven't got the breath to get out and travel around. I love to walk and visit my neighbors, but now I don't do that very often. You're always short of breath.

I've got a nephew. His dad worked in the mines, and he's in pretty bad shape, and my nephew's been in the mines about seventeen years, and now they tell him he's got rock dust, too. But he's still trying to work. I believe anybody who works in the mines for long enough is going to get it.

I quit work on January 6, 1972. When I came out of the mine that day, the boss said, "You going to be back tomorrow?" And I said, "I don't know; that remains to be seen." And I didn't go back. I took the flu again, and when I went to the doctor he said, "You better give it up; you're just damaging yourself trying to go back." So I just quit then.

I went down and signed up for disability on my Social Security. They turned me down. They had my Social Security number mixed up with another fellow named William Davies. I know the boy; he's not a relation, but he belongs to the church I belong to. Over there at Pinetop, where that boy's from, 90 percent of the people are named Davies. If you ain't a Davies, you married one!

What had happened was, they were looking at *his* doctor reports instead of mine, and they decided I wasn't disabled. I got a lawyer down at Prestonsburg, and he's got it in court in Baltimore, but I don't know what the outcome is. So I've been trying to get Social Security since seventy-two. I've had hearings, and I can't get them to change it. When it comes back, it comes right back the same thing: they've still got his doctor reports. I've seen his report. It has my Social Security number on it.

[Davies was asked about the assistance available to him or his family members under the black-lung program.]

I got my first check, I think it was sometime in seventy-four. I applied for the benefits in seventy-two. They gave me a runaround and sent me to a lot of doctors, but after I got a hearing on it, the [administrative] law judge gave it to me. I never was able to get one of my sons put on the list of dependents. When my oldest son got married, I went down to have him taken off the list because he wasn't eligible anymore. But when I got the letter back from them, they had taken my *daughter* off. I went back down there and said, "You took *her* off two years ago when she got married." They said, "Well, it's all the same." And then I come to find out they'd never had my other son on there to start with.

I had been drawing $600-some, and now I'll be getting $492 from now till the end of my life.

We get the $492. Nothing from Social Security. We got food stamps, but I'm not sure about that now. Since my youngest son got married, I went back and changed it. I didn't want to break no law, and don't *aim* to break no law, if I can keep from it. Before, we were getting $68 in food stamps a month. That's not a lot of food.

I own my own home. I've got bottled gas, and coal. Coal doesn't cost me anything. My nephew works at a mine; a boy I went to school with runs the mine, and he's a good fellow. He takes care of me. We make it pretty good. We raise a pretty good garden.

Most of the time now, I lay around the house. If my brother or sisters call, I may go spend a day with them. I watch television, sometimes. Not very often. If there's a ball game on, I'll watch it. I'm not too much for this foolishness that comes on TV. The soap operas and stuff aren't fit for young children to watch. Something that's not fit for my children to watch, I don't want to watch it, either.

This clinic is a wonderful thing. I don't have any insurance. The government gave me a black-lung [health-insurance] card, and I kept it for about two or three years. That was good to be doctored on for only my lungs. And then they decided that the coal company and their insurance was responsible for that. And now they won't pay for it.

So I come over here to the clinic. They charge $5. And the medicine we get here is at a discount price. I take some smothering pills, for when I go to smothering, you know. And I take three heart pills a day, which is $46 a month, just for the heart pills. And I take three blood pills a day. They don't cost that much.

But if I need heart pills, I come here to the clinic and they'll let me have them, and I'll pay for them when I can. They've never turned me down. I don't owe them anything at the present time, but they're awful good about it. This clinic is a wonderful thing to this community around here. Because I think they do everybody the same way they do me.

I don't try to blame anyone. Mining was a means of supporting and feeding my family and giving my children what I never had when I grew up.

One of them's driving a school bus, and the other one, he's not working at anything right now. He got a job in the mines, but I talked him out of it. I told him if the mine didn't get you one way, it would another.

After Davies had left the clinic, Eula Hall talked a bit about him and other black-lung victims. Generally, she said, the miners accepted their fates because they felt they had no alternatives. "For one thing," she said, "there're not many other jobs here for people. It's coalmining or nothing. A few have school-teaching jobs, and a few have other jobs. But the main source of employment here is coal work. If you're going to stay here, you'll be a coalminer. You put the risk behind you and hope you never get black lung. You just die a little every day with it."

The miners, she said, were not the sort of people who wanted—or even felt they needed—to resort to deceit to get their disabilities officially certified. And so they were especially perplexed by the massive bureaucratic machinery that is arrayed against them.

(F.P.—1987)

Hank Rowan's was an extreme case. William Davies suffers from an occupational disease that is restricted to workers in relatively isolated areas, all of which are poor. Their experiences contrast with those of people with kidney failure, which strikes without regard to job or class.

As of 1985, almost all of the 85,000 people suffering kidney failure were getting life-sustaining dialysis treatments. Unlike other diseases, most of the costs of kidney treatment are covered by Medicare. By law, there are no major economic obstacles to treatment.

Dialysis, in which the patient's blood is cleaned by mechanisms outside the body, is today almost commonplace; there are some 1,300 federally approved dialysis centers around the nation. In some cases, Medicare will pay for the equipment so the patient can do it at home. Kidney transplant costs are similarly covered. In 1985, almost 7,700 transplant operations were performed. Another 8,500 patients were waiting for organs to become available through donations.

Either way, the costs are high. Congress had been told in 1972 that within a few years the cost would be $200 million annually; but it turned out to be several times that amount, and the number of patients has been growing about 5 percent a year. At a typical dialysis center, a week's worth of treatment can run $600. The treatment must continue throughout the patient's life, unless there is a transplant. Medication costs are high, too, and patients often find themselves paying a great deal for transportation and lodging near the dialysis facilities. Treatment is almost certain to interfere with the patient's ability to make a living. But the alternative to treatment is certain death.

"You've Got to Stay in the System"

We talked to two people suffering kidney failure. The first was Sam Morgan,* a thirty-four-year-old man in the rural Midwest who has been on dialysis for twelve years and treats himself at home.

I don't have any problems now. I was single then, and now I'm married, and I've got a wife, and I've got a stepchild, and we've got this house, and we've got the kidney machine at home, and when I look back to when I first started on the kidney machine and all the negative things I felt, and how things are now, it's just like night and day.

We still have a lot of money problems, and there are times when it's not fun to be on the machine, but when I'm off, I don't even think of it. I'm on it three days a week, for about six hours each time. My wife's got to always be here, too. She puts my needles in my arm. But that's really all she does. Once she gets me hooked up, I do all the rest. I set the thing up and I take it down, and clean up the messes and everything. I spend quite a bit of time outside. I do a lot of fishing and a lot of walking in the woods. I just like going out.

I have no idea what this thing is costing. I've had transplants that cost $30,000. I've seen a bill. I don't know if everything was on that billing—if it was just the surgery or if it was the whole hospital stay or what. I couldn't even guess. I guess Medicare paid it. That's been quite a few years back.

Now Medicare and Blue Cross pay for most of the dialysis. I still get billed for a small part of it. I really don't know what would have happened if the government hadn't picked up their part. I mean, I've still got bills now that I'm paying on.

Blue Cross is my biggest cost right now. I've got my wife on my policy now, and together it's $270 every other month. When the month comes that we have to pay that, it really hurts. And we still owe taxes on this house from last year. We just bought this house last year. That's why I've got to try to find some work this fall— we've got to start making payments on the taxes or we'll lose the house.

I haven't looked for work for the last five or six years. Our income comes from Social Security, the disability program. We get about $1,300 a month. Most people would probably think that's pretty good money, but by the time you pay your bills and pay insurance—and if you have a car you've got to pay car insurance—there's usually just enough left for food. And we buy our food at the start of the month, so we'll be sure to have it for the whole month. But that just makes it.

I don't think we could get food stamps. They would say that we have too much income. We don't have to pay any income tax. But you still have to pay other taxes. I have to pay for all the medications except one gets paid for by the Kidney Foundation. As a matter of fact, there are a lot of times that I'm out of medicine and I just have to wait a couple of weeks until we get our checks and can go out and buy some. My [medication] expenses vary from month to month. It all depends on when I run out of something. It's maybe $50 or $60 a month. There are some medications that I should be taking but I haven't taken for a long time because they cost too much.

[Sam was asked if he thought the social-welfare system was treating him adequately.]

I guess so. It keeps me going. Keeps a roof over my head. And there are a lot of people out on the street who're a lot worse off than I am. So I feel lucky.

I don't know how I'd improve it. I don't see that they would ever change it to cover all medication, the way they're cutting back so much on everything right now. It would certainly help if they did. But I'm sure that once they did that, they'd start having a lot of fraud, too. People are always going to figure out some way to ruin things, abuse them.

Sometimes it's like a catch-22. You've got to stay in the system. Because if you go out of the system and make money, you're going to lose what you're getting now. So it kind of makes you want to stay in, because if you go out and start working and start getting ill again and then have to quit work, it's so hard to get back in the system. It almost makes you scared to want to go out and work. I've known a lot of people like that: they're scared to go out and work and then have something go wrong, and they'll have nothing to fall back on—so that's one of the reasons they stay at home. When you first start on the kidney machine, you're so ill, when you get to the point that I was at, you can't do anything. I couldn't have worked for a good couple of years there.

I know that I'm not going to live a full life. I know I probably will only live another five or ten years or so. I just take each day at a time, now. I don't know too many people who have been on the kidney machine for twelve years. I first started on the machine up here in seventy-four, and there aren't any of the people left who were here when I first started. They're all gone, now. So I just know that it's not something that I'm going to keep on doing until I'm fifty or sixty—at least I don't think so. I don't think they can do all that much more to improve the kidney machine. It does all the cleaning now. But you can only get cleaned up so much.

[He was asked if "each day at a time" was a good way to live.]

When you don't have any other choice, yes.

(F.P.—1986)

"I Still Have a Pretty Active Life"

Sarah Carter,* who is black and lives in Manhattan, has been on dialysis for five years and looks forward to the day when she can do it at home. She suffers from hypertension, which afflicts one of every four adult blacks, as compared to one of every six whites.

The kidney dialysis clinic at New York Hospital is less than thirty minutes by bus from my job as a Salvation Army social worker. It's a long hospital room which accommodates about twenty patients, each having her own private chair, dialysis machine, and TV set. Like myself, most of the patients receive their treatments after work.

It takes about twenty minutes to set up the machine and then you make your chair comfortable. You're on the machine for about three or four hours, during which you get a chance to look at TV, read, write, or sleep. Thus, the hours of dialysis, three times a week, go pretty quickly.

My kidney problem resulted from high blood pressure, which I have had for most of my adult years. Ironically, I've done some of my best work when my pressure is high. Nobody really knows what causes hypertension.

I suppose a lot of mine has to do with the extreme stresses under which I have lived and worked. As a divorcée, I've had to rear two sons alone here in New York. The older, Michael, thirty-four, is an architect and civil engineer in Atlanta who knew what he wanted to be when he was seven years old. On the other hand, Kevin, thirty-two, wanted to be everything from a tap dancer to a cowboy, and he's still trying to find himself. They're two extremes, but I love them. Kevin, who is unemployed in Washington, D.C., has put me through quite a few hard times and heartaches. I went through a lot of psychological therapy to learn how to deal with him.

I didn't become seriously ill until April 1983. I had been working for the New York Board of Education since 1969 and had become the director of a federally funded drug-and-alcohol-abuse program. I was really enjoying that, when my doctor informed me that I might need dialysis.

I took a four-month leave to look for another job, since the one I had was much too stressful. I was grateful that I had three federal job offers. But since I wanted to get away from political pressures, I accepted my current position in 1983. My annual salary dropped from $38,000 to $23,000. That was hard to take, but I had no choice. Even so, my lower-paying job has helped me to keep my sanity, kept me feeling like a responsible citizen, and given me some dignity within myself.

I had to decide which type of dialysis I wanted. Or you can get a kidney transplant. My twin sister, who is the dean of the school of social work at a predominantly white southern university, had said that she would give me a kidney, but I felt that would probably weaken her. Friends told me that even if scarce kidneys are available, transplants only last for a while.

Because my schedule allows me to be dialyzed after work, I can go home afterward, go to sleep, and the next day feel as if nothing had happened. According to how much fluid was taken off, I might feel a little weak. But as the day goes on, I always get stronger. So I still have a pretty active life. I can even travel out of town because every state has dialysis facilities. All I have to do is have the social worker call and set up an appointment.

These thoughts were in mind as I prepared to spend the 1985 Christmas holidays with Michael and his family in Atlanta. But on December 14, an electrical malfunction started a fire in my four-story brownstone in Harlem, which I have been paying on since 1976. The house was a near total loss. I had insured it for $50,000, but it was going to take at least $100,000 to repair it. That was too much for me. Since I already had my plane ticket, I decided to go on to Atlanta anyway, relax during Christmas, then return to deal with the house later.

While I was being dialyzed in an Atlanta hospital, I had a fever that I couldn't shake and they kept me in the hospital for four months. It was terrible. I lost twenty-five pounds. After release, I had to stay at my son's home for weeks to recuperate.

I worry about the massive expenses connected with dialysis. The treatments run about $40,000 a year in New York and are covered by Medicare, for which I pay a $409 annual premium. When I travel out of town, I have to pay between $26 and $32 a visit to the institution where I am dialyzed. Medications cost about $125 a month. When I was in Atlanta with my son and his family, I paid $52 a month for ambulance service. Before I got that, it was costing me $22 a day to go by cab. Here in New York, transportation to and from the hospital runs about $16 round-trip. Then too, I have the added expense of eating out quite a bit because I don't always feel well enough to cook.

(A.P.—1986)

Hank Rowan could not work, William Davies no longer can, Sarah Carter works regularly, Sam Morgan plans to start. Rowan's catastrophic ills overwhelmed the social-welfare system; it could not cope, and may even have given up its half-hearted efforts to do so. The real challenge is not the technical problem of methods and processes but the more basic test of political will. Does the country have the will to pay for the needs of the Hank Rowans?

Presidents and members of Congress should think very hard about these matters. We don't know what the public costs of Hank Rowan's operations and treatments were, but they must have been immense. So is the cost of long-term kidney dialysis or transplants. No government should practice triage, particularly not a democratic one. However, the government must guarantee that the legal ways are open for patients to choose between treatment and death, or to delegate that decision.

Politicians should also ponder the adversarial position they, through their programs, have placed Davies and Rowan in. Though black-lung sufferers may provide the clearest example, a great many people seeking to claim their entitlements are all too often treated by administrators (themselves often responding to congressional pressures) as suspect and inferior. No welfare system should be like that. Policy-planners could contrast the situtation of Davies, clutching for his lawful entitlements, or Rowan, desperately dependent on the decisions of a myriad of "helpers," with those of Sarah Carter and Sam Morgan, served by a program in which entitlements are defined clearly and received in dignity.

This look at the very sick furnishes policy suggestions that are also applicable to the situations of the less severely sick and the retired, whom we will consider later. The primary lesson here is that goals and equity should be the only determinants. When the subject is welfare or unemployment or the inadequacy of wages, other choices also rightly come into play. It then becomes appropriate and even necessary to debate which macroeconomic strategies best serve the welfare policies and goals (but not, of course, the other way around). It becomes valid also to debate which level of government is the most efficient for providing a certain type of care, and which is the most constitutionally appropriate one.

But these questions should not be relevant to the case of people in the situations discussed in this chapter, fully outside the economy's expectations of any further contribution or participation. Care for them should be regarded as a necessary charge—virtually a fixed cost—in any macroeconomic policy, and the question of where responsibility lies within our mix of public and private authorities should be answered solely on grounds of efficiency.

The only relevant *policy* questions concern goals and equity —and those are hard enough to answer. The goals should be dignity and comfort. Those are largely subjective conditions. Certainly no one can believe that the plight of the Rowan families or the William Davieses of the nation accords with either. The nation does a lot better, for example, with citizens with kidney failure, people with hardships that can afflict anyone. In any case, the path to dignity and comfort is through finding the will to spend whatever is required by our own understanding of what those qualities mean. And here, as with much of our social-welfare system, the nation does not provide enough even to meet its own estimation of need.

Equity is conceptually complicated. Traditionally, inequity has been rooted in racial and ethnic discrimination. Plenty of that still exists, but we have at least delegitimized it and are generally and institutionally armed against it. A second traditional problem of almost equal virulence lay in discrimination against the poor, of whatever race or grouping. We are a long way from overcoming this, but my sense is that, among all the ways in which we discriminate, we are farthest along toward achieving equity here, in the way we treat the handicapped and old. There is a distance to travel, however. For example, the survival rate among those with cancer is lower among the poor, in large part because they have less access to the medical systems' diagnostic and treatment services.

The claims of one person or group may compete with those of others in society. This will be related, of course, to the amounts of money society wills to spend, but even in the most prosperous of nations, that cannot be infinite. So hard choices are unavoidable. With not enough facilities or nurses or doctors for all, how do nursing homes select the illness for priority? There are many similar questions. Generally, how does a society apportion limited resources among the health needs of all its people? If choice had to be made between doing more for a Hank Rowan or for the children of that family—including family planning so they won't produce as many offspring— what would equity require?

These are issues of fairness, of what best accords with society's sense of justice. They need to be faced with clear vision, and they should never be allowed to get lost in the swirling currents of debate over process or techniques, never smothered by bureaucratic nonsense.

No recent issue has been more plagued by such problems than AIDS. The response to this health emergency has been hindered by conservative moralities that blame AIDS sufferers for their disease and by budget-cutting that made the consideration of goals secondary to dollars. Consequently, there was too little money available, especially in the crucial early years of the crisis, and therefore minimal solution.

The following vignette emphasizes again how expensive treatment can be, measured not only by medical costs but by the consequent added expenditures for disability, food stamps, unemployment compensation, and other welfare entitlements. Furthermore, the inflexibility of the health-care system may have hindered the development of new drugs for the virus associated with AIDS and the common opportunistic infections that are actually the real danger to people with AIDS (PWAs), and also discouraged preventive approaches and outpatient care.

The brief history of AIDS evidences a fault that runs throughout our health-care system: its addiction to special treatment programs for individual conditions—this one for kidney failure, that one for black lung, another for "brown lung," yet another for cancer. And thus more competing claims arise, for each disease has, as it were, its own "lobby." It is worth contemplating what by contrast might be the advantage of a comprehensive national health plan.

"They Think It's Going to End Tomorrow"

It takes just one step into the Minority Task Force on AIDS, in Harlem, to receive a deep and frightening shock about just whom AIDS is hitting hardest. Up to 90 percent of all AIDS-infected children in New York City are black or Latino. More than 65 percent of all intravenous-drug users are infected. The rate of spreading may only be on the rise; there are authoritative estimates that by 1991, when there may be up to 50,000 new cases in the country each year, 65 percent of those will be people of color.

I visited the Task Force just a few days after visiting the buzzing and sprawling downtown headquarters of the Gay Men's Health Crisis (GMHC), which is searching for a new building to consolidate its operations, including a volunteer program of nearly 2,000. By contrast, and in spite of the horrifying statistics, the Minority Task Force is a minuscule outpost—a few offices and a small dinner-seminar room—serving 83 PWAs on an annual budget of $100,000. Gregory Broyles, the director, after stressing the importance of community-based groups in providing culturally sensitive educational and intake services, says that he could readily use an expanded operation with a budget of $1 million. On top of that there is a desperate need for PWA housing. It's easy to understand Broyles's assessment: "As it is now, I'm not very hopeful."

I met Michael Waters* at the Task Force. Medium height and trim he speaks tersely, almost haltingly, but conveys a restrained dignity. He is educated and, before diagnosis, was not poor.

The last job I held was in the accounting department of a university. I earned a decent salary. I was able to support my wife and two children [age nine and thirteen]. After that, I decided to go back to school to get a bachelor's degree. I graduated in June of eighty-six. I began on job interviews. Then suddenly I began to feel strange. It was as if I was sapped of my energy, my motivation. I just lay around, because I was weak, tired. Nightsweats. Fevers. Chills. I suspected that it might be AIDS, but I didn't want to admit it. But I was feeling so terrible and was losing a lot of weight. I decided to go to the hospital to get a checkup. This was April of eighty-seven.

That evening, the doctor came out and said I had a bad case of PCP [pneumocystis carinii pneumonia, which has been the most fatal of the infections that strike PWAs]. Then he went on to say there was a possibility that I might have AIDS. So that kind of tore my life apart right then and there.

I had no insurance coverage at that time, but I had savings. I was comfortable. That's not the case now. I was in the hospital for one straight month. From then until I was accepted for SSI [Social Security's Supplemental Security Income] in September—five months—I went completely through my bank account of $800. Prior to my diagnosis, my wife was working in a school in the Bronx, but then she had stopped in order to care for me. But we needed food, materials, and so she planned to go back, but her job was no longer there. So it was a financial disaster. I was totally bankrupt and had to borrow at least $1,500 from various friends. [Borrow?] They were gifts, really.

I try to go back and trace my footsteps. At the beginning, I thought I got the virus from using drugs intravenously. Then I thought it could have been from interactions with a prostitute. And then I went even further back and thought it could have been from sharing a needle with a friend who had syphilis. I don't know for sure.

There is a certain stigma to AIDS, and prior to being diagnosed, I held a negative view. I thought to have AIDS was one of the lowest things that can happen to a person. When I was diagnosed, I felt that low.

I had no interest in living. When I came out of the hospital, I just lay in bed and waited to die. The sooner, the better. Get it over with. But I did not die. I began to gain my weight back, my thoughts. And I said, "Hey, I am not dying as they said I would." So I've decided to fight. And to go on. And to enjoy life day by day.

Actually, from July to September I did receive an amount from welfare. I would say, $67 biweekly. [Laughs.] I know, I know. That's the tragedy of it all. It's impossible—it's not impossible, I did survive it—but $67 biweekly! Going day to day without one dollar. That was really difficult to adjust to. But there is that kind of life, and I was a part of it.

SSI started in September. That's not much either, only $410 a month. Regularly, my phone bill is $40 a month. The electricity is about $60 every two weeks. The rent is $320 a month. My food I usually receive from the Task Force. Food stamps, I receive $25 a month. No public assistance [i.e., nonfederal assistance, available in New York and some other states on various programs]. No rent subsidy. My wife gets unemployment; it's $90 every two weeks. My two children are being supported on that. I'm fortunate that in the public school my kids attend, breakfast and lunch are served. However, during the summertime it's going to be that much more difficult because they're home and I must feed them breakfast and lunch out of my budget.

I don't make as many loans as I did. But every now and then I still have to make a telephone call. Because there are many days that I simply run out of money.

Surviving during that summer was the main problem. I went days with just tea and biscuits. It was a lousy existence. I remember making phone calls to public assistance, SSI. They stated that it would take a month or two before I could receive anything. I remember arguing, "What am I going to do now? What am I going to do for tomorrow? I'm completely out of funds." I remember calling and calling.

There should be agencies set up specifically for emergency funds. I don't mean perhaps they'll give you $50 and that's it. A $50 grant from the Task Force or GMHC is supposed to last for months? It's impossible. It's good for two days! So they should have some kind of government agency that would give you the money immediately. And every week.

I was fortunate in that my relatives had money to lend me. Those who do not have that are actually going under. Starving. And that's why a lot of people with AIDS die, because of lack of care, lack of food. Many people with AIDS don't have the money to eat. They believe they are going to die and don't have the drive to get out there and go on a job interview or go to an agency. So they just lay home and literally die.

When I began to feel ill, the disease was on my mind quite a bit. But before that, no. The education wasn't directed at me. It's always the belief that it applies to others and not you.

As far as informing the people in Harlem and the South Bronx, I would narrow it down. Now it's so broad. A commercial comes on TV saying, "Don't Die of Embarrassment." It's so negative. You have to take away the negative aspect about AIDS being associated with homosexuality. No one in the ghetto community, even if they are homosexual, will admit to it. The macho thing. You have to take that away. And you have to take away the stigma of it being a filthy disease. I would focus only on the facts, and I would not hit on the emotions. At schools, churches. And always emphasize there isn't anything wrong with you if you do have AIDS. And then the people in the closet will come out and receive care. Or those who are unsure will be tested. Because many people have the symptoms but they fear going to be tested. They fear they will have a mental breakdown just knowing they have something that's supposed to be so stigmatized, so negative.

I'm seriously considering going back to work. Healthwise, I've never felt better. The only thing is figuring out a way, the hiatus I have from being out of school and in the hospital, putting all that time on my résumé. A future employer would want to know what you did between this period and that period. In my case, I cannot tell them I was diagnosed with AIDS. There are people who say it's OK to tell them because they can't discriminate. But I know better. An excuse will be made not to hire the person. I have to find another way to plug that gap.

Last summer made me feel totally outside [of society], ostracized. An outcast. I felt I was some kind of maggot, really. You just don't want to live, knowing that you're that. Until you overcome that feeling, you won't live.

An interview with Ross Kurtz* suggested the extent of the AIDS underground that has developed to attend the emotional, financial, and medical needs of PWAs. They have searched out experimental drugs on their own and developed effective home-care programs. As a result, they believe they have begun to change the way the health-care system operates, forcing it to concentrate on a more cooperative, active relationship with the patients and to emphasize preventive approaches to sickness.

The thirty-three-year-old Kurtz, who was quite weak when I visited him in the hospital, described some of the financial and medical problems PWAs must cope with. He had been tentatively diagnosed as having cytomegalovirus (CMV); untreated, the virus can lead first to blindness and ultimately to death. There is an approved preventive treatment, which involves being surgically fitted with a catheter in the chest which is then hooked to a machine to insert the medication, up to five times a day. Kurtz had become so frustrated after a month's stay in the hospital that he had decided to forgo this treatment and sign himself out, so that he could carry on with alternative treatments that the hospital would not provide.

They would keep me here forever, because their goal is to stop the fevers, no matter what. But I can have fevers just as well at home.

Probably part of it is what happens when you come to a hospital. But also I'm being presented with certain choices as if they are ultimatums. I feel there are other possibilities, and the only way I can investigate them is to get out. It's just the usual story of having some kind of control over what you are doing.

I've got Blue Cross, which I got after my diagnosis. Once a year they offer policies without consideration of preexisting conditions. It's $244 a quarter. There's an exclusion of the first eleven months, which I have now lived through. You pay in but you can't make any claims at first. I've outlived their expectations.

After that, there's a $750 deductible, and you're home free. It's 80 percent, and Medicaid picks up the rest. So I'm essentially covered. But I'm not sure how it's going to work out dealing with individual doctors. They're already sending me their consultation fees—doctors who are part of the hospital. Who needs it? [Laughs.] There's just no way I can pay it.

Where would I be now if I didn't have the insurance? Bellevue [a city hospital with many indigent patients and a poor reputation]. I can see it from this window. I visited people over there, patients. You have to hide your wallet when you go to the bathroom. I knew this guy who had a couple of junkies in the next two beds. And it was like, Who wants to stay there?

To do tests, people are put in the hospital, even though it could be done on an outpatient basis. But Blue Cross just won't cover it. It's one of the major flaws in this whole system.

I'm totally broke. Technically I have no assets. I mean, I have things. But not much else. My mother and father help out. But my father's retired and my mother's about to be retired, both from the phone company. It's not like there's a lot of money there at this point. So I don't push it.

I get disability, SSI, which is $560 a month; it just went up. My rent is $350; it's very cheap. I'm able to stay in my apartment with no sweat. But under normal circumstances, especially in Manhattan, I think rent would be a real bitch. For Medicaid, you aren't supposed to make any more than $417 a month. You have to spend down, as they call it, what you receive from Social Security toward medical expenses. So I can get Medicaid because I deduct the cost of my pantamidine treatments from my SSI, which at the time brought it to $420, which they figured was close enough to $417 that they went for it—though as I said, I haven't gotten the card yet. But the idea of living in New York on $417 a month is ridiculous.

In contrast to black-lung disease, AIDS hits many people in the prime of their working lives. A recent study of the sixty-five AIDS cases in Nevada concluded that $84.4 million in real income—and nearly that amount returned to the economy through savings, taxes, and spending—will be lost. Consider then that 34,000 people have died from the illness already, and that future estimates grow geometrically.

At the same time, because so many PWAs are living longer, a new perception is developing of AIDS not as a fatal disease but as a chronic one. As a result, more and more people are going to become dependent on public assitance for longer periods. Thus there is a second contrast with the black-lung and dialysis programs: no independent federal care program. Some localities, particularly San Francisco and New York, are putting out vast sums for AIDS, but in the absence of a national strategy, there is little incentive for other cities and states to do so.

"The System Has to Give"

With more than 14,000 PWAs, New York has far more cases than any other city, and it is estimated that over a half million people there are infected with the human immunodeficiency virus (HIV), all of whom may go on to develop AIDS. Clearly the city has responded out of necessity, but it has also been pushed to do so by a number of grass-roots organizations. The oldest is GMHC, formed in 1981, which has developed into a broad-based service organization for anyone with AIDS, providing food, recreation facilities, and financial and medical assistance, as well as pursuing the lobbying functions that were its origin. Louise Quinn,* thirty, is a loquacious and scrappy financial advocate there.

New York is doing things that no other state is doing. Look at rent supplements. They are only given to PWAs, no other disability group. Also, there's the Medicaid spend-down program. No other state has that. And in other states, the cutoff for Medicaid is a lot lower.

But you really have a feeling that, even after seven years, they think it's going to end tomorrow. With each emergency, they'll bend the rules and make a judgment on the one case, but they won't standardize it.

And I don't know where the money is coming from. You can get up to $500 a month in rent subsidy, plus $300 food money. At first, they were expecting a six-month turnaround on this, but now people are living longer. But still, the $500 limit makes no sense. Let's say I'm just diagnosed, I don't have a penny in my pocket, it's going to be at least two months before benefits come in, and my rent is $800 a month. Add $300 for food, and that's $1,100 a month. They're going to say, "No way," and laugh you out the door. Fine, I'm evicted. The shelters won't accept AIDS cases. So now you've got to put me up at the Y for $25 a night. Well, that times thirty days plus the food money, and you're giving me about $1,100 anyway. But they don't look at it that way. They will actually let you get evicted.

You need AIDS units within all the different agencies. Medicaid has one, but it's grossly understaffed. Social Security has one, and they're effective. Welfare doesn't, and the people don't know what they're doing. They don't make allowances for the urgency and the seriousness of the illness.

We're seeing a lot of people now who are blatantly lying to the government. Getting their benefits, getting their cards, going back to work, and just not telling anyone. The agencies all work off IRS computers, and the IRS is two years behind reality. By the time they catch up with you, you could be dead. And if you're not, what are they going to do?

It becomes very demoralizing. All these middle-class boys have worked since they were sixteen, always saved money. Now to have to go sit in an agency for eight hours, to constantly fight on the phone for the money, to get the checks on time, to have to live on that amount of money. What most of them do is they literally freeze up. They can't do it.

The intravenous-drug cases are, on the other hand, just very accepting. Same for a lot of the Latino cases you find, and other minority cases, where you have low-income families anyway. To them life's a struggle, and this is just one more. They just trudge on with it. Their expectations are never that high.

From what I see, Blue Cross–Blue Shield is not that big of a deal. It will get you admitted to a hospital faster and get you a better room. But a lot of our clients are hooked up with clinics that take Medicaid, and it's good for the prescriptions. So to me, it [dependency on having insurance] is a real sign of a middle-class mentality. They grew up with it. And they don't understand how to manipulate the system. They don't like to play all these games.

I say to them, "Look, you've got AIDS. A cold is an emergency to you. No hospital can turn you away for an emergency. You don't have insurance? It doesn't matter. They have to put you in somewhere. You may not like the way you're treated, but I'm sorry, I think most hospitals are bad anyhow." But you can't get that through to them. They want that card; they want to understand how it's all going to work. That insurance coverage gives them such peace of mind. I say to them, "Medicaid doesn't pay for your hospital stay, what do you care? You don't have the money. You don't have a spouse, they don't recognize your relationship, no one's responsible but you, and if you die tomorrow—all those bills, the hospital gets stuck for." But you have people who are getting only $500 a month, who keep sending hospitals $50, $10, trying to pay off bills. I tell them, "What? Are you crazy? Buy yourself more food."

Many of our clients live in New Jersey and use a New York address. All you need for any of these agencies is a place where mail will come. In fact, the New York address is even necessary, because Medicaid cards are issued by the state, so if you have a New Jersey Medicaid card, it can only be used there. But most of your doctors are still in New York. In other states, there's no acceptance for the disease.

(A.B.—1988)

Gradually, the country seems to be overcoming its resistance to dealing with AIDS. Remember, though, that it was six years into the crisis before the country's president even spoke the name of the illness in public, and the current presidential campaign has brought no significant debate over policy approaches.

The lesson is clear. Just as inner-city poverty is not squarely addressed because most politicians are distanced from the problem (i.e., are white), so AIDS has shown how even a disastrous health emergency will be neglected when those in political power do not feel that they and their kind are affected.

The most immediate thing that must be done is massive education—of the population, of politicians, of those who work in the social-welfare system. Beyond that, the work lies in the research laboratories and treatment clinics. For social-welfare policy, then, the prime responsibility is in health care, and that necessarily points to an already overburdened program, Medicaid. State and local public assistance in some places and the amazing network of private help that has sprung up are invaluable; but the basic sustaining arm is Medicaid, requiring sufferers to spend themselves into poverty before they can be helped. It is an indecent and undignified policy.

THE SICK

Despite his many difficulties, Davies, the black-lung victim, does have the reassuring support of a federally created and funded clinic, though small and itself struggling, and of federally funded lawyers, kept in the field by Congress against the opposition of the Reagan administration. Institution-building has been a vital part of the best elements in our social-welfare system. There will be more on that in later pages. The following is a depiction of another small and struggling health-care institution, and the for-profits enterprise that operates in the same county, an example of public and private cooperation in extending health care.

The Sapphire Valley of West Virginia is guarded by rugged mountains, bisected by a sometimes wild river, and populated by independent, hard-working people. It is isolated from the rest of America by both geography and economics. But it is not part of the Appalachia of deep, abject poverty, of the perilous coal mines and the wasted children. Rather, the Sapphire Valley is a lovely place whose mountains are beautiful as well as rugged, whose people wave at strangers as they pass on the road. The bottomlands are not clogged with coal dust and the unregulated fumes of industry, but rather provide pasture for dairy cattle and fields for modest-sized crops.

In the higher elevations, which are never far from the narrow valley, distance is measured in minutes or hours, rather than miles. A trip of twenty miles can require the better part of an hour, and it is likely to cover one-lane roads that have many blind curves and that become impassable in winter.

Although the hills are beautiful enough to attract vacationers in the summertime and busloads of leaf-watching tour groups in the fall, and although the valley is fertile, the region is well below average in wealth. In one survey, taken by a medical organization serving the two counties that make up the valley, more than 80 percent of its patients were classified as "poor to moderately poor." The organization reported, "The local economy is based on low earnings and high unemployment," with most of the major industries and professions in a state of depression. Farming remained about as steady as farming ever does, but logging was down because of the national decline in housing starts. Mining, formerly a significant industry on the western slope of one of the counties, had decreased, and teaching, once considered the only stable part of the valley's employment picture, was endangered by a decline in the number of students.

The region's increasing median age, high degree of isolation, and severe unemployment have caused some particular medical problems. A large portion of the population suffers from chronic obstructive lung disease (a catch-all term that does not include black lung). Because many low-income people subsist on inexpensive carbohydrates, rather than the costlier proteins, there is a high percentage of obesity. Hypertension is "very high," according to one assessment, and there is a great degree of inadequate prenatal care.

Health professionals also believe that people don't visit the existing medical facilities as often as they should. The assessment explained, "We feel that many patients forgo preventive services and many treat themselves because of the lack of third-party funding mechanisms. Also, the transportation barrier causes many people to treat themselves or let the illness 'run the course' instead of going to the physician. Unemployment in the area has caused many families to rely on medical care only as a 'last resort.' "

The Sapphire Valley has a number of medical professionals and institutions to serve the population. Clarkville, the largest town, has a modern, full-service hospital. It is a for-profit institution with about 125 beds, operated as part of the LifeCare chain of hospitals. ("LifeCare," along with all other names here, including that of the valley itself, have been fictionalized.) And in the rural part of the valley there are two small facilities, operated by Sapphire Valley Health Clinics, a nonprofit institution that provides primary-care services for residents, regardless of their ability to pay.

"We Are Here to Serve Our Board"

Margaret Harris* is the administrator of the rural clinics. An energetic woman who speaks with the gentle, understated wit of the mountains, Harris stresses personal dealings with members of the community, a role she feels the hospital does not fill. The clinics, for example, choose the dozen members of their board of directors every two years by a mail ballot of the patients.

Harris spoke in the waiting room (the only space available) of the busy West Clinic, a converted home a mile or so outside an unincorporated hamlet. (The East Clinic, made up of mobile homes, is about an hour away, in the next county.) The West Clinic is reached by a narrow road that winds through hills and farmland. It was decorated with posters and drawings designed to put children at ease. Behind the building, a steer grazed.

In 1977, the area residents got together and decided they needed some health care. So they met with the federal people who were looking to start clinics in the medically underserved areas. They opened the doors of both clinics in the fall of 1978. Originally we started with one doctor, who traveled between the clinics, and a physician assistant. We've had a lot of National Health Service Corps obligees. Now we have ten employees, and we just last month started full-time hours in each clinic—thirty-seven hours a week. It's a family practice, mainly, but we also offer early pediatric screening and family planning, and we do health promotions. We try to inform the public. We go to the health fairs. We try to be community oriented.

We have some patients who come from as far as forty-five miles away. A lot of them say they know they can get what they need at a health department or the hospital in Clarkville, but they say they feel like they're just a number there, just rushed in and out.

The hospital was very opposed to us when we began. But a lot of people will not go to LifeCare. They go over to Virginia instead. They don't like the doctors at LifeCare, they don't like the way they get billed, and they don't understand how the billing works. They can go to the emergency room, and they will serve them there. But LifeCare'll give them a bill before they leave that day, and make them sign an agreement. I've known them to do that. If you don't pay, they *sue*. They send a collection agency after you. We don't do that here. There is a personal touch here. Pretty much everybody who comes in the door, we know. The receptionist knows them well enough that she can pull their chart without looking up their number.

We are federally funded. We accept all the medically indigent. We have a sliding fee scale, based on income and family size, for patients who cannot afford the full cost. Sometimes they only have to pay like fifteen dollars.

The two clinics serve 6,800 people. This year, we'll probably have six or seven thousand "encounters." We have to do federal paperwork every time somebody comes in. We have to count them as an encounter. We have to determine whether they are a first-time user ever, or a first-time user this year, or if it's the second time they have come.

[Harris explained that in the current year, the clinics expected to receive fees of about $336,000. Another $50,000, she said, "we just write directly off" because it is clear that the patients cannot pay. The remainder of the budget, $175,000, comes from the Department of Health and Human Services. DHHS requires a lot of documentation.]

We write a grant proposal every year. They want four copies. And we do a needs-demand assessment about what our patient population is, what age the population is, and what our range of health problems is, and we have to do a health-care plan. We've already done one, but they want it more in-depth and more around the life cycles, around what we plan to do for infants up to two years old and the elderly, and so on. We've had [the federal] Maternal Child Health Care here doing an audit for the past two and a half days. They're going to do their exit interview with me today and tell us what we've been doing right and wrong.

We have a lot of conversations with the DHHS people. We've been to seminars and meetings about how to write guidelines. They leave enough leeway so that we can write some of our own, but they have general guidelines we have to follow. I think they're realizing more and more that each clinic is unique. You can't write guidelines that cover us *and* an urban population.

We're part of what is called a consortia project, where they give you funds for renovations and things like that if you get together with other clinics and you bring a doctor in who will travel among all the clinics. In our case, they wanted him to travel between here and East Clinic and another one over on Cherry Creek. Sixty miles one way.

My federal program officer, Mr. Williams, came down in July. He thought it was *beautiful* country. But he told me after he'd been here a while, "We do now realize that this is unreasonable, because of the terrain and the roads." I guess they just don't believe it until they see it.

We *have* to have the federal dollars in order to survive. So we do the paperwork. It could be cut. This year they have decided to cut our grant-writing down some, but I don't think it's going to be really cut. I think it'll probably be added to. They want us to do a whole grant proposal and a two- to three-page executive summary. My question is, "Well, do you want to just sit there and read the executive summary and decide on the basis of that without reading all of the grant proposal?"

[The conversation returned to the influence of the private, chain-operated hospital that also serves the patient population of the Sapphire Valley. Harris repeated her comment that LifeCare's policies rubbed some people the wrong way, but she wondered just who was responsible for that.]

Is that the fault of the local management, or is it the fault of LifeCare's head office? It's just like the feds trying to direct us here. They're too far away, they don't know the situation, and they don't know the people and how they feel. In a way, you know they have to do that. They've had to become more cost-effective. And they have to collect all that money. The feds are requiring *us* to collect money, too.

It's a delicate balance. The feds want us to become more competitive, but we are here to serve our board. That is the main reason we're here. Yes, we can become more competitive, more cost-conscientious. But you still have to serve the board. And be sympathetic to people not being able to pay.

Those doctors down there in Clarkville are more money-oriented than people-oriented. But *we* are becoming a little more money-oriented, too, just in order to survive. And I can't disagree with that, either. We're not here to throw money away. We're here to serve the people.

(F.P.—1987)

"And Then This Community Loses a Resource"

Harvey Dickens* is the executive director of the Clarkville hospital operated by LifeCare. He is a young man with a ready sense of humor who sees his hospital as only one element in the total picture of health care. Dickens also sees competition taking an increasing and healthy role in this broad approach.

Like Harris, Dickens spends a lot of his time and resources dealing with the government. This might be expected in the case of the clinics funded directly by Washington, but not in the case of a private hospital. As it turns out, this facility is closely regulated. Many of LifeCare's patients are covered by Medicare, which uses what it calls a Prospective Payment System (PPS) to determine how many days of treatment will be covered for a specific diagnosis.

Dickens spoke in his small but comfortable office behind the admitting room at the hospital.

Nowadays we'd think twice about starting rural hospitals. But I think this one has been a good one over time. Our occupancy is higher than the company average, and higher than the national average.

I would say that the greatest change agent in health care today is government. The federal government, with the Prospective Payment System, obviously has done a lot to change the way health care is delivered. What they pay for is a procedure or a diagnosis. Through some studies, they have come up with what they figure is the amount of resources utilized to take care of that particular diagnosis or procedure, and therefore that is what they're going to pay you. This is for the federal patients, the Medicare patients. Then if the hospital can treat that patient while utilizing *less* resources, then the hospital pockets the difference. If they use more resources, then they lose.

Well, as a part of that same law, in order to police this activity, they instituted what we call a Peer Review Organization—a PRO—and those usually are provider-driven, that is, by physicians. A contract is given by the Health Care Financing Administration [an agency of DHHS] to the PRO to come in and look and see how the program's functioning.

If in fact they fear—retroactively—that a case was not appropriate for inpatient care, then they will deny that admission. And once they deny the admission, then the hospital eats that amount.

Obviously that's created a change in medical practice. In addition, they now are looking into whether you're letting out a patient too early because you want to circumvent the PPS regulation. In other words, the patient would normally be in for five days and utilize the resources for five days, but *you're* getting him out in three days because you want to pocket the difference between what the payment is and what resources you utilized.

One of the ways the peer-group review looks at whether we did a good-quality job is what we call a readmission. If a readmission happens within a certain period of time, that admission can be considered to be invalid because the patient was not well upon discharge. What's happened in the past is a physician would look at a patient who came in with pneumonia, say, and give him a course of antibiotics, and after five days in the hospital, if the patient is now afebrile [without fever], looks like he is doing fine, we'll discharge him.

But now we're saying, wait a minute: if that patient is admitted for another pneumonia within seven days, or whatever that period of time is, the Peer Review Organization is going to ask, "Why didn't you take an X-ray?"

So now the practice of care changes. Instead of the patient being in for five days, we wait until we get a clear X-ray. So all of a sudden now, we are going in just the opposite direction from getting the patient out as quickly as possible. But the problem is, I'm the one that's eating it; the prospective payment doesn't change.

I don't know if that's good or bad or whatever. But I *do* know that the Prospective Payment System is saying, "We think that X amount of resources should be expended in five days," and now I've got a patient staying here seven days purely because Medicare is saying, "We don't want to have that patient discharged prematurely and coming back to your hospital." I *do* know that practice is changing so that the patient stays in two days longer, we shoot more X-rays, and all of a sudden we expend more resources on the patient. And that almost ensures that I'm going to lose money on that patient.

Medicare is supposedly trying to reduce utilization in order to reduce the money they pay, but because of the way the physician is being reviewed, it can sometimes change practice back to increasing length of stay and increasing the amount of resources we use on a patient. And all they've done is cut my bottom line and cause me to have increased expenses, and yet get no payment for it. And, as you can see, that can bother someone!

I haven't even gotten to Medicaid yet. Medicaid is a very sore subject with hospital administrators in this particular state. We have two problems. One, the state has always had a problem figuring out which accounts they're really responsible for and which they're not. We go through this time and time again. And the other problem is collecting.

Just in round numbers, I know that we have an accounts-receivable allowance for Medicaid that is past 180 days old of approximately $500,000. It's just exasperating to me to have Medicaid—a federal-state program—tell you, "We just don't have the money to pay you." It's just hard for me to understand that.

Some of our income is from the commercial payers—Aetna, Traveler's Insurance, perhaps the United Mine Workers. Blue Cross pays a little. Not very many people pay out of their own pockets.

Like I say, this is a community hospital. Some people can't pay right away. Sure, we've got accounts-receivable policies, and we follow them. But we try to respond to all the needs. If a guy comes in here and he has a procedure done and it's $1,000 or $500, and he can pay $10 a month, we'll accept that. We'll try to work with anybody. Because we know there are people out here who don't have jobs.

[Dickens was asked about Margaret Harris's comment that LifeCare aggressively pursued patients who hadn't paid their bills.]

I will never stand back and say that good business practice is not going to be followed. We're going to try to get the money up front. If people don't pay, yes, we will put them through some sort of system where they will be called and they'll get letters. To me, that's just good business. If I took my car downtown to get it fixed, they'd do exactly the same thing to me if I didn't pay. And I'd expect them to do that.

I wouldn't say that people here aren't used to that way of thinking. They're used to it from everybody else. It's not unusual for Sears to do it. It's that people have always had the feeling that since it's health care, it should be different. Because, after all, I *need* it. I go to Sears because it's my pleasure: I *want* to buy that coat. I don't *need* to buy the coat. And sure, I know I don't have enough money, but maybe by the time the bill comes, I'll have it. If I don't, I'll try to pay it a bit at a time.

I think when you come to the emergency room, you're probably not in that frame of mind. That's probably what makes it a little different. We're going to work with people the very best we can. But we're going to do a good business. Because in a time of limited resources, you cannot *not* do that. You've got to make those efforts. Because if you don't, then you go under. And then this community loses a resource that is a very important one. If you don't have good business practice, then you're not going to have a hospital.

(F.P.—1987)

In President Harry Truman's day, national health insurance was a controversial subject of lively debate. As Truman had pressed for the Full Employment Bill and had lost, seeing it shrunk to the toothless Employment Act of 1946, so he also strove for national health insurance, and lost.

As a result of that defeat, because something had to be done, the labor unions took the case into collective bargaining. Over the next two or three decades, they negotiated employer-financed health care. What they achieved was matched for non-union employees in many establishments. The result is a multitude of plans that until very recently seemed to grow and grow in cost. If they didn't lift Americans to the best health care in the world, they did help assure the most costly. And because these plans are funded by business, the costs of health care are ultimately paid for through higher prices, and not through taxes (except indirectly).[1] Thus health-care costs have become a highly significant factor in America's competitiveness with other economies.

Under President Johnson's leadership, Medicare and Medicaid were enacted—the one to cover the aged, who could no longer benefit from workplace plans, and the other to cover the impoverished. But up to 35 million people have no coverage at all, mainly because they work for small employers, who provide no coverage, or are small farmers or farmworkers.

What should be done for them, and for the poor and near-poor generally? The War on Poverty also initiated the direct provision of medical service through community-based centers. Mud Creek Health Services in Kentucky and Sapphire Valley Health Clinics in West Viriginia are examples. Only a few were ever begun, and fewer still linger on. Though these examples are all in rural areas, others were set up, and a number

---

1. Employer-provided health and retirement plans are part of the cost of doing business. As such, they are shaped within the context of other economic factors, including taxation. Analysts have not yet sorted out the probable effects of health costs on taxes, especially in light of the Tax Reform Act of 1986. It might be pointed out also that many economists hold that such benefits don't supplement wages but replace them—that is, without them, wages would have risen to the level of the cash value of benefits plus present wages.

still flourish, in cities as well—for example the two-decades-old Comprehensive Family Care Center in the Bronx. These clinics are a better way of serving the poor than through subsidizing private practitioners—the usual method of Medicaid. The following is the story of another, larger such clinic.

"A Right and Not a Privilege"

The Jackson-Hinds Comprehensive Health Center in Jackson, Mississippi, treats more than simply diseases, infirmities, and injuries. It believes that health problems and the things that cause them are inseparable. It directly confronts threatening environments as they affect health, while delivering care to thousands of the poor in Jackson and the rest of Hinds County.

In 1974, several practicing physicians and other interested people in the area submitted a funding proposal to the old Office of Economic Opportunity for a comprehensive health center. The funding was granted, despite resistance to the project from two successive governors. Subsequent funding—directly from the Department of Health, Education and Welfare (now DHHS)—also circumvented state approval power. Thus this residual deposit of the old War on Poverty stays at its post.

Today, in modern, well-equipped facilities, the center provides dental and medical services that include family practice, pediatrics, psychiatry, and gynecology, augmented by social services, nutrition counseling, health education, and a transportation system that provides round-trip service for more than 150 people a day. The center's unique environmental program eliminates health hazards in and around homes, by such elementary means as building sanitary pit privies, correcting fire hazards, providing safe water, and controlling rats and roaches.

Dr. Geraldine Buie-Chaney, director of Pediatric Services at the center, was herself one of nine children from a poor family in Meridian, Mississippi. While attending Tougaloo College on scholarship, she decided to enter medicine, graduated in 1977, and in 1981 became the third black to complete the pediatrics residency at the University of Mississippi's medical school (the first was Dr. Aaron Shirley, the center's director).

Chaney was determined to practice medicine in her home state, although she could have secured a more lucrative practice elsewhere. "If I was going to infiltrate the system and do something about improving it, I had to be a part of it." As president of the Mississippi Medical and Surgical Association (state arm of the predominantly black National Medical Association), she has sought to improve the ratio of black doctors to white in Mississippi, now only 130 to 2,300, because the state's indigent-health-care problem is disproportionately a black problem.

It has been nearly ten years since I was a physician at the Cary Christian Center near Rolling Forks, Mississippi, but I still remember treating the family of a tenant farmer living on a rice paddy up there in the Delta. I visited them about twice a month. None of the seven children—the oldest was thirteen—had ever been to school, because no bus went out that far and they had no transportation of their own.

They lived in a shotgun house with no windows, no electricity, no running water. They had to walk a mile to the well to get drinking water. And to wash their clothes, they drew water from a creek that ran in back of their house. Their baby suffered terrible diarrhea because of worms and amoebic dysentery. As tenant farmers, they were paid for the rice crop they harvested. But by the time they repaid the plantation owner for all the money they had borrowed to live off of the year before, they had very little left and they had to reborrow.

Because the mother and father in this family were married, they were ineligible for Medicaid. [This is the case in Mississippi and the other score and more states that deny welfare to two-parent families.] When necessary, the kids' uncle picked them up in his truck and brought them to us for health care, because we saw patients whether or not they had money. Those children were in and out of our clinic constantly, always with some kind of infection—intestinal, chronic ear infection, or whatever.

Today, we have several families similarly situated in rural Hinds County, near the state's capital and largest city. Last winter, for example, we discovered one of our families living in an unheated rental home. The first time I visited, the kids had to walk around a great big hole in the porch to enter the house. Their clothes were piled up in a corner, because they had no closets. Cots were everywhere in the sleeping room shared by seven kids, ages three to thirteen, and their grandmother. They had very little food and sparse clothing, and could not afford home repairs such as screens on the front door. Flies were everywhere. The family, it almost goes without saying, had no health-care insurance. The grandmother was afraid to apply for welfare, because she was seventy years old and feared that her grandchildren, who were the children of two teenaged mothers living out of state and several fathers, would be taken from her. I believe she now is getting assistance.

In recent years, health care for indigent families like these has become a critical issue, especially in Mississippi, which has the lowest per-capita income and one of the lowest educational levels of any state in the nation. Some 24 percent of Mississippians live below the federal poverty level. In 1980, 32.5 percent of Mississippi households had incomes of less than $7,500, and 65 percent had incomes of less than $16,000. Furthermore, about 800,000 Mississippians, or nearly a third of our state's 2.5 million citizens, had no form of public or private health insurance. A fourth of our people are illiterate. To compound the problems, Mississippi's unemployment rate remains consistently higher than the national average, which means more uninsured persons, most of whom are ineligible for Medicaid.

As the major insurance source for the poor, including children and pregnant women, Medicaid has been unable to cover this population adequately. This is primarily due to its link to AFDC [Aid for Families with Dependent Children] eligibility requirements, which in Mississippi sets the standard of need at 30 percent of the federal poverty level.

Except for the elderly and disabled, and those few two-parent families covered for limited services under the Optional Categorically Needy Program, Medicaid coverage is available only for AFDC recipients. [Some states extend coverage to people who, for one reason or another, do not receive AFDC or Supplemental Security Income but who meet the income requirements for one of those programs.] Consequently, many of Mississippi's poorest, particularly the married poor, are not covered for basic medical services. In this state, less than 30 percent of those whose income is below the federal poverty level are eligible for Medicaid, compared to more than 50 percent for the United States as a whole.

I'm reminded of one old man who recently called the clinic, complaining of shortness of breath and chest pains. He had a history of congestive heart failure.

He said: "Dr. Chaney, I'm real sick."

I said: "Why don't you come into the clinic?"

He said: "Well ma'am, I'm on Medicaid, and they tell me that I can only have twelve visits a year to the doctor and I can only get four prescriptions each month. I've had my twelve visits to the doctor and I can't come in, because I don't have any money."

I said: "The twelve visits don't matter to us. You just come on to the clinic."

He said: "That's awfully nice of you, ma'am, because this reminds me of way back when they used to have the master over the plantation. He used to tell us when we could go to the doctor. It seems like to me that this Medicaid and this welfare stuff is just like that. They tell us when we can eat and when we can go to the doctor."

This old man articulates some of the problems afflicting the elderly in general. They find it most difficult to obtain the services that Medicare and Medicaid do not cover, services such as preventive checkups, outpatient medication, and institutional long-term care. Unfortunately the Reagan administration has cut back on many home-care services, including speech therapy, occupational therapy, and social-work services. Medicaid is therefore not well suited for the health problems of the older population, and our fastest-growing population, the seventy-five-plus, has the greatest need because it is the most frail. At present, 43 percent of the Medicaid budget goes to nursing homes for the elderly—that is, 43 percent goes to about five percent of the population. What Mississippi needs is an alternative system that is more comprehensive but not as expensive, a long-term care policy that keeps people at home as long as possible and seeks to maintain a reasonable quality of life through their last days. We need to define long-term care not just as institutional care but a combination of advanced home care and institutional services. I would estimate that perhaps 30 percent of the nursing-home population does not need to be there.

Access to quality health care is a right and not a privilege, and it is government's responsibility to ensure that access. Unfortunately, Mississippi, unlike richer states, simply does not have the resources to underwrite health care for all of its indigent citizens. After squeezing the maximum health care yield from our limited resources, we are still obliged to seek assistance from the federal government. If that assistance is not granted, then thousands of indignant Mississippians are doomed to suffer, at best, an impaired quality of life or, at worst, an untimely death.

(A.P.—1986)

SOCIAL SECURITY

The next two vignettes deal with by far the largest plank in the social-welfare system: Old Age and Survivor Insurance, more commonly called simply Social Security. About half of the social-welfare expenditure goes to this program, which serves about a sixth of the population. When Medicare is added on, the two programs together take about three-fourths of social-welfare costs. Since 1970, federal spending for OASI, when adjusted for inflation, has risen by more than half, and for Medicare has more than doubled. The next largest program is Medicaid, which costs less than half as much as Medicare. Although it is medical assistance for the poor, the money actually goes to the providers: doctors, hospitals, clinics, drug companies, pharmacies. OASI and Medicare tilt in some respects toward their low-income participants, though they still exclude some of the poor; they tilt in other ways toward higher-income participants. Nevertheless, they are the most nearly universal programs we have. Like public education, they come close to the true meaning of a "welfare state": entitlement to necessary services and assistance solely because one is a member of the society.

Four current debates about Social Security are touched on in the two following vignettes:

- The perceived adequacy of its financing.
- The supposed dispute between generations—that is, be-

tween current workers, who pay the taxes that provide the benefits, and retirees, who receive those benefits.

■ The notion that those benefits should be indexed to inflation (welfare benefits such as AFDC are not).

■ The question of taxing benefits if a recipient's income is high.

Current estimates are that the OASI Fund is sound and in fact will increase to astronomical size until the early years of the next century—the year 2016 is the best guess. Then the retirement of the baby-boom generation will drive it down precipitously over the ensuing two decades. Medicare's Part A fund—which covers hospital and certain followup care—is more shaky, but expected to be sound for fifteen or twenty years. Medicare Part B, which is mainly for physicians' services out of hospitals, is paid for by monthly premiums from those who choose it, supplemented by general revenues of the government. Unlike Medicaid, both are administered by the federal government.

Because this book's primary subject is those living below the American "standard of living," it can only take note of the United States's unique mix of public and private pension and health plans. It provides a comfortable aging for millions of the middle class, including union members. The private plans have played a very substantial role in reducing the poverty rate among the aged by more than half during the past two decades. That has been the clearest triumph of American welfare.

But about 12 percent of those over sixty-five are still below the poverty line; private pensions are no preventive against layoffs (as the lumber workers of the next chapter illustrate); and some 35 million Americans (and the number is thought to be growing) have no health coverage at all, not even Medicaid. Congress has been considering several approaches for those covered by no health plan, most of which would require employers, even at very small firms, to insure their employees. Apparently Congress prefers to expand the private system under governmental regulation, having the costs paid for through higher prices, rather than expanding the public system financed by taxes. As my remarks earlier in the chapter indicate, I doubt that in the long run that is the better road.

The next two interviewees represent widely diverging evaluations of the Society Security system.

"Social Security Is a Sinkhole into Which I Pour Money"

When Vincent Matthews* attended an Ivy League school late in the 1960s, he was in the middle of the flower-child generation. Matthews, the son of two physicians and grandson of an Italian immigrant, took education seriously. He earned an undergraduate degree in psychology, a master's in international development, and a doctorate in something called general systems research, an interdisciplinary degree. His training was so broad that later, over a ten-year period, he taught psychology, sociology, and anthropology to members of the military and foreign services in countries around the world. The government-sponsored classes ran for two months each.

Matthews made an important discovery while he was an undergraduate: "He who understands and can manipulate certain pieces of technology has power relative to other individuals." What Matthews then owned was a public-address system. "I looked around at the context of the sixties," he explained recently, "and I said, 'This is an era when he who has an amplification system for the voice is able to address social issues.' I shut my university down when Nixon invaded Cambodia."

Matthews is now twenty years older, but he is still manipulating technology. With his wife, the entrepreneur operates a clearing house in Boston that links buyers and sellers of used computer equipment. It is a successful and growing enterprise. The Matthewses also are becoming active in real-estate investing. There are nine employees in the firm.

Matthews has strong feelings about the social-welfare systems, and about Social Security in particular. He believes they work against self-reliance and are inadequate for the challenges that face them. Social Security, he feels, is doomed. Matthews's thoughts are nurtured primarily by his experience as a small-businessman who started from scratch.

He is particularly sensitive to the benefits—which he likes to call services—that he is expected to provide for his employees, even on those occasions when, he says, they contribute little to the business.

Back in the sixties, I was an activist. But now I find myself much more becoming a pull-yourself-up-by-your-bootstraps, it's-a-lot-of-hard-work, do-it-yourself person. For me that's a very radical transition. That doesn't mean I've become heartless. As a society we have an obligation to people to help them when disaster strikes. But at the same time, I find myself more and more thinking, "Are we teaching people a kind of learned helplessness?"

If we provide a lot of services for people, they learn to be helpless. And this strikes me as being the real challenge of this era: to provide services to the individuals who have desperate situations so we can allow them to get out of those situations, but not to provide so much service to the destitute that they learn to stay destitute.

My concern is that the system runs the risk of covertly teaching people to come to expect that society will provide a great deal for them with a minimum amount of effort on their part. And I find myself in conflict over this. I'm a radical of the sixties who's been hardened by the realities of having to run my own operations. Nobody, but nobody, comes along to make it easy for me to provide services [benefits] for *me*, let alone for my employees, let alone for people who extend beyond my group of employees.

I find myself now hiring people, and they show up expecting remarkably high levels of service. They've got a job and now they suddenly expect that all kinds of services will accrue to them simply by the fact that I exist and have given them a job.

Now, I'm a *liberal*. I believe society ought to take care of its people. But at the same time, I look around and say, "My God, there's got to be a way we can have them learn the relationship between the effort they expend every day and the services they receive every day."

I look at the world this way: Every day you've got a kind of balance between how much effort you put out and how much you receive back. My worry at the moment is that American society and its information culture have created a belief that "I have a minimum level of service due me by society. I'm *entitled* to this. It grows out of my civil rights, my social rights, my birthrights." In point of fact, in order to cover the costs of my own minimum daily resources, I have to create some utility in the world. I have to be putting it out in order to get it back in again, or the system goes into deficit spending. I think this is what's happened to our country on the whole. We've been operating not just at the governmental level in deficit spending; I think we're running as individuals on a deficit level, and we've been doing it for a long time. I don't think the average American produces as much utility in terms of what he *does* productively on a given day as he consumes in resources.

As for Social Security, I know something about that firsthand. My mother collects Social Security. I can look at her example and say, "This person, as a medical doctor, produced over the course of a lifetime a certain amount of utility to people, in the form of medical care. She socked away some bucks in the form of Social Security payments over the course of a lifetime of providing the service, and now is entitled to collect back on that."

But when you add in cost-of-living indexes, what you put in and what you pull out are no longer equal. All of the people I know who collect Social Security don't need it. This is my personal community of individuals—I can't speak for the whole system—but I certainly see a lot of people who are collecting a thousand dollars a month from the Social Security system who have a few hundred thousand in the bank and other investments and could live on interest and dividends. They are certainly entitled to something back. If they put it in, they're entitled to it back. Whether they're entitled to it back multiplied by ten times because the cost of living index has gone up ten times is a harder one for me to answer.

I think a society can't support that eternally. As I see Social Security structured, it will eventually crash. It's going to crash when the baby-boom generation hits sixty-five and the tiny population that's behind them is trying to support this massive number of what I expect to be perfectly able and perfectly adept sixty-five-year-olds. These people are health maniacs. They are probably going to be the healthiest sixty-five-year-olds in history, and they're probably going to live to be ninety. So a very small population is going to have to support them for a long time.

In my case, I have assumed for the last decade that the Social Security system is incompetent to handle my level of need. I've become accustomed to working hard and earning a standard of living that the system simply could not handle. I assume Social Security will be bankrupt by the time I'm sixty-five. I expect that even if it still exists, it will pare back its services to such a level that they will essentially be of no value to me—nice pocket change.

I assume Social Security is a sinkhole into which I pour money. Most of it goes to my mom, so I don't mind. What I put in every month is about what she collects every month, so I consider that my payment to my parent. And that gives me some mental relief.

I pay FICA taxes on my income, and I match the tax of my employees. [Taxes paid under the Federal Insurance Contributions Act which are generally spoken of as Social Security taxes, are paid in full by self-employed people such as Vincent Matthews; employers contribute half of the FICA payments of their workers.] When I think that that money I'm putting into FICA is not actually going into a long-term annuity for me but is actually being used to pay out current Social Security checks to current recipients—when *all* of the people I know personally who receive Social Security don't need it—it strikes me, a businessman trying to make a successful business happen, as unfair.

I'd kiss the Social Security system good-bye in a minute if I could. I would pull out my funds that are going into it, and I would declare that as an individual I simply choose not to have it. I'd run the risk of being destitute as an old man. I don't think it's possible to arrange it that way, though, because there would be lots of people who, given the fortunes of life, would choose out now and be destitute later and would come around then saying, "Can't I get back in again?"

So if I'm convinced that the system's going to go bankrupt, what am I doing for myself for old age?

I'm an entrepreneur; my objective is to build a financial enterprise of large proportions that has enough utility that it's generating to a community of users so that the business itself has value greatly in excess even of my wildest dreams of financial return. That is one plan.

I am also concurrently executing a series of transactions in the real-estate market. We're buying downtown buildings, city buildings that are in miserable condition, and upgrading them. I'm making them into valuable, workable space. And either of these two plans has enough room for me to create enough utility that I will be able to enjoy the long-term financial return on that effort.

I don't have an Indivdudal Retirement Account, and I don't have a Keogh plan. And I haven't paid an income tax in a long time, because I keep rolling over anything that looks like income into something like real estate. I don't play with tax shelters. I don't even have a savings account in a bank. I have an interest-bearing checking account and a couple thousand dollars in stocks.

If I were setting up a Social Security system from scratch, it would be based on an education principle—on teaching people about how their work and their utility produce value. And I certainly would want to have a level of effort tied into the Social Security system. Recipients should do something. I don't think anybody should be paid to be idle. *I* wouldn't want to hit sixty-five and have somebody say, "Here's your check; don't do anything ever again." That's a *fantastic* waste of human resources! I would much prefer for the system to say, "After you put in a modest number of hours of volunteer work in a hospital, your Social Security check arrives. And if you're destitute and can't do twenty hours of volunteer work in a hospital, then you can apply for the next level. You sign a waiver that says you're destitute."

I don't know anybody who can't make himself or herself productively useful. There are museums in the city of Boston where whole wings are shut because there's an inadequate supply of paid working guards. And that's immoral. That shouldn't happen. Schoolchildren should be able to walk through those sections of the museum with tour guides or museum workers who are there on a voluntary basis. There's no reason why a guy who's seventy, on a cane, can't sit in a chair in a corner and be a museum guard. He'd actually talk about what a good time he had.

As for the social-welfare system in general, I think we need to provide a financial incentive to people. There's a classic example right here in Massachusetts of what happens when you do that, and it has to do with homeless, bottom-of-line folks. The state of Massachusetts instituted a bottle bill which put a nickel bounty on every can in the state. Now there isn't a single can in the streets. It's normal to see a street bum, dirty and unkempt, walking from trash can to trash can, scouring the street, carrying his plastic bag full of deposit cans.

Now, the fellow's probably going to go out and buy a bottle of wine with the money he gets from those cans. That's unfortunate; that's another whole issue. But the point is, declaring that in this trash there is a bounty is all it takes for somebody to say, "I'm going to go collect that." And the net result of that, from the system's viewpoint, is that we hired all the bums at a nickel a can to go clean up the streets.

It could work in a number of other areas. How do we put bounties on clean subway cars? And how do we put bounties on picking up discarded newspapers? And on and on and on. It suddenly raises the question, "How many other places can I put a social-welfare system together in which the individual who is performing work is rewarded directly for the work, and he is not being hired by a tax-dependent system?" I think the opportunities there are absolutely boundless.

I really don't believe that any person I have ever met truly feels that he or she is happy receiving money for nothing. My reaction to most government-organized projects is that they teach you how to work with the bureaucracy more than how to solve a problem. I do believe that people who are dissatisfied with the dole would look for alternatives.

Being flat broke and unemployed is an ideal condition for producing entrepreneurship. That's when I started my business. It was like, nobody was going to hire me, so I had to hire myself.

I think it's harder and harder for people who've worked for their own money to be sympathetic with people who aren't working for their own money. From nothing, I pulled a business. It's possible to hard-work your way out of nowhere. Of course, if you haven't got the raw materials to create an enterprise out of nothing, you end up still with nothing. There's no question in my mind that the fact that I had a doctoral degree and a lot of fortunate educational background is a necessary ingredient for the success of pulling myself out of nowhere.

So my conclusion out of all that is that I shouldn't be doling funds out, but I should be encouraging people to educate themselves to prepare themselves for the hard work of being a human. My heart goes out to people who are destitute. My response to the destitution is, "Start working. Stand up and let's go. If you need a hand standing up, I'll help you stand up. If you want a push in the direction of where there's work to be done, or if you want some advice about where there's some work to be done, I can help you. But don't sit in the rocker on the front porch and grouse about how bad things are. I'm sorry. It's too bad. Life is a bitch."

(F.P.—1986)

"Social Security Was Established as a Contract"

Harold and Rose Rubenstein* retired to Florida in 1972, making a home for themselves in a sprawling condominium in a sleepy community that stretches in the shade of Fort Lauderdale.

Heart trouble slowed Harold down in his midfifties, but he remains, at sixty-nine, a man of great energy, constantly pushing his political beliefs as a city councilman. In 1984, he was a Mondale delegate at the Democratic National Convention. Rose paints and teaches painting to fellow retirees. She talks proudly of her son, a computer scientist at a state university in the North. And she talks sadly of a daughter lost in her teens to a boating accident.

Harold believes in hard work. He believes in education. And he believes in private enterprise. These are the doorways to opportunity in the America his grandfather adopted in 1915. That Rubenstein had brought Harold's father and mother, uncles and aunts, from Russia, escaping the oppression of Jews. Harold's father, like his father before him, worked as a lather on construction sites. This was no business for his son, he thought. Harold must go to college.

College was not to be. Before he finished Brooklyn Latin High School, Harold had determined to enter the food industry. It would break his parents' hearts, but in time, he believed, he would own his own business. He started as a short-order cook, went through a couple of jobs, and then bought his first business: blending and selling coffee, house to house.

He had to close down when the war came. He was drafted and sent to North Africa where he was injured fighting with the Forty-fifth Infantry against the Germans. After the war, under the GI bill, he studied food management. Within two years, he was directing the sale of 150,000 hot dogs a weekend as a short-order manager on Coney Island.

Harold was not content. He wanted to run his own show. So in 1956, he bought a small luncheonette next to a Catholic church in New York City and outsold his Italian rivals in an Italian neighborhood. "I gave them quality. I made them feel at home. And I made the customer feel important," he recalls. "You don't learn that at the Wharton School of Business. But that basically is what makes a business work."

After the luncheonette came a coffee shop in mid-Manhattan, then a stationery store, and, when he was slowed by health problems, lucrative stints selling office supplies for two large companies. Hard work held its rewards: Harold and Rose moved up. From Brooklyn to the Bronx to Mount Vernon to Scarsdale.

Today Harold and Rose draw $9,000 annually from Social Security and $6,000 more from his councilman's salary. The interest earned from their savings each year puts them, he says, a "little over" the $32,000 triggering point which makes their benefits subject to taxation. (In the first three years that benefits were taxed, beginning in 1984, $10.1 billion in revenues were generated for the Social Security trust fund.)

I always said I want to retire when I'm fifty-five. I used to see the retired people walking around with canes. And I said, what the hell kind of retirement is that? I want to have fun and enjoy it, go dancing, go running around. I want to have energy when I retire. I don't wanna retire to an old-age home.

So I worked hard toward retiring at fifty-five. I don't have a pension fund. I hadda set up my own pension fund, which was my savings. I worked very hard putting money in the bank, letting the interest compound.

And as luck would have it, I hadda retire when I was fifty-five anyway. Because I was so sick.

It was 1972. We were living in Scarsdale. I had been with my company for about a year and a half, and I'm one of the top five salesmen in the eastern division. They expected me to make twelve sales a month. I could do that in three days. It was unbelievable. I was making nearly $40,000 a year. But I was killing myself. It was stress.

One Sunday, I had a very bad pain. So I called the doctor up Monday morning. He told me I have to stop working. I got a bad heart condition. So I just quit.

That year Rose and I had taken a cruise down to Miami for the specific purpose of finding a place to buy for the winter. We put a deposit down on an apartment here. The place wasn't going to be ready until 1973.

When we got back from the trip, so much snow had fallen we couldn't get in the front door. It was terrible.

Rose said, "This is impossible. Let's get rid of the house." So I called the broker. I had no idea what the house would go for. I had paid about thirty-something.

He said, "I could get fifty-five for it."

"You could?"

He sold it immediately.

So I called down here and told them that I needed a place, not for seventy-three, but for seventy-two.

When we came down here, we had a chance of buying in a more affluent place. This salesman showed us one. You had to be a member of the tennis club. Turned me right off. He spoke to the wrong guy when he spoke to me. I don't like snobbery, showing off.

Even around here it's: "Meet my son the doctor." "Meet my son the lawyer." Nobody was ever a shoemaker. They were shoe manufacturers. Nobody owned part of a drugstore. They owned a chain of drugstores. I was the only one who said I was a hash slinger. And proud of it.

I went by my cousin's place yesterday. Luxury condominium. Probably worth $200,000, $250,000. I wouldn't pay ten cents for it. And driving a Cadillac don't impress me either, 'cause I don't like that kinda living. I'm a plain person. I like plain people.

This city is laid out very funny. Fort Lauderdale surrounds us. We're not a high-income city. Low- to middle-income. There are a lot of young families. Doing service work. Construction. Mechanics. Little businesses. I'd say about 45 percent of the population is retired.

As soon as I moved down here, I became active in the community. They wanted to make me president of the phase, or section, we moved into. I said, no, I'm interested more in getting the financial part set up properly. So I became the financial secretary. I set up the books. Instead of spending large sums on an outside management, we do a lot for ourselves on a voluntary basis.

After a while, I became president of the phase, president of the men's club. I just had so much time on my hands. Then I started going to city hall every week. One of the councilmen asked me to serve on the community development committee. It decides how to spend the federal money that filters down to the counties. I had been asked to run for the council. But I had turned it down. I was too young. I said when I'm sixty-five, I'll run. I kept my word. In eighty-three I ran. I was unopposed.

I've always thought of myself as a liberal fiscal conservative. I'm not a left-winger. And I'm not a right-winger. I'm middle-of-the-road. But, I'm a liberal. And I'm highly principled. I'm not bragging or confessing it. That's the way I am.

You would find that 90 percent of the people here would oppose any tax on Social Security on the grounds that they don't want to give up anything. I oppose it on principle alone. And the principle is that the government made a contract with me. We shook hands on it. The government said it was not going to touch Social Security. Now they're playing with it. That is very unfair.

You know, I've not yet run across one person who feels it's fair to tax any part of Social Security. Most people don't like it, because it costs them an extra two cents. It's taking some of their money. But, like I say, I stand on principle.

I wasn't asked if I wanted to go into Social Security. I wasn't given an option. I was told it was set aside for a specific thing—only. And that's why it should never be touched. It should be kept in a vault somewhere. It doesn't belong to the government. That money is *mine*. They were suppose to be holding it in good faith.

The government guaranteed COLA, the cost-of-living allowance.

When I said yes to Social Security, I had no choice. But the government said, "You can trust me! We're not going to hurt you." And they gave me a firm commitment that I would never have to worry about my Social Security. And they told me there would be an adjustment, an increase for the cost of living. I wouldn't have to worry about it. Now they not only tax part of Social Security depending on your income, they will hold back on my COLA.

Let's say you pay so much per month for your Medicare premium. That's fair. We should pay. It's an insurance program. Next year, the payment increases. But they give me a cost of living increase to cover it. That is fair. But then they say they're gonna hold back that COLA 'cause they're a little strapped for money. "We can't give you your money right now," they said. They did that to veterans and everybody else. I think they breached the Social Security contract. And if this were ordinary business, I could go ahead and sue for breach of contract.

I don't believe in ramming anything down people's throats. Look at private industry. Eastern Airlines. They said, "Look, we're going broke. We'll all be out of money unless you take a cut in certain benefits and pay until we're back on our feet." They gave the people a chance to say yes or no. Chrysler did that, too. A lot of 'em said no, and they left. But it worked out and they did ask the people.

Here in Florida, the legislators aren't voting whether to have a lottery or not. They're putting that on the referendum, and they'll let the *people* decide. The people will vote. It's the fair way. But the government never had a referendum on taxing benefits, establishing a floor, or anything else. They broke a contract without consulting with me, the taxpayer, first. That's my beef. Did they have a public hearing? Send me a questionnaire? Hell no. Simple as that.

Social Security was established as a contract. Neither the government nor I should abrogate it in any way unless by mutual agreement. It should not be done where only one party has an entire say in the matter.

The government, allegedly, is a public servant. The Congress is a public servant, allegedly. But they're not. I'm the servant. The taxpayer is the servant, because the government is telling us what to do without asking us.

I really don't lose that much to Social Security being taxed. I'm standing on principle. On rights. In dollars and cents the taxing doesn't stop me from going to the movies. But I'm still being victimized. And so is everyone else who has not been asked for their approval.

You know, I don't think it's fair to tax the interest people earn on their savings. Very early in life I was taught the value of savings. The importance of saving. And I scrimped to save. I went without a lot of luxuries to save. Instead of buying a Cadillac, I bought a Chevy so I could have money lying in the bank earning interest. I didn't work that hard so our savings could be taxed. That money was taxed the *first* time we earned it. Every penny I earned. If you tax the interest now, that's double taxation.

Taxing the interest on my savings does make a little difference. Like cutting down on donations to different causes. But it does not change the way I live, basically. I'm not giving up necessities. It doesn't stop me from getting a car. I just don't have any money to waste, because prices always keep going up.

I wouldn't even raise the floor on the level of taxation of Social Security. Again I stand on principle. Raising the floor means that you are saying people with more money can afford to have their Social Security taxed. That's discrimination. That's wrong.

Of course I've heard this business about Social Security funds being gone when the next generation reaches sixty-five. I think that's a scare tactic. That's just pure, pure bunk. The government needs to go where they created the trouble. Where they overspend. Where they mismanage.

In any good business—I don't care if you run a momma-and-poppa store or you run a multibillion-dollar corporation—the bottom line is proper management. With mismanagement, you have waste. You cut the waste, then you're running a tight ship and you got money for everything. And you can set your priorities in the right order.

Here we have the government building a debt that our grandchildren won't be able to pay the interest on. That's criminal. I think it's gross mismanagement. And if they could clean up one act alone—the Defense Department—that would be enough.

The government claims it must tax Social Security to get revenue in the trust fund. Ten billion so far? Why not get 100 billion by cutting the waste in defense?

I'm not against spending money on defense, mind you. I'm all for it. I'm against wasting money. That bothers me very much. And billions are wasted. Billions that could be used for something else.

I would put defense spending as one of the top priorities, if not the top. Our national security is our number-one concern. But that doesn't exuse funds being wasted, thrown away or stolen. I'm talking about the Defense Department paying hundreds of dollars for a screwdriver. That's criminal. That's sinful.

I just don't understand why the government is afraid to muscle the defense contractors. Why don't they put out the bids properly, give out the contracts properly, buy the right way, and save, save, save. They could save enough to pay for all the human services we need. To pay for all the social services Ronald Reagan cut out and then some. For education, job training, health. We could pay for everything from the waste in defense. Double everything.

But say that doesn't happen. Would I be willing to have my benefits taxed for any purpose? I think it would be worth it if the money went to education. It hurts me to know how much is needed for education that's lacking. I even believe that the lack of education monies indirectly harms the elderly. Where does much of the crime come from? Who preys on the elderly? Young people, dropouts. They don't have trades. So they turn to crime. If more of them could go to college, get vocational training, job training, then you would see a drop in crime.

And I believe in investing in education. For everyone. College-bound or not. Education built this nation, and education can protect its future.

The problem is I wouldn't trust those people in Washington to put the taxes off my benefits into education. I don't trust them. I know whereof I speak. I'm an elected official. I don't trust the government anymore. They lie.

They say the money they tax on Social Security is in the trust fund. Is that so? Have you seen it?

(W.T.—1987)

These should be stories enough to sketch in the policy lines the country now follows—and to suggest those it might take up to help those people who, because of age or infirmity, are now out of the labor market, or on its edges. Sarah Carter's story shows that it is sometimes possible to carry on a productive, independent life despite a severe handicap. Harold Rubenstein shows us a man plunging into community activities after retirement, and William Davies fills the pulpit of his country church despite a crippling disease. One of the old ideals of democracy was that society should assure that "careers are open to talents." That ideal should be always in our thoughts, but we should also remember that honoring it includes providing opportunities and encouraging work and service even for those from whom we expect none.

For the people at the waning of life and for the physically disadvantaged, the only real policy question has to do with society's will to meet its own standards of dignity and fairness. What would that principle suggest for the situations shown here? Our particular concern is for those in the lower income classes. A useful way to think about their needs is to imagine higher-income people in similar situations.

Consider Hank Rowan's difficulties. First he needs to be rid of the number of people coming at him from all directions, this one with cash, that one with food stamps, this one with pills, the other one with interrogations, and so on. The nation's social workers are on the whole a good lot. They know that a Hank Rowan should not be forced to beg for help from a maze of sources, and they know how much easier it would be if he had a single source of care, with service arranged according to a single plan. If Hank Rowan were a desperately ill banker, he would probably have enough private insurance to give him such ready, easily realizable care without having to suffer the indignities of negotiating our system. Maybe Hank Rowan wouldn't need the luxury of private doctors that the banker could afford, but he deserves to be able to get comfortable treatment from one source, with respect.

We would not object, in the matter of catastrophic illness, to providing the same care and service free to the banker as well. It is almost always worth paying such a price to avoid having another means test. Here and in other situations throughout this book, it would be well to consider using taxes as the equalizer in social welfare, not the means-testing of benefits. The cash value of care could be accurately calculated, and then added to the taxable income of those above a certain bracket, as is now done with Social Security.

Equally important is another principle: don't charge the victims of catastrophe, their spouses, or their families. If they have a few dollars or even if they have more than a few, let them use the money to add to the basic care offered—spending is, after all, thought to be good for the economy. Moreover, there can be no public interest in bankrupting families by forcing on them the high costs of American health care. Congress repeatedly debates and sets parameters for public spending for treatment of catastrophic illness and for care in nursing homes. What it has come up with are laws that can often require a person to make a pauper of himself before he can receive help. In no other western industrial country is that so. If the nation still wishes to shun national health insurance, can it not at the least make an exception for a catastrophe? The high costs are the results of the American way of preventing and caring for illness. And Americans freely choose to have it that way. But it is not fair to impose those costs on people who are beyond the capability of choice.

The difference in the way government assists those with kidney failure and those with black lung marks another aspect of American class bias. Kidney failure strikes rich, poor, and in-between alike; black lung happens only to coalminers—people usually hard up. Health care discriminates unfairly between the two, and only reinforces class differences. It shouldn't be like that. There is probably a case to be made, some years from now, for merging the black-lung program into the workmen's-compensation and Supplemental Security Income programs. But let it alone for now. Despite bureaucratic shenanigans, it does its job of sustaining the lives of many good men and their families, partially sustaining too the economies of many destitute mining communities. (This point is always worth remembering. Just as military expenditures sustain the economies of some communities, so the flow of dollars from welfare, Social Security, Medicare, Medicaid, and other social programs bolsters the economies of a number of our poorest areas.)

The Johnson years saw the growth of an infrastructure of institutions throughout the country, committed to the interests of the poor: clinics, legal services, co-ops for small farmers, community-development projects. In the intervening years, there has been little new growth, but some of the creations remain, scattered remnants of a good idea. Our society—Americans often say proudly—is powered by the pursuit of self-interest. The poor are ill-equipped to pursue their own interest aggressively, the aged and infirm poor least of all. The few clinics like those we visited, and legal-services projects like the Appalachian Research and Defense Fund, provide something more than a mere cash relationship between powerless people and their government. They are also effective ways for delivering other services the government has taken responsibility for, while tending to the personal interests of the recipients and treating them with dignity.

Social Security and Medicare are major pillars of the American welfare system. Undoing them not only is politically implausible but would also be economically disastrous to a nation that has by now incorporated them into its structure and its basic expectations. Improving them is always possible, and sometimes imperative if their financial underpinnings shake. An enormous surplus is building up now in the Social Security trust fund, and will continue to grow, as planned, until the early years of the next century, when demography indicates it will begin to be drawn down rapidly. More than likely, political debate will focus on the surplus before then, questioning whether it should not be drawn upon for other purposes. Obviously, that would be a momentous issue, and utmost caution is in order. One of the fundamental decisions made when Social Security was established in the 1930s was that it would be financed not out of general revenues but from trust funds built up through payroll taxes on workers and their employers. The rate of that tax and the income on which it is based are legitimate issues for argument. As now set up, it is a regressive tax; ceilings on the amount of income taxed effectively increase the rate at which lower-income people are taxed. Benefits received after retirement, however, tilt slightly in favor of lower-income people because of the way they are calculated and because high-income recipients now pay a tax on what they get.

It seems to me that Medicare, however, needs more than technical improvements. It is questionable in concept. In the first place, it forsakes what is and should be the guiding principle of all dealings by the federal government with individuals: impersonality. Social Security runs like a machine, with discretion held to a minimum; Medicare, by contrast, is shot through with administrative decision-making. In the second place, Medicare cements an invidious social distinction between classes of the elderly: between those who have it and those who don't, and between those who can and can't afford Part B. In the third place, Medicare embroils the federal government and the health professions in endless controversy. And finally, it forces onto the federal government an overriding preoccupation with spiraling costs rather than with quality of service. Medicare, like Medicaid, is a poor substitute for national health insurance, open to all, the same for all, keyed to accepted standards of adequacy.

Whatever the need from time to time for improvements or repairs, the basic way that Social Security is financed should not be disturbed, for it has formed a bond between the programs and the public that is important to the political health of the democracy. In the future, perhaps the views of Vincent Matthews will represent the majority. Today, however, the vast majority of people—especially low-income people—look upon Social Security as a dear and proudly held possession. Harold Rubenstein is right when he speaks of it as a perceived contract. I can imagine few if any changes of public policy that would be as disruptive of social stability as a weakening of the goverment's commitment to Social Security. Rubenstein's spirited defense of COLA—the indexing of benefits against inflation— is sound; most recipients have almost no control over the factors that affect the cost of living, and should be protected from its vicissitudes. (How the COLA is indexed, though—to prices, to wages, to a mixture of both, to median income—is a valid question meriting serious technical study.)

One reads with disgust the expensive newspaper ads decrying the budget deficit, taken out from time to time by large numbers of businessmen, laywers, and other prominent figures. Their prime target is Social Security—the fact that its benefits are only lightly taxed, and the fact that they are indexed—with no more than perfunctory complaints about Pentagon spending. Like our national political leadership, these economic leaders lack the courage (or desire) to challenge the sellers and buyers of weaponry, its fantastically costly spread around the world and into outer space, and the arrogant foreign-policy commitments that produce them.

I disagree with Rubenstein, however, about taxing, without being committed to any particular figures. Why should high-income retirees not pay something on their receipts? Taxation with progressivity is in order. But in the interest primarily of the poor, it is essential that the proceeds of that taxation go into strengthening the trust fund, and diminishing the need for future increases in the payroll tax. The Social Security system, as conceived by the planners of the New Deal, is a great civic bond. It may always stand in need of maintenance. But weakening the bond created by that act of marvelous statesmanship would also weaken the good order of this society.

CHAPTER THREE

A Just Entitlement:
THAT THERE
BE WORK

EARLIER I STATED my belief that the serious responses of public policy to poverty and dependence were either some form of guaranteed income for all or a guarantee of available jobs at decent pay. The odds against either being enacted are high. Both would be opposed on grounds of economics and politics. The second response, available jobs, would be more feasible to attain than adequate income transfers and would be the more ethically desirable of the two. This chapter will explore some of the effects of joblessness and some possible ways to increase the availability of work.

On the first Friday of every month, the Bureau of Labor Statistics (BLS) publishes what we think of as "the unemployment figures." These are its estimates of the number of people who were out of work the previous month and looking for work, based on a sample survey of households. This number, plus the estimated number of people employed, gives the total labor force; the official unemployment rate is a percentage of this total. But there is much more to know about the unemployment figures than simply each month's official rate. Here are six questions worth keeping in mind when you look at those figures:

- *What is the short-term trend of the unemployment rate?*
  Is it going down or up? At present it is going gradually
  downward, at least since late 1982. The unemployment
  rate has declined from nearly 10 percent six years ago to
  a little under 6 percent in early 1988.
- *Who do the figures includes—and who gets left out?* The
  BLS counts as employed anyone working, even if only an
  hour or so a week. It does not count as unemployed those
  not looking for work because they don't think they can
  find it. The bureau does publish estimates of the numbers
  of both these groups, calling the first group (those who
  want full-time work but can't find it) "part time for economic reasons" or "involuntary part time." The second
  group are called the "discouraged." The numbers in both
  groups declined in the mideighties, but as of January 1988,
  there were still nearly a million discouraged workers and
  over five million involuntary part-timers. Adding these
  people to the unemployed that month resulted in a so-
  called real rate of unemployment of 10.9 percent, as compared to the official rate of 5.8 percent.[1]
- *What are the variations around the country?* They shift
  constantly, with different regions faring better at different
  times. But it is hard to remember any time when unemployment was not severe in some large section of the
  country or another.
- *What are the variations by race, gender, and age?* Here
  the differences are extreme. Black unemployment usually
  runs two or two-and-a-half times that for whites, while
  Hispanics fall somewhere in between (in January 1988,
  the figures were 12.2 percent for blacks, 7.2 percent for
  Hispanics, and 5.1 percent for whites). Women's unemployment rates tend to be about the same as men's but
  their spells of unemployment tend to be longer—that is,
  it's harder for them to find new jobs. Unemployment of

---

1. This and other arcane matters wrapped into these statistics are well
   explained in an August 4, 1986, report from the House of Representatives' Committee on Government Operations, *Counting All the Jobless:
   Problems with the Official Unemployment Rate.*

white teenagers, ages sixteen to nineteen, runs nearly triple the general rate; for black teenagers, it is usually five times as high (officially it was 25.0 percent in January 1988; the real rate was 43.6 percent).

- *Are wage levels moving up or down?* Wages are virtually stagnant. Real wages, adjusted for inflation, have not improved since the early 1970s.
- *What has been the long-term trend?* Unemployment levels have slowly but gradually increased. The economy has ups and downs, with plateaus in between. Since World War II, the trend has been that after each downward period (or recession), unemployment does not decline all the way back to its prerecession rate. The result has been an inch-by-inch rise in the levels regarded as "normal."

One barrier to full employment is fear of inflation. So strong is that fear, and so accepted has become the conviction that the two things are causally connected, that some analysts have actually redefined their idea of full employment. "Full employment" has traditionally meant that every physically employable person wanting to work was doing so, allowing for the amount of unemployment inevitable at any time—"frictional unemployment," assumed to hold at around 2 percent of the work force—workers moving from one job to another, out of work for the season or other temporary pause, and the like.[2] The Full Employment and Balanced Growth Act of 1978 (the Humphrey-Hawkins Act) adopted an unemployment rate of 3 to 4 percent as a "medium-term" goal.

That law has since been ignored. Nowadays, full employment is often defined in relation to the level of unemployment

2. The Full Employment Bill of 1945 (S.380), which in emaciated form became the Employment Act of 1946, had defined full employment this way: "All Americans able to work and seeking work have the right to useful, remunerative, regular, and full-time employment, and it is the policy of the United States to assure the existence at all times of sufficient employment opportunities to enable all Americans who have finished their schooling and who do not have full-time housekeeping responsibilities freely to exercise this right" (section 26). So spoke an earlier era of liberal thought.

believed not to stimulate inflation. There is no unanimity, but the estimates for this tends to range from 5 to 7 percent. The old goal has been tacitly abandoned within the government, because inflation is regarded as worse than unemployment— worse, in fact, than almost anything.

No one likes inflation. It hurts nearly everybody. With un- employment, on the other hand, only a minority suffers di- rectly. All the democratic slogans—"majority rule," "greatest good for the greatest number"—seem to reinforce the econo- mists' current preferences. In light of this, it's worth looking at what the suffering means.

ARE THE UNEMPLOYED NEEDED?

"What Is He Got Forward to Look To?"

The troubled look, the whiskey-laced breath, the baritone voice angrily indicting a ubiquitous "they," all sum up the aura of hopelessness radiating from fifty-one-year-old Jimmy Morse.* His plight mirrors a larger crisis that, since 1979, has beset Gary, Indiana, and other cities on the southern tip of Lake Michigan. During that time, the region has lost some sixty- five thousand manufacturing jobs, including more than twelve thousand at US Steel's Gary Works, where Jimmy was once employed. Beginning in 1981, he was sporadically laid off for varying periods until 1983, when at forty-seven and with thirty years' seniority, he voluntarily retired rather than risk a firing that he feared was imminent.

Today, he is part of an unemployment crisis that has dev- astated the entire city. Because nearly one-fifth of Gary's work force is unemployed, the city's services have been drastically curtailed. Fortunately, unlike many in his shoes, Jimmy has not lost his home, a five-room frame house that he purchased in 1978. But he has no money for needed repairs. "I can't buy a nail," he says. "I got bright ideas, but they don't spend at the hardware store."

In ungrammatical but eloquent words, Jimmy talks about the hopelessness of his future.

My mother and father separated when I was about three months old. My father left us in Mississippi and came to Gary. School days there was limited to me, like maybe two months out of the year. I came to Gary so I could help my mother and help my own self.

When I got here, my father asked me, did I want to continue to go to school or go to work. I said I prefer goin' to work. If I had went to school, I would'a been somethin' like a couple years behind the other kids. I chose to go to work, because that's what I left home for. I worked in the canteen at the Gary Works. I got paid once a week with pure cash money in a little brown envelope. After taxes, I had $26 for forty hours' work.

When I got eighteen in 1953, I went in the mill as a laborer like everybody else. I worked hard for thirty years. The last two or three years the bottom was fallin' out of everything. They was lookin' hard at anybody with more than ten years' seniority. They was settin' us up to be fired. Like you didn't have no certain job. The man tell you do certain things that you know you not supposed to do: you go and do it or else. If you tell him, "Hey man, I'm not gon do it"— that's it! That's it right there! You got fired.

Only thing you could do is say, "Well, I'm gon' do it, but I'm workin' under protest. I will file a grievance." He'll tell you, "Gon' file a grievance." Anytime a man can tell you, "Go get your union man," that means you ain't got nothin' to back you up. The union's hands was tied. No more callin' on the phone talkin', "I can't make it to work." When things was nice, you could call up with two hours' notice. But that had never concerned me. I didn't have nothin' to do with that part. Now if you laid off, if your baby swallowed an open safety pin, wife slipped on some grease in the kitchen, you yourself was on the way to work and had a car wreck—whenever you come back to work you better make sure you got all your papers signed by somebody else. Otherwise, they'd fire you.

When they got ready to lay you off, they just put on the bulletin board NOT SCHEDULED NEXT WEEK. Then you go to the unemployment office and start signin' up. You might be signed up two or three months. One time I was out here a year and a half; that was when I was laid off in November 1981. That's when the bottom fell out of everything. I did get $141 a month unemployment [insurance] and $162 TA [Trade Adjustment Act Assistance].

Only thing saved me from rock bottom is, I been blessed by the Almighty to have my thirty years. Jes' think 'bout the peoples that was tryin' to do somethin' for they self, holdin' they jobs—younger peoples with only fifteen, seventeen years' seniority. They got nothin' comin'. I was jes' blessed that I was as old as I was and had stayed on the job. When the bottom fell outta everythin' like it is right now, I just accident had my thirty years.

When I came out of the mill on my retirement, I thanked the Lord that I got out before I got fired. I had to take what the company offered—take it or leave it. After I signed the papers, I stopped off at Mr. Lucky's Lounge. I bought about $42 worth of drinks. I said: "Hey! This is my retirement. Drink, boys, till it run out. Don't take nothin' wid ya now. Just drink!"

Since 1981, I been takin' the bitter with the sweet. What I do to keep from goin' stone crazy? I fish. When the mills started goin' bad in 1980, I went to the store and bought me some fishin' equipment. If I have good luck some days, I come back and sell the fish. The only thing I want is enough money to go back fishin' tomorrow. I might have a fish two feet long and tell somebody to give me two dollars. He got eight or twelve dollars worth of fish. He's happy and I'm sho' nuff happy, because the next mornin' at five I'm gon' fishin'. When the winter months come, what am I doin'? I'm sittin' up watchin' television. I have a $190 to $215 light bill and I gets $552.63 a month for my thirty years' service. Now, you get the light bill outta there. You get the water bill outta there. Buy some food outta that plus $131 we get in food stamps. You're about $40 short.

That $552.63 is no money considerin' the way that they charge you for everything. It's five of us here—wife, myself, and three boys. The one who is twenty-two is still here with me, because there's no jobs. The eighteen-year-old is in his last year in high school. Them basketball trophies over there belong to him. I enjoy watchin' him play basketball at Roosevelt High School. That helps me look toward another day, otherwise I might flip over, the way things are goin'. [His third son is fourteen.]

I'm glad that you can wear long hair now, because I don't even have to get it cut. I can go a year if I want to. My wife does her own hair and my eighteen-year-old son cuts his. I don't have money to do nothin' like I used to do. I can't afford to put clothes in the dry cleaners. I had to sell my 1974 Ford the other day for little or nothin'. You can't hardly do too much without a car.

I love to drink sociably. I don't go out in the street and fall down. I don't drink to forget all these troubles. I do the same amount of drinkin' that I did when I was workin'. I hope that I never come up with a problem that I jes' got to drink to forget it. I wouldn't want to get in that state where I jes' gotta go and get me a bottle. Where I'm going' then? I ain't goin' nowhere! I drink when I go fishin'. I take a bottle with me, if I got enough money, and wets my tongue. I don't try to drink no fifth in no thirty-five or forty minutes. I ain't interested in that. That don't concern me. My biggest hangup right now is the cigarettes. I'll light one cigarette with another cigarette.

I tried to find work. You get in your car and you drive in your area—we'll say twenty miles in radius—you drive to all these corporate employment offices. They got chain-link fences around them with a guard standin' there. The office is closed. If anybody can tell me right now where I could pick up an application lookin' for a job and they're hirin', I will be there. Instead of hirin', they're layin' off the people they got.

I can't move to another city either. I'm a family man. I'm not a drifter. I got kids here in school. I can't jes' reach and grab everything and go to another city. It doesn't make sense. You take your kids to another place, they got to get familiar with everything. They'll be two years back. My boy comin' out of school this year wants to do somethin' for himself. What is he got forward to look to? Not a thing, because it's nothin' gonna change here in the United States in the next twenty-five to thirty years. Who gon' send him to college? You can't get nothin' from the government. What's my son gonna do when he come outta school? He can't borrow nary a penny from the government.

I'm fifty-one years old now. I won't try to go to Chicago and let the man hire me makin' $3.75 an hour and I got to get back and forward to that job. I will not go to Chicago to put no application in at nobody's office. That's jes too doggone far [thirty-five miles]. If I went to Chicago and got a job, I'd be payin' nothin' but highway. At the end of the year I wouldn't accomplish $400. That's alright for young men like my sons. I'll tell them, any day the sun shines, go and try to get you a job. I'm fifty-one years old. I think I did enough in my younger days. Only thing now, I jes' think I need some help. I need the head man [President Reagan] to quit jazzin' around. If the head man would open up then everybody could breathe a little. But he got everything tight and steady pullin'. People gettin' laid off every day.

If the mills was to open up again, I'd be the first one to get me an application. Oh yeah! But I'm not goin' nowhere from Gary. And I'm not goin' to be standin' up on no corner waitin' for some sub-contractor that I ain't never seed before, come by and say: "Hey! I need five men. We gon' pour a basement today." I'm not gettin' in that line. That's for younger men. I look like a fool, jumpin' out there in the line. Let the man that ain't gettin' nothin' do somethin' for himself. I'm gettin' this little $552. Why would I cut off somebody that ain't gettin' nothin'?

I don't see very much hope for the future for me or my sons. I don't feel real sorry for myself. It hurts like heck, but I'm tryin' to get used to this. My forty-seven years was too young for a man to come out of the mills when he wants to work. I always wanted to keep me a car to ride in. I always wanted to be able to go to the store and buy what I wanted to eat and have ten or twelve dollars in my pocket when payday come. Or else I could go to a friend and say: "Hey man, let me have sixty dollars. We get paid next Wednesday." I can't go to nobody that I been knowin' ever since I been in Gary thirty-five years and say: "Hey man! Let me have seven dollars so I can go to the store and get a carton of cigarettes." I ain't got no friend that I can go to now and can't nobody get nothin' from me, because he can't help me and I can't help him.

I know I ain't gonna work no more in the mills, because it ain't no such thing as that anymore. Ain't but four or five departments workin' out there. You could play football on the parkin' lot. The country is in badder shape now than it ever been in my life. What is a depression if we not in one now?

I ain't caught nothin' but wax since Reagan been in there. I know President Carter signed for this foreign steel that's comin' in that made us start workin' down to two shifts and four to six hours a day when you supposed to be workin' eight. Foreign steel was takin' our man-hours away from us. And it ain't no racial thing either. That blue-eyed soul brother is catchin' jes' as much hell as I'm catchin'.

The government is breakin' his back, jes' like its done broke mine. Either you already got it or you ain't gon' get it. That's all!

I'm jes' livin' here in the United States. I got no power to voice myself or nothin'. We don't make steel for our own self anymore. Everything come over here. They got people overseas workin' for twelve and fourteen cents an hour. We might be over here makin' ten or twelve dollars an hour. Reagan, the boss man, gon' catch hisself right out in the middle of the ocean. He won't be able to take the stuff back and he can't bring it here, because can't nobody buy it. Ain't no jobs. I'd have a brand-new car sittin' out there in my driveway if I was workin'.

The people that would be buying brand-new cars to keep this country goin' is the ones that's laid off. The people that would be buyin' clothes to keep the cotton fields goin', the people that could be buyin' things, using things, them the ones that ain't got a buck. I can't see how Reagan figures he's pullin' the country up so fast. I haven't paid federal taxes in four years, but I used to pay as much as $2,500 a year. The government has lost all them taxes.

I don't think about gettin' in an elevator, riding way up to the thirty-fifth floor, get off, step on the landin', and jump. I don't think that way. That don't even cross my mind. I don't think about spinnin' my revolver around, lining up all the peoples in my house and cut down on them, then cut down on myself. I don't think like that. They'll have to get nineteen Mr. Presidents before I do that.

(A.P.—1986)

Moralizers have always been in the front ranks of social-welfare planning, never more so than now. Such people may disapprove of Jimmy Morse. He still wants his whiskey; he chain-smokes; protected by a modest pension—what contemporary critics would term a moral hazard—he refuses to relocate; and he won't work below his skills.

Others will see Jimmy Morse differently. Unschooled, because America did not school him. Unemployed after thirty years at the only work he ever learned—and at the age when other men are at the peak of their earning capacity. Owner of nothing, except a house on a particular street of a particular city where he is a familiar and his children are at least not strangers. And in his own way, capable of some quite respectable macroeconomic analysis.

Are the Jimmy Morses correct when they see no work ahead in their futures? And is it in the national interest that this should be so?

All over the industrial world, evidence grows that the economic machinery can run with fewer and fewer workers, especially blue-collar workers. It's hard to predict what the future, even the next decade or so, will bring, but quite obviously a new global economy is fashioning itself. It is fitting itself to scientific and technological changes, to the surge in entrepreneurship in a number of national economies and its slackening in some others, to a tidal wave of population growth, and to massive uprootings and consequent shiftings of populations. The restructuring is obvious, but the architecture of it is still too much to comprehend.

It may well be that the probability of the unexpected provides our only hope that more rather than fewer persons will matter in the production of goods and services. Perhaps military spending around the world will be substantially reduced, and capital and talents will be redirected toward rational, human use. On the other hand, the unexpected may just as likely be malign. I make my policy suggestions assuming that there will be no worldwide war, broad depression, or rebirth of 1960s-style social-activist movements.

Regardless of the future, it is important to hold as a firm principle, political as well as ethical, that the costs of change should not be paid disproportionately by those who can least afford it, as they are by the Jimmy Morses of the nation. That is unjust; it violates the social contract that underlies our nation.

Economists have fallen on a standard theme to justify this unfairness. Whenever the subject turns to jobs, toward looking out for the Jimmy Morses, the warning flag of inflation is waved. Later on, we shall have something to say about training and reemployment. First, however, we need to look at the economic argument.

Let us try to understand the public costs of unemployment.

There are the out-of-pocket costs to the Treasury and to state governments, principally unemployment insurance and increased welfare and Medicaid payments. These figures can be estimated, though they are bound to be quite speculative. That's because unemployment insurance is strictly limited to those previously employed, and that number fluctuates as the causes and nature of unemployment change (in 1987, for example, this insurance covered only about one-fourth of the officially unemployed). Furthermore, these costs are shared by employers and governments; the financial responsibility shifts among these institutions as Congress thinks urgency requires; some of the cost is taxed back from recipients. Nor can one be quite sure of the magnitude of unemployment's impact on welfare and Medicaid costs. Nevertheless, some plausible calculations are possible. A respected estimate is that a 1 percent rise or fall in unemployment costs or saves the government about $36 billion in aid payments. What governments lose or gain in taxes as unemployment fluctuates is also considerable.

Other costs are much more difficult to estimate, though there are those who try. These may very likely be far higher than direct dollar costs, and lay people, out of their own observations and experiences, may well be as qualified as social scientists to estimate the order of magnitude of the following:

- Lowered demand, because of lower purchasing power.
- The drag on other people's wages, as those with jobs face competition from the unemployed, who will of course work for less. Unemployment has always been a very effective means of wage control; therefore, it is anti-inflationary or even deflationary.
- The so-called social costs—crime, neighborhood deterioration, family disorganization—that often accompany joblessness. These intangible losses translate into added dollar costs of public services.
- The drop in the education and other training of children, as parents can no longer afford the investment. This is a cost to the economy that should not be underestimated.

Against costs like these, one could array others, such as:

- The direct governmental outlays for creating jobs and retraining workers.
- The growth of allegedly worthless jobs, created by the government to stem unemployment, which lead to a two-tier job market, with the "redundant" lower-tier workers (and the bureaucrats who manage them) locked out of economically "useful" upper-tier work.
- A general lowering of incentives as highly competitive conditions fade.
- An inflationary spiral of both wages and prices as a result of government-created or market-induced high employment.
- As a result of the above, the loss of the country's international competitiveness.

Let's say that all the concerns on both lists are valid. Where do they leave us, in weighing the costs of unemployment against the costs of an active employment policy? Is the presumed connection between inflation and employment levels real, or is it but another detour in the long search for a science of economics? It is interesting to note here that the Full Employment and Balanced Growth Act of 1978 is so permeated by fear of inflation that all of its full-employment goals are effectively subordinated—but the word *inflation* is not even used in the Employment Act of 1946. The closest it came is the broader term *purchasing power*. This is not to suggest that in the 1940s people were not worried about inflation; there had been price and wage controls during the war, and horror stories abounded about German inflation in the 1920s, commonly believed to have done a lot for the rise of the Nazis. The real difference, though, is that inflation and employment were not seen as so closely tied together then as we think of them today. And in fact, the United States had much less inflation—as well as less unemployment—in the 1950s and 1960s than later.

Some analysts have argued, on the other hand, that the inflation of the 1970s was caused by the boom in military expenditures that began under President Kennedy and has leapt upward with all his successors. That may be true. It is certain that there are many other causes of inflation, including ones that only partly and indirectly are affected by labor costs (such as import prices and the value of the dollar) and ones that have virtually nothing to do with domestic labor costs (such as foreign oil prices).

When factored for inflation, hourly earnings—and therefore disposable income—declined slightly in 1986 and 1987. Through lower labor costs, the working class is now shouldering much of the burden of defending other classes against inflation, as it has since Reagan came into office. Labor costs have not risen as much as consumer prices (nonlabor costs, such as interest rates and imports, have risen even faster than consumer prices), and this stagnancy may principally account for whatever productivity gains—"competitiveness"—the economy is experiencing. Executive salaries rise, legal fees and Wall Street commissions soar, and the spread between upper and lower incomes (and between levels of wealth) widens, as the gap between American workers' wages and those of foreign lands narrows. But to expect the United States to regain its "competitive" edge by wage competition with other countries, especially those of Asia, is chimerical; even were the United States to mobilize its unemployed (and even those regarded as "unemployable") into workfare or other means of depressing wages, there is probably no way the country can produce goods at labor costs as low as those elsewhere.

Therefore we cannot look to market forces alone to realize the goal of full employment at adequate wages. An active labor policy that at its core includes a readiness to create jobs is essential, both to provide enough jobs and to put a floor under wages.

IS FULL EMPLOYMENT POSSIBLE?

"The Sense of Person"

In another time, John Godfrey* would have been a hero to his country and to himself. Although badly wounded, he gallantly directed his men against enemy fire. He captured an enemy officer. And he won a clutch of medals for bravery. But John Godfrey went to the wrong war.

John was a big, gangly youth when he arrived in Vietnam in 1969 to join the Big Red One. Until then, nothing out of the ordinary had marked his first twenty years. His father, a printer, was replaced in the household by a stepfather who was a pharmacist. The family moved from Philadelphia to the suburbs, and John played second-string tackle on the suburban high-school team. When he graduated, he went to work for the FBI in Washington as a file clerk. Without a college degree, the job led nowhere. So he took a better paying job with the Chesapeake and Potomac Telephone Company at its nearby offices in Maryland. Then he was drafted.

The army trained him as a telephone-cable splicer, but when he got to the First Infantry headquarters at Dian, he was assigned to a rifle platoon. Thinking his chances for survival were better in reconnaissance, he volunteered for duty on the long-range reconnaissance patrol (LRRP).

One night, fifteen kilometers inside Cambodia, his team surprised a small enemy force, and John snatched an officer for interrogation. Another night he was not so lucky. His team was ambushed, and John was shot in the thigh and knee. When he came home, John was wearing three Bronze Stars for valor, a Purple Heart, and the Vietnamese Cross for Gallantry.

The America he found was bitterly divided over his war. No one embraced him. The right saw men like John as the first Americans to lose a war. To the left, men like John were losers of another kind, at best pawns, at worst killers.

He brought home no marketable skills. In time, the demons escaped his Pandora's box, and he was beset with guilt, anxiety, resentment, and depression. He could not hold his family. He could not hold his job. And he could not find peace.

His first marriage lasted two torturous years. His wife disappeared with their only child. She couldn't handle John, and John couldn't handle Vietnam.

He tried work in a chemical rosin factory. Then at the phone company in Jersey. At a Seven-Eleven convenience store. At a Woolworth's. At the fast-food joints. Ten jobs in ten years.

Until, in desperation, he visited the Vet Center in Philadelphia for readjustment counseling. John was diagnosed as suffering from posttraumatic stress disorder (PTSD) caused by exposure to catastrophic events in the war. And he qualified for training under the Veterans Administration's Vocational Rehabilitation, a program designed for veterans whose service-connected disabilities affect their ability to hold a job.

The Vet Center program, which struggles annually for Congressional authorization, has assisted more than six hundred thousand Vietnam-era veterans since its inception in 1979—eleven years after the Tet Offensive.

"If we don't get vets like John employed or trained in the next few years, we'll lose them in the work force altogether," warns his counselor in Philadelphia. "We know that when men are unemployed at forty-five, they are likely to stay that way. If you were nineteen in the war, you are thirty-nine now. And if you are a veteran, your chances of unemployment are much greater than your peer who stayed home." John spoke to us at his home.

I don't know if I believed in the war. I think at that time I felt that I had a responsibility to go. It was a way of repaying my country for the freedoms that we enjoy and so forth. You know, at nineteen, you really don't know a lot about life or have a full understanding of what's going on around you. But I did feel I had an obligation to go.

The service wasn't an escape for me. I didn't come from an underprivileged neighborhood per se. I grew up poor, but my stepfather was affluent. Let's put it that way. We moved to suburbia. Too many Vietnam veterans came from underprivileged neighborhoods, especially the black guys. The service was supposed to be a chance for them. It really wasn't a chance. It just made matters worse for them when they came home.

I got out in January of seventy-two. I was glad to be out. But I felt different. When I left home I was sociable. I got along with the people around me. When I came home, I felt numb. I felt isolated. I stayed within me. There was a sense of detachment. And I had no real goals or even desires. My mother didn't ask me about Vietnam, and I didn't bring it up. Then it started to hit home about how people were feeling about the war. I felt confused. There was a lot of heavy antiwar feelings and a lot of antiveteran sentiment, like we were responsible for the whole thing. It was like our fault the war happened. I really couldn't understand it. I thought I had served my country honorably. Yet I was getting no respect or courtesy.

For the most of us there was no adjustment to the civilian world. No way for us to understand our feelings about what happened to us in Vietnam or what coming home meant. We would leave 'Nam and within seventy-two hours we were on our front doorstep. And you can't send eighteen-, nineteen-, and twenty-year-olds off into a very hostile, violent, brutal situation and expect them to come back and pick up their lives like nothing happened. If there had been some kind of adjustment program from the start, it would have given us a chance to at least start out even—instead of having to spend so many years trying to deal with feelings that we really didn't understand about ourselves and about what we had had to do in Vietnam to survive.

I did feel that I had to try to do something positive with my life. And at that particular point college seemed the obvious thing. So I registered at Glassboro State College. I lasted one semester.

College didn't seem to meet my expectations or meet my needs. But to be honest, I didn't have any goals. And I just wasn't able to cope with the structured environment. Plus I was dealing with a campus environment that was basically antiwar. I felt extremely out of place. Then I began to feel worthless.

You start questioning yourself. Questioning your actions in Vietnam. Questioning reality. And when you can't find the answers, then you start to lose faith.

I was drinking too much, too, the first couple of years. Drinking heavily. Beer. Hard liquor. Or both. Then I recognized that it wasn't doing me any good. More harm than good. That the drinking would bring on feelings of anger and hostility toward other people basically because of how I was treated.

When I left college, I went to work. I guess I more or less started an odyssey of jobs. Changing jobs. Quitting jobs. Months of unemployment. A lot of it was Vietnam. The animosity toward authority. The nervousness. The instability, or the inability to adjust to a structured situation. And I kept regressing as far as sociability went.

I found myself less and less interested in becoming a part of an environment where it was necessary to make money, to make a living.

I remember leaving Bell Telephone because the job was becoming more and more stressful. I was becoming more and more a loner. Less and less sociable. And my tolerance for the customers was getting less and less and less. That's nowhere for an operator.

I remember this gas station. I was the station manager. And the station was robbed. It was really an attempted robbery. The individual pulled a knife on me and tried to hold it to my throat. I beat him off. Afterward, I requested a transfer to another station. I didn't need the extra worry, whether this guy was gonna come back up there lookin' for me with a gun. I did not want to have to come to work packin' a piece, lookin' over my shoulder, worryin' about whether I was gonna blow some fool's head off because he was gonna mess with me. See, ever since I had returned home from Vietnam, I went to great lengths to make sure that I never owned a gun of my own. Having the Vietnam experience, I knew that if push came to shove, I would use it. I didn't want to be put in that situation. They refused to transfer me. I had to quit.

In 1982 I got a job I really liked. It had a future. I was an assistant manager at a catering company. That summer we had a contract at a university, feeding one of the dorms. We provided the students with their three meals a day. I supervised about fifteen people. Cooks, servers, cleanup people. And I was in the process of being promoted to my own unit. Well, we were working six or more days a week. I came in one day and was told that I was gonna be losing my day off. I lost my temper. I slammed a door. I threw a pencil. And the district manager saw it all. Suddenly I go from the manager-to-be of my own unit to someone who's unstable. From someone who has a promising future to someone who's dangerous. They said, "Give me the keys." And that was it.

I was extremely upset. Irritated at myself as well as at the catering company. I felt that I had a career opportunity taken away from me, for whatever reason. So this time I went to the Vet Center to get some help. I talked to a team leader. I thought that if I didn't talk to someone I might do something detrimental to myself.

The counselor is a veteran like me. That made it easier. He helped me find something positive in myself. Good things in my life to look at. He showed me that Vietnam had taught me a survival instinct. Finding what I need to get by. How to get to the better day. To use my intelligence. To think things out instead of just reacting without real thought. And to appreciate the simple fact that I had returned from Vietnam. Returned in one piece.

At the time I was having flashbacks and nightmares. They would come in stressful periods of my life. When I lost a job. During periods of unemployment. Basically I would relive an experience, such as when I blew away a kid, eight or nine. The big thing was to throw candy to the kids. Well, this jeep with three guys in it was doing it. And this kid threw something back. A hand grenade. Took out the jeep and the three guys in it. There was no even thinkin' about it, you know. I just turned and let loose. M-16. There was no possible way that kid survived.

Even though that child was a threat, it was difficult to deal with when I remembered it. I began to think something was wrong with me because I had done that thing. People here don't understand war. "You killed a kid? How could you do that? Baby-killer!"

With the help of the Vet Center I got over most of it and got to realizing that to survive I had to do what I had to do.

Meanwhile, I was assessed for PTSD and started collecting a 10 percent disability for it. And I was awarded with Voc Rehab. So from October 1983 to August 1984, I went to an institute in Philadelphia to become an electronic technician. One thousand hours.

When I got out of school I sent résumés out to every major firm in the Philadelphia area. Close to a hundred firms. And people just weren't hiring. I had a stack of letters at least four inches high, each with, "Thanks for your résumé. We'll keep it on file."

I tried working in a pet store. I got some work at a gas station, but the owner let me go when a relative needed work.

By now my wife was pregnant. And I was unemployed. Without unemployment compensation. I didn't qualify from the last job. So push came to shove. We went down to welfare. I needed medical protection for her and the baby. It was a sobering experience. I felt— I don't know how to put it into words—I was totally disgusted with myself. I felt like I had failed myself, because I was unable to take care of myself and my family.

Then I began to feel like my country had left me out. Left me out to dry. Here I was with a certificate of study. Finally ready to launch a career. After all those different jobs. But I can't find work in my field. It was like the country said, "Fine, you went to Vietnam. You did your thing. You came back in one piece. But we don't have a responsibility to you. Adiós."

I don't know whether or not you call welfare the last straw, but I just felt like it was. I thought, I gotta do something. That's when I sat down and I sent Ron a letter. President Reagan.

I wrote, in part, something like this: "I cannot find work in my field of training. Electronic technician. My degree [certificate] is worthless. Wherever I have sent a federal application, the story is the same. There is no job for you because of Gramm-Rudman. I was recently married and we are expecting our first child in November. But the beauty of both occasions is tainted by the frustration of having no money and being unemployed. Our emotional well-being is sorely taxed by the frustration and uncertainty of our future. Neither of us wants the public assistance but our options are nil. I don't think it's too much to ask to have a career opportunity and be able to provide for the well-being of my family. For I have served this country honorably in Vietnam and have endured the rejection from society for serving in 'Nam.'"

Three months later I got a reply from the local labor and industry office [perhaps the Private Industry Council]. They had been instructed by Washington to assist me, because of the letter.

By then I had been working as a seasonal employee for the Internal Revenue Service, and I had got an offer from the Transit Authority which I took. Electrician. They hired me based on the electronic background from the schooling. From the Voc Rehab. So I'm doing maintenance on the commuter cars that run from Philadelphia through the suburban areas. It pays $438 a week. And I get $128 a month for PTSD and for my right knee. So I'm hanging on moneywise.

But I would probably be a lot more advanced as far as financial gain is concerned if I had not gone to Vietnam. I would probably be completing my eighteenth year with the phone company in Maryland. I don't think I'm anywhere near the peers of my generation who did not go to Vietnam, in either accomplishments or personal satisfaction. I feel like I'm ten, fifteen years behind them. I had to pay a penalty for going to the war. My life should have been more stable. More full.

I know there are changes going on in the public mind about the Vietnam veteran. How deep it goes, I don't know. Somehow the memorial in Washington and the parades ten years after the fact just seem a little hollow to me. I know it's part of the healing process. But somehow to have occurred so long afterward, I . . . I don't know whether it's just cosmetic acceptance or whether it's genuine.

Vietnam cheated me out of the opportunity to live a normal life. I'm grateful to the Vet Center, the guys who are trying to help me live a normal life now. They have shown me I have nothing to hide as far as my experience in Vietnam is concerned. Yet I still think about the child. I know I had to do what I did for myself and my squad. I had to stay in one piece. Yet I know how I feel about my own daughter, how precious she is to me. Then to turn around and have to kill another . . . child.

I wasn't the best soldier over there. I wasn't the worst. I just did my job. And now I've spent all this time trying to get back the innocence of my youth. The sense of person. The things that a man loses when he goes to war.

So many years. So many years.

(W.T.—1987)

John Godfrey's story emphasizes the need for an economy that provides enough work to go around, of a sort that makes a genuine social contribution and pays adequate wages. Vietnam veterans provide a particularly graphic example of the combination of the same alienation and unemployment that many people experience. The most common response to their problem is simply to talk about the need for "growth," which presumably will solve it. Certainly in the face of a growing population plus continued technological displacement of labor, growth is essential. Rapid growth, in particular, can spawn unskilled jobs that draw in many who are not employable in slacker times. But it is also true, as recent experience in America and western Europe has shown, that growth alone cannot

fulfill full-employment needs; that growth without good planning can wreak environmental and aesthetic havoc.

There are not enough jobs now; what in addition to growth
might supply them? Full employment alone as a goal, just like
growth alone, has many problems. Suppose the law somehow
guaranteed that everyone physically and mentally fit could
have a decent-paying job, which is roughly the case in controlled economies. The presumed result would be lower incomes throughout the work force, because productivity would
drop without the incentive of feared unemployment. Full employment might thus penalize those already working, unless
other things, such as prices, were also controlled. Something
like this does happen in controlled economies. Conservative
economists have long contended that planned economies lead
to political despotism. That aside, the question for those who
believe full employment is an important goal is whether legal
guarantees are the only acceptable way to reach it.[3]

But it was said earlier that all policy is a matter of choice.
What do we choose, and who does the choosing? The prevailing
economic opinion is that full employment—the traditional 97
or 96 percent of the work force—would impede growth by pro-
moting inflation and other conditions inimical to productivity.
The other side of that proposition is, of course, that growth
alone cannot erase unemployment. We are back then to the
five possible responses discussed in Chapter 1: do nothing;
rationalize the problems away; ameliorate things; guarantee
incomes; or make jobs available. And if the last is politically
unacceptable because it threatens "freedoms," and the first
three are deemed unacceptable because they are morally de-

---

3. For a vigorous presentation of the cases both for and against full employment, see Robert Lekachman, *Greed Is Not Enough* (Pantheon,
   1982), pages 200–203. He concludes: "Full employment is the most
   efficient agent of equitable income redistribution politically conceivable
   within the parameters of market capitalism. Full employment sucks
   into the labor force individuals who now strive desperately to survive
   on welfare, food stamps, Social Security, and unemployment compensation. Full employment improves wages for low-paid workers. . . . It is
   a particular boon to blacks, Hispanics, teenagers, and women, last hired
   in good times and first fired in recession." I agree.

based, then must our national policy favor guaranteed incomes, with guarantees more comprehensive and expensive than our present large bundle of income-transfer programs?

But who should make the choices? Social scientists like to propose "thought experiments" that set out scenarios and their consequences. Let us suppose that low-income citizens voted in the same proportions as the rest of the citizenry (which is not now the case); or suppose the even more extreme case, and *all* low-income citizens actually voted. Would public policy continue to tolerate an official unemployment rate of 5 to 12 percent—up to 14 million unemployed—and even more by the more inclusive real rates? Obviously not. Must it be acknowledged then that growth—which was supposedly impeded by full employment—depends on an incomplete democracy? To put it another way, must it be said, as de Tocqueville might have put it, that full democracy is no friend of freedom?

Yet on the other hand, perhaps there is still truth in the democratic-socialist thinking that spread over western Europe in the 1940s and 1950s, which held up the goal of both political *and* economic democracy. Some truth still in President Roosevelt's 1944 message to Congress, where he proposed a "second Bill of Rights under which a new basis of security and prosperity can be established for all," some truth in the conviction that a free people can be its own destiny, and not merely the product of supposed economic and political inevitabilities.

These are all hard issues, and I am sure others could be added to them. To raise them here has a primary purpose—to emphasize the seriousness of the issues our interviewees are speaking of. When social-welfare policies are debated, it is not merely a question of whether a certain benefit should be raised or a regulation tightened. Though they contribute nothing else, at least the Novak social scientists acknowledge that in these debates there is much at stake. And that is the quality of people's lives and the meaning Americans attach to citizenship— not just in the present but in the future we are creating for later generations. We sweep all these matters into a mixture called "welfare state," but that is a poor rubric. We are debating what the common interest requires, what our constitution—

in the Aristotelian sense of a way of life that bonds a society and defines its character—will be.

I believe that high among those requirements is the opportunity to work, and through work to be self-reliant. One cannot talk as we have done to a cross-section of Americans without discovering their agreement with that. Jimmy Morse said, rightly, "My forty-seven years was too young for a man to come out of the mills when he wants to work." People want work, because without it they feel not only dependent but alienated and, in John Godfrey's words, without a "sense of person." For them, the fundamental issue of social-welfare policy becomes, How do we enable people to work and support themselves? Can the marketplace itself do it? Must government do it?

The answers suggested in this book draw their strength from confidence in the federal system. As much as the Bill of Rights, it gives substance to the hope of kindling a thorough and full democracy here. The state governments in the past have often been bad actors, particularly in the South. The great constitutional achievement wrought by the civil-rights movement and simultaneous legal victories is that, through the application of the "one man, one vote" principle, they need not be. This book relies heavily on the possibility of states enacting constructive economic policies in behalf of social welfare and the employment of their people.

There have been few years since World War II in which the United States reached what used to be the desired index of full employment—at most, 3 to 4 percent unemployment. Moreover, there are other fracturing trends within the national work force—an increase in part-time work, a shift toward lower wages—though apparently these do not disturb those who believe that American labor is overpriced. The economy does not run at a pace sufficient to provide adequately paying jobs for all those now in or preparing to enter the work force. And experience shows that it cannot be expected to do so.

The curse of past federal jobs programs has been their frequent change, their failure to convince the public of their desirability, their typical separation from the needs of the market, and their niggardly funding. So predictably, they have failed to accomplish even their announced objectives. Their shortcomings can be lumped into two categories: instability and inadequacy.

Part of that reflects the indifference of the electorate, and a good bit of that has had to do with two political facts. It is probably accurate to say that the public never comprehended the Comprehensive Employment and Training Act (or CETA), the major federal jobs program, begun in the Nixon administration and carried on through the Carter, never knew what it was getting for its tax money, never translated those dollars spent into results it could perceive and more-or-less approve of—not as an earlier time could "see" that the CCC built parks or as people now can "see" that Head Start does a traditional and acceptable service.

The second political fact is that interested constituencies are the best guarantors of stability, and jobs programs have seldom had them. Head Start, both a child-development and an adult-jobs program, does have an effective constituency now, made up of workers, administrators, and local merchants and other business interests, who can attest to the program's continuing and visible "product." It has, in short, become a "special interest." Politicians and editorialists claiming to be conservative use that term to spare themselves occasionally from being more direct in their assaults on the poor, minorities, and liberals, but that is merely conventional cheap demagoguery. Like any political order ever known, this republic is composed of interests, and as in every political order the problem is to weaken those which do not accord with the common interest, and to strengthen those—like this one—which do.

But building a constituency in behalf of adequacy is even harder than building one for stability. American social-welfare policies have been long cursed by tokenitis and demonstrationitis. It is better that federal and state governments do nothing at all rather than act on a scale designed for failure and therefore receive public disdain and disapproval. Politicians like to show they "care," like to "take a step forward," "make a beginning," "get started and show success," "establish the principle"—but in the long run, all that caring is of little help to those in need: The program stalls or fails, and the public decries the expense.

Adequacy in social-welfare programs remains elusive because total governmental spending greatly exceeds revenues. It will continue to do so as long as Congress, led by the Pentagon and White House, spends as it does on arms and—following the precedent set during the Johnson administration, which fought the Vietnam War without tax increases—pays for its profligacy by borrowing. An economy as dependent as ours on loans and investments from our trading partners abroad and on the willingness of its residents to incur mountains of private debt, is not predisposed to invest in public improvements, including an active jobs-creation program. So considerable pessimism is called for, until self-interested constituencies come into being and press for change.

There is also an underlying attitude that militates against adequate social-welfare programs. At bottom, American national optimism—our prevailing ideology—expects growth to solve all problems, if not now, surely soon. Americans have traditionally assumed that larger production will sooner or later lead to better distribution of income and wealth, and that earnings are preferable to savings. It is an attitude of immense convenience, since it simultaneously exhorts self-reliance and excuses selfishness and inequality.

On the contrary, all experience points to certain conclusions. They are that:

- Welfare reform will not cure poverty.
- Moralizing harangues will not cure poverty.
- Only money in hand will cure poverty.
- Jobs are probably the best if not the only feasible way of putting money in hand.
- There must be a governmental readiness to create jobs when fiscal and monetary management prove insufficient stimuli for the economy.

The key word is readiness. Job-creation plans should always be in place, readily applied when employment falls. There is nothing novel about that. The Pentagon keeps ten or so weapons assembly lines running pretty steadily by always having new designs ready for Congressional funding. The Corps of Engineers maintains a cornucopia of plans. There is no reason a different kind of planning cannot also be done. What might be its general characteristics? I suggest three:

- Plans and programs should be for work demonstrably useful to the public.
- They should give preferred hiring status for a portion of their jobs—say 10 to 20 percent—to persons unemployed or working below the minimum wage, but otherwise should hire the best available persons at prevailing wages and salaries.
- They should be largely run by state governments.

The second point may seem the most controversial. "Poor people's programs" have more often than not been flawed in principle and in outcomes. Programs need to demonstrate publicly observable and appraisable achievements. I do not, therefore, propose a "jobs-creation program," in the usual sense of a revived CETA. I do propose expanded governmental undertaking of needed public works. These would drain some workers from other employment; so did the interstate-highway system, so does weapons manufacture. But only in a tight labor market, such as exists today in some states, is there a realistic possibility of putting the unemployed to work and the poorly paid into adequately paying work. And if a tight labor market must be paid for by some inflation, that is a matter for democratic choice. It is morally wrong for millions to be kept in dependency in order to control the prices others pay; unemployment is a callous substitute for price regulation by government. At the very least, inflation's other causes should be brought under control first.

An old refrain lists public jobs that need to be done in the United States. Oldness does not invalidate, any more than triteness makes a statement untrue. We might group many of those jobs under the term, *maintenance*. That is a concept easily graspable by a middle class long committed to "keeping up the property." Maintenance can be increased or decreased relatively simply, and can be variously applied in different areas. Flexibility is important, because of the ups and downs in the private marketplace and the varieties of regional experience. Maintenance is also an unending need.

Consider a work program that also brings a new approach to federalism. It would thrust most of the responsibility for planning—for *thinking*—and for execution onto the state governments (not city or county governments, which are mere legal creatures, but the states, those big underutilized chunks of our constitutional mosaic). It would also depend on the federal government to define large goals, to set and enforce standards, and to participate strongly in financing.

These days we seem to see more sprightly intellects, more inventiveness, more clear definition of problems within the state governments than in Washington. Witness the impressive public-service projects, the widespread conservation concerns, the more compassionate response to the homeless. Carpe diem; it may not last long. The great reforms of the 1960s energized a voting population of most effect close to home. The federal government, on the other hand, is so benumbed by what it conceives to be "national security"—the functional equivalent of the southern states' one-time obsession with segregation—that it may for yet a while longer be a stranger to either energy or wisdom.

Consider a new development of the potentalities of federalism (though in a two hundred-year-old government, nothing is altogether new). Each state might develop its own maintenance plan and transmit it to a designated federal office for review, approval, and later monitoring. The plan would cover the state's natural and capital resources: forests, shorelines, bridges, sewers, waterworks, school buildings, mass transit, toxic-waste disposal, public-housing upkeep. The plan should describe the state's own intentions and expected funding toward the needs set forth over a period of years, say a decade or so. Federal standards as to each state's financial capability could he established and periodically revised. Federal funds might then flow, adding to the state's normal program, when triggered by falling employment and wage levels within the state, and could taper off as those levels rose. For examples, federal aid might commence when unemployment in a state exceeded 4 percent or when average wages were less than half the national median, and it could be in amounts, based on a state's plan, estimated as sufficient to bring the state's employment picture up to those indices. The states could, in their best judgment, perform the work directly, or through contracts with their municipalities or counties, or with private businesses.

Improvements on such an approach as is crudely suggested here are, of course, endless. The basic intent is to yoke together the powers of federalism. And through the role accorded the state governments, a constituency of great influence would come into being, one inherently interested in program stability and adequacy. It would also establish the principle that the constitutional authorities of this country—the federal and state governments—have primary and joint responsibility for the "general welfare."

The approach cautiously put forward here both does and does not conceive of publicly supported employment as "jobs of last resort." They are so only in the sense that employment added over and above a state's normal maintenance would not occur until certain unemployment and wage indices triggered it. On the other hand, "last resort" does not imply that the jobs would be undesirable. The challenge is to stimulate employment, not degrade it.

It seeks also to avoid the bad consequences that flow now from certain great founts of jobs created by the public fisc: military expenditures, space exploration (which is largely military, too), and such high-technology edifices as the projected multibillion-dollar supercollider. My earthy maintenance proposal would not, as these others, create hordes of jobs that have minimal transfer utility for satisfying consumer wants; would not create a class of workers insulated from competition; would not be expected to enlarge the already swollen ranks of executives paid Hollywood-size emoluments; and would not, therefore, further widen the gaps in our national income distribution.

WORKERS AT THE MARGIN

So far we have spoken only of *new* jobs, to drain off the army of unemployed and inadequately paid. There are things that can be done to strengthen the existent work force, and in doing so benefit not only its members but national productivity too.

Demographic trends determine the composition of the work force, and the economy adjusts as best it can, because it has to. One of those trends in particular presents special problems related to social-welfare policies. The large number of women entering the work force demands a greatly increased availability of day care. This service can be expensive, whether paid for by the public through taxes, by employers (resulting in higher prices), or by parents' fees (which they may then seek to recover through tax deduction or wage improvements). No one knows accurately how many children now are in some form of day care, no one can predict how many would be if all needs were satisfied. But day-care services are an essential part of any realistic employment program. The next chapter will discuss the place of day care in a welfare program.

Some people now working have a day-care benefits "package," sometimes won through collective bargaining, though as of 1987 the Bureau of Labor Statistics estimated that only three thousand companies offered any kind of child-care assistance to employees and only 1 percent of workers had facilities for child care available in their workplace. And as with other forms of children's education, many parents pay for private care.

We don't know to what extent society in the future will want to include younger ages in the normally provided public education. Kindgergarten is almost universal now, and though still at parents' option, it has carried the public responsibility down to age five. Head Start is for poor children, but will non-poor parents of three- and four-year-olds soon begin to covet that service? And, will they then want day care, too, all the way down to nurseries for infants? (Some high schools provide this now, as a way of bringing teenage mothers back to school.)

What, too, about day care for the many women like Kim Ellert,* neither on welfare nor much above it, making out as best they can and doing what they can for their children?

"There's Too Much Malarkey"

Osceola County, Florida, is literally the crossroads of many worlds: Disney World, Sea World, Circus World, and Disney's international showcase, EPCOT—and the world of visitors lured to them.

Once a landscape dotted with Brahman and Angus cattle, and great pine, oak, and cypress trees twined with drooping Spanish moss, this area has undergone a startling change in just two decades. Now concrete has rolled over the old grazing pastures as if it were molten lava, while neon lights and billboards for fast-food restaurants and motels compete for tourist dollars.

Native Floridians of this former "Cow Capital" and "Fisherman's Paradise" reminisce about the good old days when life was slow and quiet. Descendants of the area's pioneers recall when steamboats were the mode of traveling and transporting goods. This was the territory that the legendary Indian leaders Osceola and Billy Bowlegs once tried to defend against the white man.

Some say that the development has been good for the area, others that it has profited only newcomers who had not even heard about the area until Disney World came along. They speak out about the lowering water table, destruction of wildlife habitats, and other ecological impacts. But all the debate doesn't really matter. For the modern reality is that there is a world of service jobs in Osceola County to take care of the world of tourists in all those motels and restaurants. Kim Ellert, an attractive and articulate twenty-one-year-old white woman, usually fills one of them in order to scrape out a living for herself and her two children.

Kim's story sounds like enough bad luck for at least three people. In spite of it all, Kim has an air of confidence that, come what may, she'll lick it in the end. "That's the way life is; there's no help in crying about it."

When I was almost sixteen, I met Phil, my husband. I looked at him as an escape. I thought, you know, get married and get away from this whole family and I'll never have to bother with them again. We dated for several months and then I got pregnant. On purpose. So we could get married. 'Cause he was in college and he didn't want to give that up. He said he didn't want to get married for years. Which was smart, but I didn't realize it at the time. I wasn't looking at things as far as reality. I was looking at: get married, have a happy family, give my kids what I didn't have. You know, the old story. And so we got married and it was just the opposite. Four years later, we were still living at my grandmother's—with two kids. Nothing ever changed. There was no escape. With the kids coming so close together, there were so many bills to pay. There was no way to get ahead. Phil had quit college when Christopher was born and got a job paying $4 an hour. But you can't make it on $4 an hour, especially when you're paying hospital bills, which are so unbelievable. The hospital bills are what kept us down so much. We had to pay $700 up front for the doctor, and the hospital bill was $1,000 for each kid.

Christopher was ill a lot and had to be hospitalized. Sarah did, too. The doctor and hospital bills just kept piling up. I've got a file cabinet full just of medical bills. We had insurance through Phil's work, but we still had to pay 20 percent and the bills were in the thousands, so it was a lot.

We just never could get ahead. There were always medical and insurance bills—and truck payments. Phil had to have his four-wheel-drive truck, and that was $225 a month, plus insurance. I never had a car. You know, it was like, "Why am I married?" I began to say to myself, "You were really stupid, Kim." I started wondering if I could do it better on my own. Because Phil didn't want me working, he wanted me just like his mom—stay home and raise the kids. [After a frightening emergency with one of the children, she insisted she must have a car, and got one.] I'm not really talking against Phil. He really loves the kids. That's one thing you can say about him. He is the best father that these kids will ever have. No one will ever take his place as far as that goes.

You know, I didn't get to graduate from high school because I was pregnant and then married. I only needed four more credits to graduate. After Christopher was born, I wanted to go back. I was still only eighteen, and a lot of my friends were still in school. I went to talk with the principal. But she said that she couldn't let me back in because my grades were not all that good in the last school year. I told her I had been sick much of the time, that I was pregnant, and I was worried about being able to get married, that I was just too involved with Phil. But she still said she couldn't allow me back in. I asked what she expected me to do, and she said I would have to go to night school. I told her I couldn't afford to go to a night school. But she said, "I'm sorry." I was crying my eyes out, begging her to let me back in school. Because I wanted to learn. And yet these kids who don't want to learn, messing around smoking pot and doing anything they want, are in school. Here I was wanting to learn and couldn't get back in. And I couldn't afford night school. So I gave up. I was so discouraged. I never expected her to say no, not let me back in. She knew I was smart.

I had three different jobs when Phil and I were still together. But whenever I got wrapped up in the job and seemed to be enjoying my work, Phil would get upset, and I would have to quit. My first job was at a fast-food place, and after a while they wanted to train me to be an assistant manager. Then I got one at a motel. I was pulling "doubles" [two shifts] over there, and I enjoyed my job. I was doing night auditing plus working at the front desk. Then I got a job at a regular restaurant as a waitress, and that was my best job. I was sometimes making up to $300 a week. I had to pay a babysitter about $75 a week; sometimes I was working doubles there, too.

I always gave everything I had in a job. I took pride in doing well at whatever job I had. Eventually, I figured I could make it better on my own. So we separated. I continued living with my grandmother, and he moved to St. Cloud [a small town ten miles away].

This spring, after we were separated, things went from bad to worse. I hurt my back—bad, very bad—in a car accident. The X-rays showed that I had broken some vertebrae, completely destroyed them. Five and a half hours of surgery later, they had put in two stainless-steel rods and I was in intensive care for four days.

There was 80 percent insurance coverage on me because, even though Phil and I were separated, I was still on his insurance from work. But I was in the hospital a long time, so the bills mounted up.

Then Phil lost his job, so the insurance coverage was canceled. The hospital administrator had said that he thought Medicare would take care of the 20 percent if you're single, with kids, and no job. [Not so. Medicaid might, in some states; confusion of the two is widespread.] But I wasn't divorced yet, just separated. Medicare figured Phil could pay, but he couldn't either. The car was totaled and we didn't have insurance for that because we hadn't been able to keep up with the premiums; so the coverage had been canceled.

The doctor told me I could never lift anything heavy—not even a five-pound bag of sugar—and that I really shouldn't work for a year while I healed, with the rods and all. On top of that, I accidentally got knocked down about a month ago and it jolted one of the rods loose a little, but I can't afford to have anything done about it. And I can't not work. Now, though, I can't be a waitress because of my back. I can be a hostess in a restaurant but I don't get tips. Also, after I stand a little while my back gets to hurting.

Right now, I don't even have a job. I did have a hostess job, but they found out about my back and wanted me to get a doctor's form—you know, because of workmen's-compensation concerns—but my doctor won't give me that because he doesn't think I should be working yet. So my girlfriend and I are trying to sell these super-duper vacuum cleaners. We use her car and go to people's homes after calling and making appointments. Don't know how long that will last; depends on how much of a commission I can make—which means a lot of vacuum cleaners will have to be sold. Actually, I'm hoping to get another hostess job soon.

You asked me what I thought about welfare, if I had ever thought about getting on welfare. Well, I actually applied for food stamps and AFDC after the accident. But because I am living with my grandmother and not paying rent, they said they could only give me food stamps. But if I moved into my own place, I'd really be worse off even with AFDC. Also, the only way I could get AFDC was if I sued Phil for child support. I just couldn't do that. He didn't have a job then himself and was waiting to get into the army.

Besides, when they found out my grandmother had assets and property, I was told that as long as I lived with her I wouldn't qualify for even food stamps because she could always liquidate her assets. I can't ask her to do that. She's done enough for me.

So I just said, to heck with that, I don't need it. There's too much malarkey. You know, you have to do this, then that, and then we'll review you and get back to you in a couple of weeks. Well, in the meantime during those couple of weeks, I don't have any money. 'Cause to qualify even for food stamps, you can earn only so much. I would have to get something that pays real low—like as a maid, which I can't do because of my back, or some other kind of job that nobody really wants. I could never get ahead. So it's either stay in the same bracket, the same level, by getting welfare, and not work so I can stay home with my kids—which is supposed to be the American way—or get a job and *try* to get ahead. 'Cause here, most people look down on you if you're not home with your kids.

It's just weird, it's like a catch-22. If I went out and got an apartment, they would give me AFDC and food stamps, but there really wouldn't be enough to pay my rent and everything else. If I worked, then I wouldn't be eligible for anything. Yet, even working I wouldn't have enough to pay a babysitter and everything else without some kind of help, like food stamps.

So as it is now, I keep living with my grandmother in Davenport, which is ten miles from where all the jobs are, and she takes care of the kids when I work. I borrowed money from her to buy a used motorbike to get me to and from work until I can afford to buy a car. She's well enough now to take care of the kids, but sometimes she gets sick. My grandmother is seventy-five years old and she has emphysema. She can be fine for months at a time, then all of a sudden she'll get so sick that she can't get out of bed.

Phil finally got in the army, so once he gets squared away, I'll start getting some child support. Right now, though, it's rough.

Even so, I really can't understand anybody going on welfare in this area if they're healthy. Because there are so many jobs. I could walk over there to Dunkin' Donuts and get a job. There are just so many job opportunities. It might start at minimum wage, but it beats welfare. It's a matter of dignity. I really wouldn't want to be on the dole. When I see people standing in line for welfare, or at the unemployment line, I think it's crazy. Because you could go anywhere down the street and get a job. You might have to lie a little. Like at ————, where you could say you graduated from high school when you really didn't. They never check.

You do what you have to do.

(C.B.G.—1986)

Women at work bring up other issues, such as maternal or paternal leave during infancy, and "flexible time," enabling parents to be at home with their children at desired times. Flex-time may be an idea whose time has truly come. The more options there are within any social-welfare scheme for people (not for administrators), the better. Not all parents want to place their young children in day care, because of their own views about parenting, because of a child's particular needs, or for whatever reason. Yet our society and economy are shaping themselves around the pattern of two-worker families. The workplace, consequently, ought to reshape itself to allow flexible time in most occupations as a normal privilege. Workplace practices such as these should be formed through the give-and-take and trial-and-error of personnel procedures and the negotiation of collective bargaining, rather than through governmental guidance. Uniformity does not seem a weighty value, and agreements arrived at through collective bargaining are almost certain to be sounder than legislated plans.

Some of the conservatives' faith in "privatizing" is merited, and collective bargaining is one of the finest forms of it. The United States does through regulations (such as minimum wages) or exceptions of law (such as the earned income-tax credit) a plethora of things that workplace agreements among equal bargainers could do better. A heavy federal tilt in favor of the right to organize and to bargain collectively would, if accompanied by strict governmental enforcement of democratic procedures within unions, be of more worth than almost any bundle of welfare and work reforms one could think of.

If collective bargaining could be brought to bear, it might assure some lasting solutions to the sore problem of illegal immigrants and their participation in the labor force. Collective bargaining would be an effective form of workplace self-regulation, far better than border patrols and employer sanctions.

"Better Than Anything I Can Get Back Home"

We talked to José Martín, an "illegal" residing in Houston; when we returned with some followup questions, he had disappeared. Here are some things he said when we did talk. Read them for what they signify regarding the labor market wherein he competes with U.S. citizens for jobs. After crossing the river from Mexico, he had gone to where friends lived in El Paso.

They found a job for me washing cars, but it didn't pay much. After about two years, I came to Houston to find a better job. I started working for a company that does all of the construction and remodeling for a hotel chain here. I do all kinds of things. I put in drains for air conditioners. I fix small appliances. I do concrete work, plumbing, anything.

When it comes time to fix up one of the rooms in the hotel, I help strip down all of the wallpaper and take up the carpet. The carpenters come in and do whatever they have to do. And the paperhangers put up new wallpaper. Then I help put the furniture back in. They pay me $5 an hour, which is not too bad, but a Mexican-American friend who works here told me we're worth twice what they're paying us. He says we could be here fifty years making $5 an hour. He says one man worked here four years and every time they laid him off they rehired him over and over again at the same wage. Me and my friend don't like it because we don't get vacations or any other kind of company benefits. He says we're caught in a bind because we can't sue the company and it's not easy for us to get other jobs. But I'll probably keep this job because, as bad as it is sometimes, it's better than anything I can get back home.

To earn more money, after I finish working at the hotel, I drive my van to different places around Houston to mow lawns and do other landscape work. I work about fourteen hours a day, seven days a week, so I don't have time for girls. For recreation, I just stay in my little one-room apartment drinking beer and watching TV.

I haven't been back to Mexico in six years and I sometimes get homesick. I never know, maybe the police will give me a free trip back. If I'm ever arrested as an illegal alien, I would choose to be sent back voluntarily rather than ask for a long court hearing. When you agree to be deported, they usually take you to one of the international bridges and release you on the Mexican side. If that ever happened to me, I would be right back in a few hours, just like a lot of other Mexicans. We know that if we keep on trying there's just about no chance that anybody can stop us from working in the United States. How do you say in English? It's a piece of cake.

(A.P.—1987)

There is widespread attention being given to training—especially basic skills and job readiness training and retraining of workers idled by plant closings or severe production cutbacks. Training in basic skills, of literacy and numeracy, is a public function and responsibility. If the public doesn't achieve it through the normal twelve years of school—and it should—it ought to keep trying. Training in basic skills should also be kept separate from welfare administration. Ordinarily, job training is a function best carried out by employers. The main exception to that is the case of workers unemployed by reason of plant closing, relocation, or severe employment cutback because of technological innovations or loss of markets to foreign producers. Here private employers can help with retraining, but in most cases have less self-interest in seeing it done well than has the public. In all kinds of training, decentralized administration, and consequent flourishing of diverse methods, offers the best possibility of achieving results that meet high standards.

The need for retraining most often arises from loss of job, when a business fails or sees its share of a market reduced. Job protection has seldom been a priority, as an essay reprinted in 1986 by the Department of Labor explained:

We Americans pay an unconscionably high price for our lack of interest in job security. . . . Frequent use of lay-offs can be financially costly to the enterprise, disruptive of operations, destructive of morale, and detrimental to productivity. . . . We need to follow the examples of those few exemplary employers in the U.S. and our European and Japanese trading partners by adopting the basic philosophy and principles of job security—

that hiring an individual carries with it the responsibility to manage the affairs of the business well enough that the employee will always have a place in the enterprise, assuming he or she performs well.[4]

"The Government Ought to Be Helping the Little Man Down Here"

Title III of the federal Job Training Partnership Act authorizes programs to train and give related employment assistance to dislocated workers who have been laid off because of the changing economy or other conditions beyond their control. A program operated for three years by Lane Community College of Eugene, Oregon, served 539 of an estimated 10,000 dislocated workers in Lane County, where the lumber-dominated economy has been in severe and steady decline since 1980.

When forty-eight-year-old Mort Thatcher* signed up for the dislocated-worker program at the college, he completed a two-week job-search workshop which schooled him in application and interview techniques, résumé- and letter-writing, and methods of researching specific employers. Thatcher honed his personal self-management skills, learning how to relax, increase his self-confidence, overcome procrastination, promote positive attitudes, and thus build and enhance his feelings of esteem and self-worth. His fellow-trainees were a support network, an "extended family" that exchanged job information and helped Thatcher cope with the very difficult and stressful circumstances that surround unemployment.

While Thatcher applauds his job-search workshop, he wishes that there could be federal subsidy that would prepare workers for shifts to new careers, ones now in demand. His own thoughts focus on becoming a refrigeration specialist. When

---

4. Gary B. Hansen, "Preventing Layoffs: Developing an Effective Job Security and Economic Adjustment Program," (Dept. of Labor, Bureau of Labor Management Relations and Cooperative Programs), BLMR 102, pp. 28–29. A report of the Secretary of Labor's Task Force on Economic Adjustment and Worker Dislocation of December 30, 1986, makes a strong case for ample prior notification of plant closings or relocations and workers' participation in their planning.

interviewed, he had no job prospects in sight and was uncertain about what would happen to him in two months, when his unemployment compensation would end.

When you're forced to resign after twenty-five years as a lumberman, you hardly know what to do with yourself. I saw the end coming at the company back in April 1985, when they shut down the plywood department where I worked. I had enough seniority to go on a swing shift as a permanent laborer, but I had to start at the bottom with no seniority. Even so, I was pretty happy because they were teaching me how to operate all kinds of equipment—lumber stackers, chop saws, forklift. I really thought: "Boy! I got it made right here." But then they laid off some welders in the machine shop who bumped me out of the permanent-labor pool because they had more seniority.

So they made me a temporary laborer in September 1985. I didn't know whether I would be working the day or graveyard shift or how many days a particular job would last. I was just kind of roving around from the barker-chipper to a cleanup detail to working on particle board. I would work for three days, then be laid off for three days. Because I missed about five weeks of work during the five months that I was a roaming, temporary laborer, the unemployment office let me draw unemployment compensation.

Most of the guys knew that we would soon be out of jobs. The wife and I had been getting close to the point where we could save some money because our four children were finally gone. We had been paying off old bills, not making new ones, and getting down to where in the next two or three years we would have been able to save.

Then my job ran out, and the union went to bat to get severance pay for us. The fellows at another branch got forty hours pay for each year of service. But we got only twenty hours for each year. The union didn't really accept that, but the company said that was what we were going to get. They said: "You will take this by the end of February 1986, or we'll assume that you're not going to take severance."

In other words, if you didn't take the severance pay then, it was gone forever. With me not knowing when or how often I was going to work and with rumors of some more layoffs, I quit at the end of February. My severance pay was almost $5,400, and I cleared around $5,000 after taxes. After paying off our house mortgage and two bills we owed the credit union, the wife and I had about $900 left in the bank. We felt this would be a good time for me to get out of the lumber industry because we just couldn't see much future in it.

My wife works at a greenhouse where she makes $3.70 an hour grading and packing roses for shipping. Sometimes she works eight hours a day. But other times she only gets four to six hours, depending on whether her boss needs her. Right now she averages six hours. With her salary and my unemployment compensation, our income is pretty close to $1,000 a month. We can live off that.

When I resigned, the company gave me two pension choices. If I waited until age sixty-two, I would get $392 a month. If I took my pension right then, I would get $120.69. I decided to take it then so that I could put it away and draw interest. But the government started holding my retirement money out of my unemployment pay to the tune of $56 every two weeks. Right now I get $366 every two weeks. Without that $56 penalty, I would receive $422. What gets me is that the unemployment office allows you to earn about $60 a week without penalizing you. But they penalize me for my monthly pension, which works out to be under that $60 a week. What's going to hurt even more is that I'm going to have to pay taxes on my unemployment money. That means I'll have to somehow dig it up at the end of the year.

Meanwhile, I've been applying to my job search much of what I learned in a two-week course at Lane Community College for dislocated workers. They helped us write up a résumé, which is a good deal because you need one nowadays. To build your confidence, they have you get up in front of the class and talk. They also want you to go out and shake the hands of complete strangers. That's great because when you walk into a job interview, you're kind of nervous. This exercise helps you to overcome your fright. They also give you a video interview. After you fill out an application form, they interview you on camera. You get to see how you look and get constructive criticism from the whole class on how you can improve yourself.

All of us had to set job goals. They had a book telling us about various jobs and which ones matched our personalities. I didn't really know what I wanted to do because when you spend twenty-five to thirty years doing one thing, you don't know what else you want to do. We had access to a resource room equipped with telephones, newspapers, and guides to industries and local businesses and information about how many people work there. Also, we learned how to write cover letters.

I've always thought that I wanted to work in refrigeration, so I went to one of these businesses and talked to the owner for about twenty minutes. He informed me that I would have to go through a four-year, union-sponsored, apprenticeship program.

That means I have some big decision to make. I'm forty-eight years old. If I start an apprenticeship now, I would be fifty-two when I completed the program. How much of a chance am I going to have with only ten working years left when I finish it?

On the other hand, within two months my unemployment pay will be out. Right now I would like to go to school while working on a swing-shift job, if at all possible. However, if I could get a good job with one of the school districts around here as a custodian, that would probably be secure, and would be my first preference. Most of them pay around $950 to $1,100 a month, and they have good benefits. At forty-eight, I would have time to get into a halfway decent retirement plan.

But I don't have any experience in anything outside of plywood and lumber. This means that when I walk up to a school district and put my application in, I don't even have experience as a janitor. That's frustrating to me.

I would be willing to take a night janitor job with a little company paying $3.25 an hour and go to school studying refrigeration during the day. At least I would get experience as a janitor. Then I could go back and update my application in the school districts and at the University of Oregon.

If I have to relocate, my children have told me that they would rent our house. I know that they would take good care of it. It's a three-bedroom house and we could probably rent it for $250 to $275. My taxes and insurance would be $100 of that, and there would be some upkeep expense. If I come out with $100 extra, that would help.

The wife and I definitely aren't in as good financial shape as we once were. But we're probably not hurting as bad as most people because we do have our place paid for, and our children are grown and gone. We'll just have to learn to live with a little less.

When I was working, we went out at least once a week to eat. That's a rarity now. I do a little archery hunting, but this year I haven't bought anything for it. Mostly, we go to some friends and talk and play cards and things like that. My wife enjoys going to ballgames and she usually takes her parents, because they don't get to go anyplace.

I can't really say I'm bitter because I've had a pretty decent life and the wife and I have gone on good vacations and we do have our home paid for and our children are gone. I didn't even get too bitter with the company. I feel like I got paid for a day's work. Then things got tight for them and got tight all over.

I think the government ought to be helping the little man down here. I'm not talking about deadbeats. I'm talking about people who have worked up to thirty years on the same job. The government ought to help out on retraining people like this. The backbone of this country, the guys that paid their taxes, are guys like me that worked in that mill. The wealthy people get out of paying taxes.

The man who ran our job-search class told us to make out a check to ourselves and write in $3,000. He said this is what it costs the government to send us to this two-week course for dislocated workers. I believe it's a good program, but I also believe that the federal government could allot money for me to take a refrigeration course. I pay taxes and I never complain. The government could help me by putting me through school. It seems like the government is dragging its feet on mill workers.

I'm at the point where I've made too much money to receive an education grant. Last year, the wife and I made $26,000. This year, with my settlements, it might be more. If I was to die today or tomorrow, we have our burial plots and our headstones paid for. But still the funeral and the casket and whatnot are going to cost $2,000 to $5,000. We decided that with my pension, it might be good if I got some life insurance, so I bought $25,000 worth, with a variable yield. We're sticking a lot of our pension into it.

(A.P.—1987)

"Are the Jobs Going to Be Out There
When the Kids Finish School?"

Another recent graduate of the Lane County program is forty-one-year-old Jerry Douglas,* who was laid off after sixteen years as a dryer-tender. He completed three months of warehouse and parts-counter training that prepared him for an entry-level position. But he turned down one such position because it offered a salary that was less than his unemployment check. Then he accepted a plywood-processing job paying a bit more in his new field.

Fired! That's what happened to me and several hundred coworkers in September 1985. I had worked there for sixteen years. But the bottom fell out of the lumber industry in the Pacific Northwest because of competition from Canada and the Deep South and because of high interest rates, which slowed housebuilding. It was quite a blow for me. Here I was in my early forties with a wife, two teenage kids, only a high-school education, no job skills other than what I had picked up at the mill, and no job prospects.

I only had about $2,000 in savings because I was one of those people who would get money and spend it. If you lost a job six or seven years ago, you could get another one with no problem at all. But now there are so many people unemployed that it's almost impossible to get a job.

My severance pay after taxes was $1,600. Without it, I would really have been hurting six months ago. Even so, the company only paid us half of what it originally promised. Through our union contract, I'll be getting the other half eventually—I hope.

When I was working, I grossed $920 every two weeks. But for eight months my family had to make do with the $411 that I received every two weeks in unemployment compensation. It ran out at about the same time that I completed the dislocated-workers program at Lane Community College. The retraining program was funded by our local Private Industry Council under the federal Job Training Partnership Act.

I would have gone crazy if I didn't have that schooling because I was tired of sitting around the house doing nothing and feeling like a bum. I even felt that way sometime around some of the instructors in the program who acted like I was a dummy or something because I couldn't get a job.

From April 3 to July 11, 1986, I received warehousing training that was supposed to prepare me for an entry-level position. For an average thirty-five hours a week, I attended classes taught by two instructors and various job specialists from the community. We learned warehousing procedures, forklift operations, supervisory skills, how to identify automotive parts, and how to operate a ten-key cash register. We also learned business math, the basics of microcomputers, and a software program for setting up a warehouse inventory and controls. The forty hours we spent on warehouse security and safety covered housekeeping and fire protection, the handling of hazardous materials, and loss prevention. And we learned how to sharpen our oral and written communications skills.

When we graduated after three months' training, eleven of the fellows landed entry-level jobs paying a minimum of $4.50 an hour. I wanted to get into a behind-the-counter automotive-parts job that was available, but it started out at $5 an hour and that's about as far as it was going unless you got into outside sales. No way could I afford to work for $5 an hour. The job had medical and dental benefits, but still, $5 an hour is about a dollar less than you get in unemployment compensation. In other words, that job would have amounted to an extension of my expired unemployment compensation. The main difference would have been that I would have been on payroll.

I was lucky enough to find a job about a quarter of a mile from my home in Crestwell at a small plywood mill where they just happened to need a dryer tender. I earn $6.23 an hour. Even though that's way down from the $11.40 I earned before, it will hold me until I can land a better-paying job in warehousing. [Douglas is thus once again working at his old craft. The lower wage probably reflects the change from a large to a small company, and from a union to a nonunion plant.]

I'm lucky that my job situation hasn't strained relations with my wife. I married her sixteen years ago, and even though it might sound like bragging, we get along super well. I've told her that I might not get a good-paying job and we might lose everything we have, but we have each other and the kids and we can make it somewhere.

But I like it in Oregon so well, I don't know if I would want to relocate. A friend of mine who took the warehousing class with me relocated to Reno, Nevada, and got a job within two days. I want to take my chances here.

Before, my wife was satisfied to stay home and take care of the kids. Since she has never worked, it's hard for her to go out and get a job at age thirty-six. I think her staying home paid off because my son, who is thirteen and a seventh-grader, and my daughter, who is a fifteen-year-old high-school sophomore, have B averages in school.

Since there are so many things they need and want, this is a bad time for me to be having job problems. My son had a newspaper route to earn extra money, but it was pretty rough for him because some of his customers couldn't pay him. With her work permit, my daughter is trying to get a part-time restaurant job. That will be a big help.

I sometimes tell the kids: "I'm not preaching to you. Just look at me. I don't have any other training. Do you want this when you get older?" I think they're learning something from my experiences.

I quit high school halfway through my senior year in 1964 because my mother, who my father deserted in 1950, was in her sixties, couldn't work, and we were on welfare. So I quit school to work and help my mother.

I always had it in mind that I would pass the GED test [General Educational Development, the high-school equivalency exam] and maybe go to a junior college or something. But when I got a job in plywood, it paid so much that I said the heck with school. Without a college degree, I earned more than school teachers. I never looked to the future. I thought that because of our lumber, the Northwest would be the last section of the country to be in trouble. In 1982 I made almost $30,000. This year I'll be lucky to make $12,000.

Before, our family ate out sometimes two and three times a week. Now we don't eat out hardly at all. Neither I nor my wife have bought new clothes in more than a year, and when the schools reopened in September the kids had to wear clothes from last year. We used to go to the movies about once every two months. But it costs something like $12 for the whole family, and we can't afford that anymore.

What really helps is the video recorder that I bought several years ago. We rent movies for a dollar or so, make popcorn and stuff, and enjoy movies together at home. In other words, much good has come out of my misfortune because it has brought our family closer together.

However, we're not carrying any insurance—hospitalization or otherwise—and that worries me because we're really taking a big chance. I'm at risk because I had open-heart surgery to repair two valves when I was a freshman. That was another reason I quit high school, because I had so many academic credits to make up.

Recently my wife felt a tingling numbness in her leg. The doctor told her she had high blood pressure. She said we couldn't afford for her to keep going to the doctor. I said, "Hey! You going to the doctor is more important." I think her high blood pressure might be related to all of the stress we've both been under. I try to make the best of our situation, but sometimes I get irritated and holler at the kids when normally I wouldn't. I apologize to them and explain that I'm worried about something and that seems to help.

I worry about the 1985 Plymouth I bought about a year before I got laid off. Keeping it is the hard part. I hate to let it go back. I've never been behind on the bills, but sometimes it's hard to keep up with them. Right now, a monthly payment is past due on our car. I'm going to have to call up the car people and say I'm going to be late.

Fortunately, other than the $13,000 I owe on the house, we have no major bills. My monthly house payments are $250. The car is a little bit over $200. And a few smaller bills come to maybe $100 a month. You're talking about $700 to $900 a month for main expenses. That leaves only a couple hundred for food, clothing, and other things. It's a struggle. Maybe we'll learn something from it.

I'm not bitter about what has happened to me. I think lot of us saw the layoffs coming. I feel bad for the people that live around here. Some of them will have to lose everything they have and relocate or maybe go on welfare. I know some people whose house note is $500 a month. There's no way that they can be unemployed and still keep their homes. Already, people with as much as $15,000 equity in their houses are just abandoning them. I could probably sell my house for about $40,000 without too much problem. So I guess I'm fortunate. I'm not hurting like some, even though I might have to lose my car.

I worry about the future of the country. Are the jobs going to be out there when the kids finish school? The children of some of my friends have gone through four years of college and have not been able to find jobs. Maybe down the road it won't be so bad. Maybe I can get used to $6.23 an hour. Maybe the lumber mills will pick up or something.

If there was some way that the federal government could adjust the economy so that failing companies could be saved, that would help. The government could also help people who want to relocate by paying their expenses for maybe a month. And maybe Oregon could consider starting different industries so that we would not have to depend just on lumber. That would certainly help a lot.

(A.P.—1986)

Both these experiences illustrate the maze of decisions that surround those who seek to realize their entitlements, from governmental programs for unemployment compensation and training assistance, as well as from corporate pension plans.

With his severance pay and wife's earnings, Thatcher in 1986 was still at about the median income level. But he had no good prospect of staying there. Douglas was already well below the median, down nearly to the official poverty level. Both men and their families are recruits to a historically new class of Americans, that of declining living standards and lowered expectations. That may be the desired project when some speak today of making American industry "lean and mean." But the forebodings of *New York Times* columnist Tom Wicker seem more prescient:

If those entering the work force also are finding themselves in demand mostly for low-paying, low-skill jobs—in many cases they also are either temporary or part time—the real bad news is for society as a whole: a declining standard of living for the working and middle classes; fewer or weaker benefits such as health insurance and pensions; less disposable income for consumer spending; more working wives hence more "latchkey children"; fewer young couples able to buy houses or afford such elements of the good life as weekend cottages, boats, or second automobiles; probably a drop in those seeking expensive higher education. Some of this is visible already.

Sooner or later, a falling living standard will be political dynamite too. When it dawns on enough Americans that they can no longer expect to do better economically than their parents, or even as well, their reaction is likely to be outraged, maybe even dangerous.

"You Cut Back in Other Ways"

It is not only blue-collar workers like Thatcher and Douglas who have to cope as well as they can and take the pain for readjustments in the economy. We interviewed a Houstonian, Edgar Acton*, who until recently had been a $90,000-a-year oil-field supply-company vice-president. When we talked to him in 1986, he was unemployed, with a huge house mortgage.

Imagine never being out of work for twenty-four years then losing two executive positions within nine months. That pretty much sums up my situation and hints at how topsy-turvy the Texas oil economy is these days.

I firmly believe that if you work for a company, you should give it the best you can every day. And by the same token, you should demand the best from the company because it's a two-way street, and the system can always continue on and protect you. So when my unemployment came, I wondered, "Well, what happened to this plan?" Ultimately, what you find out is that you couldn't control this set of circumstances. There's nothing you did or didn't do. It's just the way it is, and you learn to live with it. Ultimately, you find that your strengths must lie within your own abilities.

I had to deal with the immediate problem of securing income for my wife and two college-age daughters [one attends Texas A & M University; the other has taken time off from college to work and live with a girlfriend in Denver]. I was not the least bit ashamed to apply for unemployment compensation, since any kind of income whatsoever would slow the erosion of my personal savings. I qualified for the maximum $203-a-week payments. I collected for eight weeks after I was laid off the first time. Since the second job fell through, I've been receiving unemployment again. It will run out in December. Besides that, we have a little money in the bank, and we'll be able to hold out for a while.

When you lose a job, the first thing you do is cut expenses. Certain things are fixed, of course. The house note is fixed. Fortunately, that is the only money we owe. Our two cars are paid for. You do simple things. You start instructing your kids to turn the lights off when they leave a room. I grew up with that. It's funny how you get away from that.

You cut cable TV. When I called them to cancel it, the lady said: "I take it that you've lost your job?"

I said, "Yes. Interesting that you should ask that."

She said I would be surprised by the number of calls her firm gets from people who have either taken salary reductions or lost their jobs.

You cut back in other ways. You don't go out. When it comes time for the car to get a lube job, you do it yourself. We're talking about borrowing money to put our daughter through the rest of college. Her college costs are running something like $7,000 a year. She has two and a half years of college under her belt. From this point on, we'll borrow money and that will create a debt that she'll have to repay. In other words, we're not borrowing the money. She'll be borrowing it.

Other than life insurance, I don't have any kind of insurance at all. That scares me. We're gambling and trying to get by without hospital insurance for a few months.

If it would solve my employment problem, I would relocate. I'm looking for a job by networking all around the country. I let my friends know that I'm out of work. I chase ads that come up in the local papers, the *Wall Street Journal*, or pursue any other way that I can to turn up a lead. I'm focusing on jobs in the oil-field supply industry because I would hate very much to turn my back on twenty-four years of experience, even though I know that an awful lot of my talent is transferable to other areas. So I'm also job hunting outside of the energy industry, but so far nothing has turned up.

I have a very expensive home that's not likely to be sold very quickly. It has been on the market for eight months, and we have had several lookers but no offers. Some neighbors in the same position have had offers so ridiculously low that they were not worth considering. I have $280,000 in my house and that's basically what I have it listed for. It's a four-bedroom, three-and-a-half bathroom house with a two-and-a-half-car garage, a workroom, living room, dining room, den, kitchen, and breakfast nook. It's a nice house.

I'm not bitter. You know, you have a choice in life. You can go through it being bitter and mad at everybody. If you do, it's going to impact on what you do in the future. You'll evolve into something that won't do you or anybody else any good. I think you simply have to say, this is a learning experience. I don't like it, but maybe I can learn something from it.

My wife, who hadn't worked in twenty-two years, has been picking up occasional typing work, part time; she used to be a secretary before we married. I've been getting a few nibbles from companies in the oil business, but there are so many of us in my condition that the companies are offering terms you would have to be desperate to accept.

The house is the only thing I'm in debt for. If worse comes to worse and I lose it—well, I lose it. I'll just go back and start over. It'll make me mad. I don't have the energy at forty-five that I had at twenty-two. But I'll do it because I know I'm going to come out on top sooner or later. It just makes you kind of mad to have to work all those years and save and play by the rules and then there's no payoff.

Sometimes you lie in bed at night, staring at the ceiling and saying to yourself: "The money is going to run out on such and such a day. If I don't find a way of getting some income between now and then, what's going to happen?" In the back of my mind I always know that I'm going to make it. There's going to be a way for me to make it.

(A.P.—1986)

Maybe the oil business will recover. Maybe the Northwest lumber industry will. Maybe even the steel mills Jimmy Morse worked in will. In the meantime, or in case they don't, or in case they do but discover they can get by very well with fewer employees, what about retraining?

Here again the primary role should go to the state governments, for both retraining and basic-skills training. They have an unsurpassed interest in the abilities of their resident work force, and they have the political strength, if anyone has, to secure the necessary financial and other support from Washington. Continuing in the direction taken by the Joint Training Partnership Act, and with a bow to the old NRA, state governments should work with businesses and labor organizations on a continuing, institutionalized basis, and should keep working to improve their outreach and service.

Joint committees could be formed in each state according to broad, federally defined criteria, small enough to allow effective decision-making, large enough to be able to represent all the concerns adequately. They could take on very large hunks of responsibility for designing and administering programs to provide people with useful and marketable skills. They should have federal aid on a matching formula, but one that does not dictate the particulars of the programs. The aid could, however, encourage regional cooperation.

The committees could be entrusted with directing all training and job-placement programs including the discontinuation or modification of programs we've grown used to, such as Job Corps and the employment services. They ought to have privileged access for making recommendations to Congress regarding such legislation as the present Targeted Job Tax Credit, Trade Adjustment Assistance, and Fair Labor Standards, and such oft-proposed legislation as wage subsidies.

When the Fair Labor Standards Act of 1937 began the practice of setting a minimum wage, it furthered two main objectives: it bolstered purchasing power at a time when demand was very slack and, by setting a floor below which wages could not fall, it strengthened the bargaining position of employees and their unions for still better wages. Today, the minimum wage is of very little if any benefit to unions, its enhancement of total purchasing power is problematic at best, and even liberal economists question whether it helps or hampers workers at the lowest end of the wage scale. Unions continue to defend the minimum wage, partly because it relieves them of some of the obligation of organizing low-rung workers. Throughout the 1980s, while everything else was rising, Congress held the minimum wage constant, which has to be seen as but another of the time's endeavors to depress labor costs. In constant dollars the wage, which applies to as many as 7 million workers, was at mid-1950s level. To help keep the wage up to date, some have proposed indexing it to the cost of living or some other standard. Whether or not indexed, equity and also considerations of family life should require that the bottom wage always be high enough to keep a worker and one dependent above at least the poverty line; that is not now the case.[5]

But for low-income workers, unionized, collective bargaining power would be much more in their interest than minimum-wage legislation. One advantage of the proposed committees, with their strong participation of labor unions and businesses and their broad authority, would be to get the minimum-wage issue out of the debates of economists and the maneuverings of politicians and into the arena of managers and worker representatives, where it belongs.

The state or regional committees could also undertake a far more basic task. Someday the insanity of the arms race must end, if America and the other world powers are not to crush their peoples and lands first. One factor driving it is the industrial and laboratory base it fuels, and the workers they employ. The country has to figure out how to afford peace. It is time to revive interest in conversion, from military research and production to socially useful work. Back in the 1970s, Senators Charles McC. Mathias and George McGovern cosponsored a bill to establish worker-management planning for conversion at all installations. The bill exemplified a burgeoning interest, but one which did not put down deep roots. There would be tremendous problems in a conversion process. The planning committees, away from Washington and aligned to

5. A very good discussion of the minimum wage is a June 1986 staff working paper of the Congressional Budget Office, "The Minimum Wage: Its Relationship to Incomes and Poverty."

their home needs, could possibly revive interest and find solutions.

The committees could also help design youth policies. The nation throws away too many of its young people—especially minority youth—and perhaps most recklessly and destructive of all, rejects young men. The statistics are appalling. Unemployment rates for sixteen-to-nineteen-year-olds in 1973, 1983, and 1985, respectively, were: overall, 15, 22, and 19 percent; for blacks, 32, 49, and 40 percent; for Hispanics, 20, 28, and 24 percent. Nor does schooling always help; only 34 percent of the black and 40 percent of the Hispanic graduates of the class of 1985 in the central cities of the eighty-two largest standard metropolitan areas were employed by March 1986.[6] If for no other reason than national self-interest—national security, if you will—these youths have to be given the necessary training and then put to work. For the time being, Job Corps is the nation's best youth-employment program, but it's only a start.

"These Was What I Was Good With"

At twenty-two, Michael Goddard* is an apprentice bricklayer, a high-school dropout, and a graduate of the federally sponsored Job Corps program. Originally from an unincorporated town in tidewater Virginia, he is the second of four children. His father has worked at the same poultry company for thirty years, while his mother and some of her children from time to time worked as seasonal farmworkers, picking crops.

A Job Corps counselor spoke about the kinds of young people the program tries to serve. "We target young people with specific needs, the 'hard-to-employ' and kids who have behaviors that make it almost impossible to keep them employed once you've found them a job. It's a very difficult group to work with, very few social skills. I would call them in some cases socially retarded or socially deprived. Some come from a rural environ-

6. Figures from William J. Spring, "Youth Employment and the Transition to Work; Programs in Boston, Frankfurt, and London," *New England Economic Review*, March/April 1987.

ment that may be very nutritive, nurturing, and family-oriented—very strong family ties. Others come from the inner city and have a very survival-oriented mentality. They don't necessarily have the goals educated people have. They've been raised with a different system of values that are sometimes in conflict with society.

"With a lot of the rural youngsters coming in—I might be wrong about this, but this is what I see—they come in with our values but are blocked from achieving their goals sometimes. The education systems out there just don't work for them. They don't have the jobs available to them or the means to acquire the skills. Some Corps members have almost everything going against them, but they have a drive, an overpowering will to get ahead.

"The city kids come from situations that are not typical U.S.A. There's a subculture where it's OK to fight, where you have to fight to survive. The strongest survive. What we do here is show them that there's also a culture where that's not so. And not only is that not so, but that there are other means that you can use to survive."

Michael makes $7.50 per hour, with take-home pay of $280 per week for a full five days when the weather is good. He lives with his girlfriend, Ruth, also a Job Corps graduate, their eight-month-old son, and her three-year-old daughter in a dilapidated, $275-per-month row house apartment on Baltimore's west side. The apartment has two bedrooms. The second is reserved for Ruth's brother and girlfriend, who are currently in Job Corps and spend the weekends there. Michael and Ruth's Job Corps graduation pictures are displayed prominently in their living room.

The city is great. There are jobs here. Something to do if you want to do it. Sure, sometimes the work can be slow or a job is finished and you got to find another one. But if you know how to do something, if you have a skill, you can find work, make some money and survive.

The country is so much different. I'm a country boy. In Horntown—that's where I was raised, where my folks and sisters still are—you can't walk anyplace hardly. It's a long way to go to the store, a long way to go anyplace. There aren't any jobs either. Not jobs that pay anything or have a future. My old man has worked for a poultry company for almost thirty years. He catches chickens, puts 'em in crates and on the trucks for shipping. He don't make nearly enough to pay the bills most of the time. Now that my brother and me ain't there no more and they got some things paid off—like the refrigerator and the furniture—it's a little easier for them. But things are tough there, real tough. There are lots of people that don't have jobs at all. And my old man's old, tired. He looks real old, older than he is. His hands are old, beat up, scars and all.

When I was growing up, my folks would get to arguing—seems like all the time—mostly about bills. The gas and electric and the rent—by the time you pay them, there wasn't much left. And there'd always be car trouble—need fixin', need parts. You needed a car, too, couldn't get anyplace without it. So the money'd be tight, always tight. We'd grow our own vegetables, beets and greens, some corn; get cut-rate chicken parts from the poultry company.

But there was never enough. And so we'd go work in the fields, my mom and me, and sometimes my sisters. My older brother wouldn't do it. He was too good for it; that's what he thought. Pick cucumbers, pick tomatoes, sometimes strawberries. That's when I was young, real young, in grade school. We'd start when school got out in the spring. Work all summer. Sometimes we'd work after school till it got dark. We got paid in cash. They had your Social Security number, though, and they'd take out for that. That was part of the contract you signed [with the recruiter]. It was hard on your back. Sometimes I can still feel my back. We used to shuck oysters, too. There's a trick to that, and I got good at it. I'm not sure I liked that much better.

I always knew I wanted to get outta there, had to get outta there, find better opportunities. I didn't want to live in Horntown my whole life. I wanted to better myself. When I was about fourteen, I think, I went to live with my aunt in Florida. Stayed there for about two years. I thought maybe it would be better there, see the world and all that. My cousin William there is the first way I learned about Job Corps. He went to Job Corps in the mountains someplace—Ohio, I think, maybe Kentucky. He became a welder. I don't know what he's doing now. But Job Corps seemed like an opportunity to me then.

Florida really wasn't much different than Horntown. We picked oranges in Florida, that's all. Five dollars for a big bin, about three-feet high and six-feet across. And you climbed trees with a bag over your shoulder. You needed the money to buy clothes and stuff for school. Books would cost you eighteen or twenty dollars every time.

I be truthful with you. School was hard. Some people, like they say, either they get it or they don't get it. The most difficult thing in school for me was learning. *These* was what I was good with [he raises his hands up, palms facing out]. In the city schools you have people who help you out, help you to understand and give you time. Where I grew up, either you get it or you don't get it. If you don't get it, you drop out, you go to work, you work all your life, and by the time you get twenty-two, twenty-three, it seems like you're old, real *old*, old with your hands [he raises up his hands again, turns them around in front of his face, looking at them]. From picking things, they get scratched and cut up, they get hard and the scars build up. I didn't want that but I didn't know what else to do either.

After I dropped out of school, I really didn't do anything at first. My old man was always on my back. I knew he was right, that I should do something with my life. My parents had always taught us, from the beginning, that you have to work hard for what you get, never take anything that's not yours. We don't get and wouldn't take welfare. There were others that did I suppose, but not us.

Back in Horntown, there was this ad for Job Corps on TV. It made me think of what my cousin William had done. But I didn't want to be a welder. I did know you have to have a skill, a trade. Back then I used to wear a tie and a coat all the time. I wanted to look nice, sharp, you know, and clean. And so that's what I wanted to do, work in an office maybe. When I talked to the Job Corps recruiter, she told me that there was an opening in business [clerical training], so I decided to try that. They sent me to Woodstock [a Job Corps center operated by the RCA Corporation, approximately fifteen miles west of Baltimore on the grounds of a former monastery]. Baltimore seemed like a good place to go, up north, near a city, near opportunities. They gave me tests when I got there, and I tried business for a while and learned some data-processing, too. But I wasn't really too good at that.

It took time for me to adjust. The kids were different there, rougher, a lot rougher. The night that I got there, one guy got stabbed. That made me want to leave right away, but one of the counselors spent some time with me and we talked it out. And then I got on the football team and that was a lot of fun. We took trips to play other centers. I was a running back, and scored some touchdowns.

With the business classes I also started to work for my GED. I stuck with that, and then I also took to the bricklayer trade, masonry. They told me I could get into an apprenticeship and how much money I could make doing that, and I knew that I would work with my hands better. Mr. Randall [the masonry instructor] really knew his stuff, really taught me a lot: the different tricks that you need to know to get the job done. I'm still learning tricks and developing some of my own, too. The education classes were important, too, mostly math. There's a lot of math in bricklaying, a lot of metrics, a lot of geometry. Miss Jones [the GED-preparation instructor] would say, "Michael, you *can* learn. You *can* do it." She was really patient with me, and I did learn a lot.

When I did take the GED, I came up short. I did all right in math and science and social studies, I think, but English I was short three points on. I'm going to take it again, someday. I don't know when. Maybe take classes on Saturdays to study for it, after I finish my apprenticeship. We go to classes now two Saturdays a month for the apprenticeship. That wouldn't be too much different. Maybe I'll take a break first, though.

I graduated from Job Corps last March—almost a year ago. I used to go back there a lot on weekends or days that I couldn't work 'cause of the weather. Ruth, the girl I live with, was there then, but I used to also see Mr. Randall and other staff, see how they're doing. Ruth graduated last May, in food services. She had Michael junior in June. We get along pretty good, most of the time. She had a baby before, Rachel. She's three now. At first I didn't like it that she had a baby. I stayed away from her then. But we kinda got to know each other and it didn't seem so bad that she had a baby after a while. And then we had one, and that made things better, made us closer, I guess.

We don't fight about bills too much. It's her working that bothers me. She really doesn't make much money, just the minimum wage and tips. Sometimes on Friday and Saturday night she can make thirty-five or forty dollars in tips. That's pretty good. I don't mind taking care of the kids when I get home and she goes to the restaurant. But I'd rather she was here to cook for me. That's the way it's supposed to be.

Ruth's brother Tyrone is here on the weekends, most of the time. He graduates from Job Corps next month [also in food service]. Tyrone's sharp. He's into martial arts, fights professionally, gets paid and all that. Got a bout coming up next Saturday night in Philadelphia. He's teaching me, too. We work out together on the weekend, lift weights, practice positions. Maybe I'll go professional some day. It's a dangerous sport, you know. You gotta be careful, exercise cautions. Not something to fool around with.

Job Corps was just about the most important thing that's happened to me in my life so far. It gave me a trade, a skill, something to start with. You gotta have a strategy. That's what I'm working on now. Buy some tools, first; establish yourself. Job Corps helped me get my first job in Baltimore; that was with a construction company. We did the new [he named a recent skyline adornment]. You should see it. I got a set of the blueprints at home. I'm studying them. I learned a lot on that job, different tricks for different tools, different kinds of stone. Worked way up high. First, it was scary. When you work on scaffold, you got to be aware of what you're doin'—you can't be snoozin', dropping off to sleep on a scaffold. Body start sagging, start feeling comfortable while you're laying brick, stone— fall off and that's it. No more *you*.

That job lasted eight months. It took me most of December and January to find the next job, where I am now.

At first, this company was the pits; I was getting the shaft. I wasn't using my tools. Until my papers came through, they had me hauling, carrying stuff, filling and dumping a wheelbarrel. An apprentice boy is supposed to be using his tools, learning the different tricks the bricklayers know, the bricklayers try to pass on. Mr. Wilson, my union representative, told me to be cool, the boss was being fair; the papers would come. After a while they hired some more people, and they did the carrying.

I go to union meetings, once a month. Apprentice boys don't have nothin' to say. You can't do no arguing or nothin'. They talk about different kinds of jobs coming up, talk about benefits. I got a book right here that talks about all the benefits I get. They talk about who's not getting enough money; talk about what are nonunion jobs. Next November I'll have a year in, get my vacation pay. I want to go back to Horntown, maybe buy a truck. They say if you work all year you can get close to three grand vacation pay. I don't know if *I* will. That's a lot of money, but construction takes a lot outta you, too. But it keeps you going. Sometimes the union meetings get so boring, last two, three hours. Arguments going across one side of the room to the other side of the room. The reason we go is 'cause when you're a bricklayer, you have to know these things—who's paying what, the benefits, where the jobs are, where they're gonna be. You have to try to get involved.

I haven't ever voted, yet. We had citizenship in Job Corps and I was going to vote, but I got sick that day. I pay taxes and all, but its like money you never see, 'cept for the refund I'm supposed to be getting, they say. Politicians supposed to help you out, do the right thing. Not sure they do—for me, at least. I hear Job Corps gonna be shut down. That don't seem right. But Reagan's kept us outta war. I don't want my brother to have to go to war. [Michael's brother is in the army, stationed in West Germany.] That's important to me.

I miss the country, walking in the grass, feeling the ground under your feet, space. Not much to do down there, and all, but I wish I could be there sometimes. I want my sisters to come up here this summer. I could find them a job doing something. My mother says, "No. They're too young." Ruth, she wants to be near her family in Baltimore. Maybe I could find construction work down there sometime, set up my own business or something. Got to be patient, I guess. That's what they say.

(C.G.—1986)

"I've Come a Long Ways, I Think"

Naomi Walters* is twenty-five, the third eldest, with a twin, of seven children. She grew up on the west side of Baltimore. Her family, though not poor, had severe problems, which she is ready to describe in detail. She spent two years in a foster home and several more living with either her grandparents or an aunt. She is a high-school graduate. She is also a graduate of the Job Corps program.

Her story is both unusual and typical. Unlike her, few Job Corps members are high-school graduates when they enter. Also, Naomi stayed in Job Corps for over two years; the average stay is six months. On the other hand, most don't know what they want to do with their lives; Naomi didn't either. Many others also come from troubled homes. Sometimes they are from single-parent families. When Naomi lived at home, she did have both parents; her parents are now divorced. Most have never had a steady job or any job at all.

Since graduating from the Potomac Job Corps Center in 1981, Naomi has had three progressively more responsible and higher-paying jobs; all have been with nonprofit organizations. The Potomac center is operated under contract to the Department of Labor by the RCA Corporation. Naomi lives in a $325-per-month apartment in a suburb close to Washington. Over the phone, she describes herself as short, wearing glasses, and heavyset. In person she comes across as pretty, articulate, and determined.

The junior high I went to was a terrible school, rough, really rough. It still is. Fights every day. They'd beat up on the white kids. Gang fights. They'd beat up on the black kids. The teachers were afraid, too. I didn't dress up nicely because I was afraid of getting robbed on the way home. I had to fight. The classes were a joke. We went through one whole year without a math or a science teacher. The subs would come in, and they just didn't have any control. There was this one supposed to be a permanent science teacher. The way he talked you just couldn't learn from him. Always saying "you people," you could just tell how racist he was.

High school was a lot different. Western was the best high school in Baltimore. I picked it. The academics were high. And one summer my twin brother and I got to go to a paired school, Cardinal Gibbons, for the arts. That's where I really developed my love for music. I really want to be a singer someday. I've talked to some people in the business, gone to auditions, sang with some groups. You just have to get the right breaks—and practice, really train yourself.

I was way behind in a lot of areas when I first got to Western. The kids were nicer and the teachers knew what they were doing—they were qualified. I picked up a lot, until my senior year. Then I was just skating—just getting by. Things had got crazy at home. Sometimes I think I just made it through Western on my personality. I was always nice.

I knew I had to leave home when I was eighteen. I didn't know where I was going to go. My father wanted me to go to college. But I didn't know where the money was going to come from.

I heard about Job Corps on television. Nobody wanted me to go there. My Aunt Lena said it was for bad kids. They tried to scare me. My main reason for going to Job Corps was to get training so I could get a job and be independent. I didn't want to work at McDonald's or any other fast-food place. And I didn't want to do domestic work. I wasn't interested in working when I was in high school. I could not go to work and go to school at the same time. There was too much going on, my attention was always being distracted by my family. So what was I going to do?

I decided to go to Potomac. [The Potomac Job Corps Center is located on an isolated patch of land overlooking the Potomac River in far southwest Washington, about fifteen minutes by car from downtown and not easily accessible by public transportation.]

When I first came in, I told the recruiter that I was interested in physical therapy. But Potomac didn't have that; they had nursing assistant. They told me to go through that first, and then I could go into physical therapy assistant. It was a lie. They never did have it. Nursing assistant took me five months, but they made me stay for six. Wasting my time. If I had had a choice I wouldn't have taken it. I didn't want to be a nurse.

I made up my mind at the beginning I was going to stay for the full two years. I was going to get the most out of Job Corps that I could. So after nursing, I went into BRAC [a program run by the Brotherhood of Railway and Airline Clerks, which is under contract to provide clerical training]. This was to teach you to be a railway clerk, but you could use it for other things, too, which is what I wanted to do. BRAC gave me the skills to get my first job after Job Corps.

I learned to type, do keypunch and data entry, and office terminology.

Job Corps taught me a lot of other things, I suppose. We spent a lot of time cleaning up. I had never stripped a floor in my life, never waxed, never buffed. I could have been a full-fledged maintenance person after I got out. In a way, Job Corps is like living in your own little town—but you gotta share your house. Sharing and being a part of everything. But Job Corps is a rough, rough place. Fights. Harassment. Boys fighting over girls. Girls fighting over guys. People stealing other people's clothes right out of the washing machine—taking your dirty underwear. You have to be prepared, be ready when somebody comes at you. Don't let it be a bluff. Defend yourself.

My first jobs really weren't jobs, because you didn't get paid. [Job Corps officials say that unpaid work experience provides an important exposure to the "world of work" and teaches good work habits.] But I was doing real, regular work at a geriatric hospital [at the end of her nursing-assistant program]. I worked at the reception desk, helping people out and doing paperwork; they wanted us to come back at the end. Then BRAC placed me at the Labor Department on the sixth floor, answering the telephone, typing, and everything. They placed seven people in different areas over there. I didn't do that much where I worked; that job I could have done without. But I had my typing book there, and I practiced a lot. And I got to learn what it was like to go to work every day. I guess I liked it.

The basic rules they have in Job Corps are just like the ones you need in your own home. You need to get up at a certain time. You go to sleep at a certain time. That's what you do. Especially during the week, because you don't have no business being up half the night. Job Corps should be really disciplined to help introduce people to this. I never had any problem with rules. If I think they're unfair, I'll work to change them.

In general, I'm supportive of Job Corps. If they used Job Corps for what it was designed for and stopped using it as a trash can—if judges would stop making Job Corps a jail—it would be more effective. I feel that you get what you pay for. If they pay low salaries to RAs [residential advisers] and instructors, any old kind of instructors, then that's what they're going to get, garbage. [Job Corps officials say that the salary range for residential advisers is in the "midteens," and that it has presented difficulties in recruiting competent staff.] Many of the Job Corps instructors I had in comparison to my high school were not as competent as they should be in dealing with the type of people coming through those gates. A lot of times [the trainees] were slow learners, *slow*, real slow. Then there were others that didn't have a learning problem at all. And the instructors had to deal with both. Most of the time they couldn't, not effectively. I have seen some of the people coming in there—they come in troublemakers and they have no intention of taking advantage of the opportunities being afforded them. They have a disciplinary system there, but they don't always follow it. They should. Some do change. Doing really well, not getting—not getting drunk and messed up. Some of them do turn around and end up benefiting. Changing the environment is really important.

[Job Corps serves a difficult population, many of whom are high-school dropouts and many have had contact with the juvenile- or criminal-justice systems. Job Corps officials insist, however, that they discourage the use of the program as an alternative to incarceration.]

After Job Corps, I lived with some friends in the District. I had some interviews, job referrals, before I left the Corps, but they didn't get me a job. Then one girl told me about a private placement agency. They sent me on several interviews, and I got a job as a secretary [at a child-advocacy agency]. I made up my mind right at the start and I told them that I was going to stay for two years, and I did. Even when I had to move back home to Baltimore, because the apartment broke up, I commuted every day by Trailways. It seemed like I was always leaving in the dark in the morning and coming home in the dark at night. That didn't last too long, less than a year. My mother was always fussing with me, but it took time for me to save up the first month's rent and the last month's and a deposit in order to move out. And time to find my own place that I could afford.

Then I heard about a secretarial school on television. [It is a private, for-profit vocational school.] "Be the secretary to the boss." That was a waste. The only thing I got was shorthand and bills. They charge all that money, but they have old typewriters, with typewriter ribbon. They don't even have Selectric Ones. I don't even use shorthand now. They taught other things—"Dress for Success." I already knew how to dress. And I'm still paying for it. It cost me a hundred dollars and something every month, when I pay it; sixty to the school and fifty to Citicorp. I liked my psychology class, though. I got a lot out of that class. You could bring your problems from work and talk about them. They would give you tips on how to handle them. They didn't have anything like that at Job Corps. However, I did have a good counselor at Job Corps. He helped a lot. Sometimes that place got you depressed. Most people in administration weren't really listening to the problems. They went home every night. But he really knew what he was doing and he cared about people.

After working for another youth-serving agency for about a year, I just didn't feel I was getting anyplace. I went to another private placement agency and they sent me to USO [United Services Organization]. I've been here for four months. It's challenging. It's heavy, but it's challenging. This is a move up, because I'm in personnel. People at my last job saw it as a move down, because then I was supposed to be in an executive [paraprofessional] position—recruitment. But that's no money: $13,500. As a personnel secretary, I make $16,500. That's more of an executive position to me.

I do all the correspondence and keep up the benefits—attendance and leave records—for all employees in the United States and overseas. Everywhere—Guam, Germany, you name it. It drives me crazy, all the questions and work to do, but I like it. I like the people. There's only three of us in the department, including the director. They need more. They could split my job in half, with all the questions. People coming to me all the time asking about leave days or insurance or dependent coverage. But I like it. This will probably be the job I'll stay at, for at least five years. I'm beginning to make changes, set up my own systems on how I want things done. And they seem to be pleased.

When I was home I had friends at school, but not that many in the neighborhood. The girls there I couldn't understand. They were getting pregnant. Their boyfriends would beat them up. I'd say, "Why'd you just stand there and let him beat you up?" She'd say, "He loves me." Bull! Somebody's sick.

My friends have changed a lot in the last five years. It's not that I pushed them away or told them I was moving up the echelon. They just dropped off. Right now I don't really have that many friends.

Before Job Corps, I hated a lot of people in my family. After, I don't like them, but I don't hate them anymore. We've talked. They've told me about things that happened. I don't like it. But now I understand more.

One reason I didn't stay in touch with some friends from high school was I wasn't really proud of going to Job Corps when I first went in. To me it was a step back from Western. Now I don't think it was a step back because Job Corps enabled me to get my first job.

Now I have my own place, my own home. I want my place to look a certain way. I'm fixing it up. It takes money, for furniture and everything. I do believe that you should plan for the future. I do. As soon as my rent gets put as high as $400 or $425, I'm going to a condo. That's where I'll be in five years.

I've come a long ways, I think. My skills have improved, I talk better. I'm more sophisticated. I dress better [laughs]. I communicate with people better. Then, I'd go ahead and say what I had to say. Now, I still say what it is I have to say, but I might not be as blunt or curt. Change my words a little bit and think about it before it comes out.

The United States should be moving more toward spending on education, helping those coming after us. I'm thinking about going back to school myself, and I know its going to break me. I'm going to go into debt. But it's what you have to do.

(C.G.—1986)

Naomi and Michael are young people who took hold of an opportunity that came their way. What could have served them better than Job Corps? What would they have done, where would they now be, without it? Would they otherwise be on the road to becoming self-sustaining contributors to society and the economy? Like any governmental program, Job Corps has faults, and the appraisals by these two veterans are probably as much on the mark as any. But a society bent on its own self-interest should think long and hard before dismantling it. Young people haven't time to wait on macropolicies. There must be programs to meet them where they are and to help them get on with their lives.

Naomi and Michael are both black. Kim, the spunky young white woman in Florida, might have been better off had she followed their example, rather than consign herself to years of low-wage, low-horizon jobs. But what would she have done with her children?

CHAPTER FOUR

To Receive in Dignity:
THE POOR

"Stepping Stones"

When Luis Rodriguez* moved from Puerto Rico to New York in 1973 in his early teens, his family had expected the South Bronx to be a "brand-new land of opportunity." The reality was starkly different. The "poverty and corruption" that Luis found on the neglected streets and subway tracks just north of Manhattan have confounded U.S. presidents as well as generations of social planners, local politicians, and low-income residents. Generations of promises have not been kept. But some individual phoenixes have risen.

Like many Puerto Ricans here, Luis found himself on the short end of numerous sticks—in housing, in education, in employment opportunities. And discrimination became a part of his life. But Luis, an attractive, articulate young man, believed that education promised a way out of his dilemma, and while he was working as a stock clerk in an electronics store, he enrolled in a community college. Then he met and fell in love with Vilma; they were married three years ago, and Vilma became pregnant. Business at the store slowed down, and Luis was laid off. He left school to find another job to support his

152

new family, but he couldn't find one, even at the minimum
wage.

There was a question about whether she was going to have this
baby. We weren't economically prepared for it. But our relationship
was very strong, and we decided to have the baby. We only had
$400 and I couldn't get a job. We did have an apartment. She started
working in a Burger King, and I was staying home. I couldn't find a
job nowhere. I was going out of my mind.

We didn't want the baby to end up staying with my wife's family,
because it was not a good situation in that home. But we had no
money.

We sat down and decided that one of us had to go to school and
try to make it, to see if we could get a better job; to see if we could
support our life. We decided, me and my wife, "Let us survive. We
have potential. And the only thing that we're lacking is education.
We've got to go to school in order for us to educate ourselves in
order for us to survive."

I think I first realized that that was true when I was in college. I
was taking nothing but remedial courses. And I looked around me,
and I saw friends of mine who had gone into the service, and now
they were coming back and becoming dopers. And I was also getting
into drugs, getting high and stuff like that. And that's when I started
observing myself and I said, "My God, what am I doing to myself?
I'm getting nowhere." And it is a terrible thing to become aware of,
that you are young and you very easily could destroy yourself, by
choice.

I wasn't corrupted yet myself, but I saw corruption. I've seen
somebody being killed on the street. I've seen people being stabbed,
being shot, being hit by a car that was a hit-and-run, buying drugs.
I've seen my own brothers getting into crack, into the habit of co-
caine. And dealing it themselves, and stuff like that. It is these things
that I have seen that changed my feelings.

We wanted the baby to have enough food and to be covered
medically, but my wife couldn't get help from welfare if we were
still together, and we didn't want the baby to grow up in my wife's
home. So before the baby was born, we had to play the little games,
the little paper tricks. Which means that since I was without a job,

it had to appear that I wasn't living at home, in order for her to get the food stamps and the Medicaid. It had to appear like we were separated. So I said to her, "This is what we're going to do: You go to welfare and tell them you got pregnant and you're going to have a baby, and I abandoned you and you don't know where I am." [New York is one of twenty-four states, plus the District of Columbia and Guam, where welfare might be paid even though the father was at home and unemployed. But he would have to stay unemployed, except for a four-month period, for his family to stay on welfare. As a first-time mother, Vilma would have been eligible for Medicaid even before receiving AFDC.]

That's what she did. She told welfare the same story that many people tell, that I was gone and that she never saw me again. It got me scared that we did it, because I was doing something illegal. I was scared that I might get caught and then we wouldn't get paid the money we were getting. But we did it anyway. Everything we did was for the sake of the kid.

It was terrible doing it. It made me very disoriented. I felt like it was the right thing for me to do, but at the same time I felt irresponsible. I was becoming a father and yet I wasn't financially prepared to be a father. I didn't have furniture or a crib or anything like that, and I wanted those things for the baby because I'm a father. But besides that I felt very, very *responsible*.

It was very difficult, what we did. But you do it because you're trying to survive. We thought to ourselves, "We're facing this now as young people because our parents weren't prepared for this. They didn't bring us security. And so we don't want to go through the same vicious cycle to provide this kid with the same corrupt environment, the same problems."

I watched my son being born at the hospital. It was tremendous. It just changed my life totally. I never thought that it was going to be like that. I was a different person leaving the hospital. I felt very, very good. I felt mature; I felt responsible. I said to myself, "This is the sparkle; I have to do something for my son to give him happiness."

We decided that my wife would go back to high school, and later on I would finish college. She went to a special program for mothers. [The Eleanor Roosevelt Teenage Parent Program is part of the Bronx

Regional High School, one of the city's eleven alternative schools for "students who want a second chance to earn a high-school diploma." The program for parents is a comprehensive effort to provide young mothers, and those fathers who will come, with child care while they receive training in parenting and job skills, as well as courses leading to a diploma.]

My wife heard that there was an opening for a worker at the school in the day-care center, and she talked to the people at the center about me. I saw them, and they liked the attitude that I had, and I got the job. Now we have enough money to survive on, and she's able to break away from welfare. We've been able to have a normal life. I bring in about twice as much as we could get from welfare. Breaking away from welfare is good, because you are forced to use your full potential, so you don't become limited. I believe that if you get conditioned to being supported by public assistance, and if you just lay back and let things happen—if you say, "Well, the government is supporting me, so I will take it easy"—then that will create a burden.

Some of the people around here see it different from the way my wife and I see it. They see the system like, "You're welfare and I'm me, and I need your money, and so as long as you give me money and forget about me, I'm OK." They don't see into the future. They don't plan. It's like a wheel that gets stuck in the same place and spins over and over again. And what happens is that the system gets abused, because it's not getting results. It *would* get results if people would take the system and use it as a stepping stone so that they could help themselves and get a job and education, and then leave it, not to let themselves be addicted to it, like people all around us here.

I guess it's the person himself who has to make the stepping stones. I have seen people who use these welfare monies to get high, to do anything but improve themselves. I see this in my own building. How come these people aren't doing anything for themselves? How come they don't search for other social services that could facilitate their lives, that could help them to make it, instead of always complaining that they live in a miserable place, and that they are getting corrupted, and that their kids are getting messed up, they're not going to school, they're dropping out.

I guess it would be hard to make the stepping stones if the person doesn't have the right help from the system. But it wouldn't be hard if the person would go to his social worker and say, "Look, I need this; and how can you help me evolve out of this?" But people do not do that. They just go to welfare, and, like my mother, they go in for their appointment, and the only thing they do is they present the documents they have to present and go home.

I think the system should make conditions. It should say, "Yes, we will help you if you go back to school. Or if you take a training course." It should help them support themselves, with money and food stamps, but then at the same time it should make a condition that they will not receive a certain percent unless they go to school, or go through training, or something like that. *Force* them somehow, so that if they want to get this help, they will have to do something for themselves.

[Luis's son, an energetic three-year-old, bursts into the room with a fistful of crayons and a drawing. He shows it to his father, who carefully elicits the names of the colors and shapes and generously praises the boy for his creativity. The child beams, and he plunks himself down on the floor and starts another drawing. Luis beams, too, a very proud parent.]

My wife graduated from high school last June, and she'll probably go to college next September. I'm going to try to go back to college, too. We both want to get into some kind of work where we deal with people, to express our experiences and to get poor people to think. Especially young people. We want to get information out to people.

If you want to survive, the information's out there. We never got any training in how to bring up a child, but we got the information. Somehow we got books and we read, and we saw programs and we saw films, and we explored this and that way of doing things. We did a lot on our own. The knowledge is out there. You have to move to get it.

(F.P.—1986)

THE SYSTEM

Luis and his wife *used* welfare to stabilize their family life, even violated its rules to do so. They didn't like being on welfare, but they clearly assume that something like it is necessary. They have an almost naïve faith in the availability and quality of social services. They see these services as part of the opportunity network—along with libraries and schools—that can lead to self-sufficiency.

Recent times have seen recurrent bouts of welfare "reform." It is unclear why they come along when they do. Always they are accompanied by assertions of novelty. They announce a new understanding, new ideas being let loose.[1]

In the early 1960s, there were first the Kennedy reforms, predicated on the belief that improved social work and services were basically all that was needed. A couple of years later, and with much publicity, it was discovered by Washington that the black family structure was collapsing, and a national "family policy" was said to be required; what that could have been remains obscure, buried in the ensuing bickering. In the mid-1960s, war was declared on poverty, and until a war more to the government's taste intervened, some promising campaigns were indeed begun. Some of them, like Head Start and Legal Services, continue to this day; none has ever been given enough funds to begin to fulfill its goals.

In the early 1970s, there was the so-called family-assistance plan. It claimed to provide a way out of the hodgepodge of existing welfare "systems," which were indicted for discouraging work and encouraging irregular family life. With the blessing of many liberals, congressional conservatives killed it, though as an afterthought they did extend important new assistance to the blind, disabled, and aged poor. In the late 1970s, President Carter sent to Congress a more extensive revisionist plan, without the hype given the earlier plan, but nothing came of it. Surging inflation dimmed any chances, probably slim at best, it might have had.

There were sound by-products of the War on Poverty and the family-assistance plan, so it cannot be said that these re-

---

1. For an outstanding review and analysis of past and present controversies regarding welfare, see the essay by Piven and Cloward in *The Mean Season*, by Fred Block, Richard A. Cloward, Barbara Ehrenreich, and Frances Fox Piven (Pantheon, 1987).

current reforming ventures are of no benefit. But they haven't reached deeply into the real problems of poverty, and it remains to be seen whether possible reforms of the late 1980s will leave behind anything worthwhile. In the meantime, although expenditures for all federal means-tested programs have more than tripled from the late 1960s to the mid-1980s, federal spending for the two largest, AFDC and food stamps, has declined by as much as a fifth, when inflation is taken into account. Contrast this with the rise in entitlement programs that include the middle class—that is, are not means-tested. Moreover, unlike Social Security and Medicare, which are truly national programs, these "welfare" programs vary so greatly from state to state that generalizations about their size have to be carefully qualified.

A terminological distinction has passed into common usage among those who administer or study the programs that shape the American welfare state. It is usual to say that ours is a "two-tier system," one tier being social insurance and the other being means-tested programs. Quarreling with terminology is tilting with windmills, and is even more futile when, as here, the term is more or less, for the present, apt. The social-insurance plans—Social Security and Medicare principally—differ from the welfare plans in that (with the exception of people on dialysis) only people who pay into them receive benefits from them: hence, "insurance." It is a good concept, at least for Social Security (Medicare is another story), although it does somewhat resemble chain-letter schemes: people generally receive more than their contributed funds have earned, especially with COLAs in effect since 1975, because the way the system works, retirees are supported by current workers. Many reformers who, as I do, put a heavy value on jobs do so with the hope of moving more people into the social-insurance system; if the jobs are there, that is preferable. But it is preferable on economic or other utilitarian grounds, not because it represents a move upward from the invidious "lower tier." The two parts make up one whole, an income-transfer system presumably chosen for no other reason than that the national interest requires that these redistributions of income be made.

And that—redistribution—is what both are. Both transfer money from the productive agents of the economy to the non-productive. And as long as the national interest requires this, those who receive should do so in dignity, with public respect.

Readers may take different lessons from the story of Luis and his wife. As a teenage couple trying hard to hold together a family, they dispel the ugly stereotype many people have of welfare recipients. Are they unusual? Possibly not. Certainly they share with many welfare recipients a dislike of the system and a desire to leave it. They also understand that they must cope with, even manipulate, the system as best they can.

System. The word is everywhere: capitalist system, communist system, educational system, legal system, political system, "working within the system," and on and on. The word can be used to explain: "The 6 percent unemployment is a necessary cost of the benefits of our economic system." Or to justify: Shabaka Sundiata Waglini, an innocent man, spends fourteen years on Florida's death row, coming within hours of execution, before being exonerated and set free in 1987, "proving that the system does work." It can be used for almost anything especially "welfare system." It is, nevertheless, a useful word, but now and then another might do better, for example, *method. System* suggests that a regularity of procedures is contained within a whole, but the practices of welfare in the United States are hardly like that. They go off along many paths with countless deviations; our social-welfare *methods* are uncountable if not infinite. They are at least as complicated as the American political structure itself and prove once again our astonishing capacity for turning our back on efficiency in preference for securing the interests of those groups strong enough to make their interest count politically.

Welfare is, then, less a system of interrelated parts than a crowd of methods—a gridlock of them sometimes—congressional, executive, state, local, and the charities of many private bodies and individuals as well.

"I Don't Think I'll Be Able to Find an Apartment in the Near Future."

Westchester County, New York, has for decades signified "affluent suburb." Adjacent to New York City's northernmost borough, the county promised a pastoral haven for those who wanted to flee (or would commute to) the city and who could afford the costs. Westchester offered green spaces, safety from the "bad element" of the big city, and the sort of zoning laws that guaranteed privacy, comfort—and the unlikelihood of low-cost housing. There were even tree-lined parkways alongside rivers to make the commute more pleasant.

Now Westchester has homeless people, too. The county simply doesn't know what to do with them. A 1985 report by the Homeless Crisis Action Group, prepared at the request of the county's chief administrative official, declared the situation in Westchester a "disaster," comparable to a fire that leaves hundreds of families suddenly without their homes. Such a situation, said the report, was "largely a result of the failure of the Westchester community to meet the housing needs of people with low and moderate income."

Controversy has been heated and often bitter. In August, 1987, with an estimated 3,500 people, including 1,647 children, homeless and many of them being housed in motel rooms costing as much as $3,000 a month, a responsible county official said that eighteen agencies were involved in administering what program there was. That year, a county known for its prosperity had to budget $32 million for emergency housing, and there were predictions of several times more than that for 1988. In the spring of 1986, Grace Fredericks,* who with her family had been housed for seven months in a motel in an adjoining county, spoke of her situation. She is a white woman, in her midthirties, mother of three. She was living with two of her children and her common-law husband in a single room.

I am not originally from Westchester County. I am originally from the city, from the Bronx. I lived there all my life until we became homeless last April. We were evicted from our apartment in the Bronx.

My husband was working "off the books"—he was a taxicab driver—and he was held up twice at gunpoint. He was scared about going back to work. So we were evicted for nonpayment of rent. When Eugene was driving a cab, we weren't what you'd call *stable* financially, but it was helping. I also get widow's benefits from my first husband's Social Security, and the two boys get the child benefits. With that, I was paying the rent. But when Eugene lost his job, I couldn't afford to pay the rent. And so we just couldn't make it.

My husband's parents live in Westchester County now, and we came to stay with them for a while, to see if maybe we could find a place up here. What happened after that was that my father-in-law is an older man, and he just couldn't deal with children anymore. We had to leave. So I came to the county Social Services and I explained the situation. That was in September. And on October 10, we moved into the Elm Ridge Motor Inn.

It's a nice motel, but I think living in a place like that really damages a child. We're literally stuck there. We don't have a car. We have no way to get out, nowhere to go, because everything is so far to walk to. There's not a bit of public transportation. Every place we go, we have to go in a taxi that Social Services sends. If it's a medical appointment or something to do with school for the children, I would have to call Social Services a day to two in advance so they can make arrangements for the taxi. There is literally nothing to do in the motel. You can't even walk around and window shop because there's no stores. Not even to buy a quart of milk. The transportation is the big problem with everybody. If you want to buy groceries you have to plan ahead and get it on a trip to Social Services.

We don't get to eat very nutritious food. We eat sandwiches. We don't get many fresh vegetables. They give you a small refrigerator at the motel, and they supply you with a toaster oven. But you can't cook vegetables and stuff like that in a toaster oven, and to make things like soups and meals that would be beneficial nutritionally, you can't. So you eat a lot of grilled cheese.

And the children have a very long commute to school. You see, they will not be accepted in a Westchester County school because the rules are that a motel is a temporary residence, and they have to be in a permanent residence. So they have to go to school in their last permanent address, which is the Bronx. So Social Services transports them every day to school and back. They send a cab for them; it's about fifty miles one way. [The county pays $150 a day for the round-trip taxi fare.]

One thing that bothers me a lot is the fact that my family is all uprooted. One thing I hoped was that when we got on Social Services up here, there might be some kind of program, work incentive or something like that, that my husband could get into. They haven't done anything yet with him, though. He's not willing to do work for the minimum wage. He *would* do it, you know, if it came down to supporting the family without welfare. Because we are getting older, and I definitely don't want to live in a motel for years and years. And I think that we should all be together as a family. I miss my older son [he is in high school, living with friends in New York City]. I don't like the idea of him being in the Bronx. I'm lucky if I see him once a month. When he comes here to visit, like on the weekend, I have to let the office or Social Services know that he's coming, because they would have to know that we have a guest.

I'm worried about the lack of privacy in the motel. I know that a boy and girl, after they reach a certain age, should not share the same bedroom. And all these children here, not just ours, are in one motel room with their mother and father. To me, that's not healthy. And there are *so* many children at the motel—*young* children. There are people in this motel who have been here two years. What kind of life is that for a four-year-old child, or even an older one?

I really have no complaint with Social Services. But I do think they should do more in terms of trying to get permanent residences. It must be astronomical amounts a year that Social Services is paying for motels and taxis.

There is nothing wrong with me physically. There's nothing wrong with my husband physically either. Being on welfare itself is degrading. You tend to stagnate. You have no initiative. And you just look forward to your check coming in every two weeks.

If I was in charge of the welfare system, the first thing I would do is take everybody who's on welfare and evaluate them to see if they were able enough to go out and work. Because there *are* jobs out there. There are. Whether you're going to work scrubbing floors or you're going to be an executive down on Wall Street, there are jobs to be had. And then there's a need for a means to get to the job. If you're going to find a job, you definitely need a way to get there. You have to have some sort of transportation.

I don't think I'll be able to find an apartment in the near future just because I don't have transportation to get out to look for it. As long as people are unable to get out there and look for a place, they're not going to find it. How can you find something if you can't look for it? And my husband has no way to look for work.

I have to keep thinking of this as something that's temporary. I want to be independent, self-sufficient. Because I never really was. I was a young mother, and I never finished high school.

I *do* want to go to school. Because I had the kids young, I missed my teenaged years. I was a mother before I was able to be a teenager. I was sixteen when I had my son. I have no regrets about having my children, none of them, but I do feel that I want to do things now that I didn't do when I was a teenager. I want to go back to school.

(F.P.—1986)

There are two particularly interesting things to note about Grace and her outlook. The first is her optimism. Like Kim, Luis, and others encountered in this book, she believes the jobs and opportunities are out there. The United States is indulged by an enormous sentiment of good will from even those citizens who seem to be getting the least in return. To the continual amazement of critics and leaders of the left, throughout the nation's history it has been rare for those "least among us" to direct their discontent at the "system."

The other thing to note is how unforgiving life can be. One mistake, and you can be doomed, with scarcely any good way to climb back. Kim got pregnant and dropped out of school, and her life's course was set; so too with Grace and with too many others. The system ought to be refitted to provide hand-holds for recovery, through schools, job training, or whatever is needed.

THE PROBLEM

"I'm Not Working Now"

Here follows another story, a view of the "system" from some-one within it. The story speaks to the maddening, even cruel, complexity of the system—indeed its features often do seem *systematically* interrelated for the stifling of lives.

Alice Grady* is a black woman in her early thirties. She has three children—daughters aged eleven and fourteen, and a twenty-one-year-old son. They live in southeast Washington, D.C., across the Anacostia River. They have been there only a few months, having come off a spell in shelters for the home-less. It is a multistory apartment house, not very old but with an ugly design, set on a bleak street. The project was built with a subsidy provided under Section 236, a means-tested program whereby renting families pay 30 percent of their income, after some adjustments. Mrs. Grady's rent is $438 a month; the balance after her contribution is paid by the Consortium for Service to the Homeless (Conserve), a private group. Conserve gets money for this from the local Department of Human Ser-vices, through a special program intended to get families out of shelters.

Alice talked in her living room, neatly and plainly furnished. (During her homeless period, her furniture had been stored with friends; the city also provides a family storage system, free for ninety days.) On a wall hung a plaque that read: "We Believe Everyone Should Work. Especially Those Who Have Jobs." Her husband and older daughter, plus an unidentified teenage boy, stayed in the room throughout, without speaking. Had they not been there, the interview might have been more probing about some references (how many fathers, for one example), but the essential truth of her life and situation would not be changed.

I've been receiving welfare about ten years. There were breaks in that, because I'd have a job. But when I'd have babies I'd have to stop working because no babysitters. I worked at the Washington

Convention Center as a security guard for about three years. I've did a little bit of everything. Nurse's aide, maid work, fast-food waitress, been a cashier. My longest period on welfare has been this one, three years.

I liked my nursing, and the Convention Center was very nice. I liked the people there, and my boss. I just couldn't make it on what they were paying me, though. None of my jobs ever paid more than minimum wage.

I was having trouble finding a place to live, and I wasn't married then, and so I went in a shelter. I stayed there for eight months, first at the Capital City Inn and then the Pitts Hotel. It was rough.

They fed you; that was about it. It was mostly like prison. If you've ever been to prison, this is what it is. Prison. Things you could do, things you or your children couldn't do. You can't go to work if you're living there, because of your children. You must be with them at all times, one parent; that's the regulation.

Finding a place wasn't easy. I lucked up on this one. It's pretty far out.

I'm not working now. Right now I'm pregnant with my husband's baby. ["Has it been a long time since you have had one?" I ask. She laughs.] Eleven years! My first husband is dead.

As soon as I can get a babysitter, I intend to go back to work. But it won't be easy. There is a bus stop right out front, but according to where your job is, you'd probably need two or three buses to get to work. You'd have to leave early in the morning, and you'd be leaving your children because they're not supposed to be at school until eight or nine o'clock. Then you'd have to find a babysitter for them in the evening till you got home.

I get $350 a month in AFDC and $127 food stamps, but they never last out the month. After I have my baby, I'll get WIC [Supplemental Food Programs for Women, Infants, and Children, for which she might also have been eligible during pregnancy]. Because I'm on welfare I get Medicaid, and it's been very helpful. So I'd have to make better than minimum wage to make it worthwhile to leave welfare.

But I'm hoping to get off welfare and get me a good job. Right now they're helping me, but it's just making ends meet. You don't have anything left.

I've had no help from the Welfare Department in looking for a job or in job training. They don't provide that. They'll send you to WIN [the Department of Labor's Work Incentive Program], but its just like looking on your own. You go in a little class one or two days and the next day they put you on a computer, and you look down it and find your own job. They'll call the job and say they're sending you out. It never worked for me. But I am signed up for WIN.

You can't go to work anyhow, if you're getting welfare, unless you get a babysitter for your children. They still say I must have one for my fourteen-year-old daughter. I don't have that kind of money, to pay for a babysitter. So I have to stay home. And by the time the rules allow you to leave your children alone, you're off welfare anyhow. My eleven-year-old could go to day care, if there is any around here, but they don't have any for fourteen-year-olds.

I'll be willing to put my baby in a *trusted* [she emphasized that word twice] day care at six months. I'd like to raise my child until he gets a year, but as you know, the money is slim so you have to get out there earlier if you want to make it. You have to pick a good babysitter or day-care school. Children catch so many germs. You have to be careful. I would even like to work while I'm pregnant, but don't too many jobs hire you when you're pregnant. So I'll be ready, when the baby is six months to a year.

I've always lived in D.C. I went all the way through the twelfth grade, graduated, Cardozo High School. It didn't train me for work. I just took the regular courses.

I was raised in foster homes. I didn't know my family until I was twenty-one. Then I met my mother and father. Didn't know who they were before then. I stayed back and forth, was moved about six times in foster homes. When you are a child, you can't do anything about it; you have to live with it. Just like the shelter. When you don't have anywhere to go, you have to abide by their rules or else you'll be doled out.

I don't know whether my parents were ever on welfare; when I met my mother she was working. My sister and brother were raised by my mother. I don't know the situation, why I was raised in foster homes. My brother lives in Virginia, my sister lives in Maryland. With the passing of my mother, I see more of them than before, but we're not too close. She is a nurse, at D.C. General, and my brother does floors; he is a big contractor.

I hope all my children finish school. The girls didn't do very well last year, because we were in the shelter. Their grades fell down. They were worried: "Where are we going?" "How long can we stay here?" I'm hoping they'll do a little better this year.

My twenty-one-year-old son is in Job Corps, in Philadelphia. He likes it. He says there are no jobs unless you get training. I don't quite know what he's taking up. He hadn't finished school. He went to the tenth grade. I couldn't keep him in; that's a boy. Now he's got his GED from Job Corps.

Right now my husband is looking for a job. The shelter program put him out of a job, the way they were running us from place to place. He likes truck-driving. He's also a cook. He's like me, a jack-of-all-trades.

We vote. This year we couldn't, because we were homeless. You know, the homeless here can't vote. You have to have an address.

It's just rough on welfare. It's just not enough. What can I do for school clothes for the kids? When my husband gets a job, we'll be cut back on welfare. I may still get a little help, because my two girls are not his. But not much.

I pray every night. Right now we haven't been going to church, but my children go. A bus comes and picks them up.

(L.W.D.—1987)

From talking with a good many of America's poor and also with those who work with them every day, I feel fairly confident about a few conclusions.

First, the common knowledge that youngsters, from their midteens to their midtwenties, usually do foolish and often do bad things has strong policy implications. The surest way to improve upon the problems associated with welfare is to have a sound youth policy.

When youngsters from the middle and upper classes get into trouble—pregnancy, drugs, drink, dropping out, or a bad car accident—there is usually a family, and enough money, to help them through. Economically and culturally short-changed youth need similar supports; they need to be society's special concern. Our society needs to build a "second chance" into its education and social-welfare methods. Americans are sometimes shocked by European procedures that effectively assign youngsters at early ages to career tracks. In West Germany, children are separated after primary school into those going to the academic high schools that can lead to universities and those going to trade schools. In Britain, examinations at age fifteen determine who will go on to university. The United States, to its credit, is much less rigid. Yet our social order is such that youngsters of lower income pay harsh lifelong penalties for youthful mistakes.

A second conclusion is that the world of work and the world of welfare are separate. They don't and won't mix well. Trying to force them together inevitably cheapens both. Welfare can be fruitfully combined with school or with many kinds of training. It cannot be combined well with work.

Here is the story of one combination that *is* successful, because it involves realistic training for an acceptable job. It makes one wonder why policy can't always work this efficiently and sensibly, or why in this case it did not succeed even earlier.

"What with the Daycare Center for the Kids and All"

You have to be poorer in Kentucky than in almost any other state to qualify for AFDC. Each state has the prerogative of setting its own "standard of need," and in Kentucky this results in welfare eligibility so restrictive that a family of four is cut off when its income is not even half the poverty level.

Of those receiving AFDC, two-thirds are children; one out of every four children in Kentucky depends on AFDC at some time, though only very few remain on the program all their childhood. Kentucky families on welfare average about the same number of children as the general population. Divorce, unemployment, or other temporary adversities are the main causes for turning to assistance; more than a fourth of the receiving families stay on for fewer than thirteen months.

Marsha Adams,* who is white, shows the dilemma of many women with children who are temporary recipients of welfare benefits. She wants to be self-sufficient and is taking advantage of available programs in hopes that they will eventually pull her out of her personal quagmire.

Petite and demure, Marsha describes herself as being very soft-hearted, emotional, and shy. She says she tends to be anxious much of the time, can't be still, has to keep busy. After her parents' divorce, she was raised in her native eastern Kentucky mountains by her grandmother, graduated there from high school, soon got married, moved to Lexington, and is now divorced. She is twenty-five, with two children, four and eight.

My ex-husband was helping me with a little money for the kids until the April before our divorce in June. Then he left town, and I don't know where he is now. For a while I was doing OK. I was working an average of thirty hours a week at K-Mart, getting the minimum wage of $3.35 an hour, and my younger sister was taking care of my kids in the apartment we shared. Later, though, K-Mart cut my hours down to about twenty a week, because they were having budget problems. On top of that, my sister got a job of her own and moved into an apartment with a friend. Suddenly, I didn't have my built-in babysitter, and I was having to pay the full $240-a-month rent. I tried to find another job, but there just didn't seem to be anything available for which I was qualified, even though I had taken some business and typing courses before I graduated from high school.

It was then, four months after my divorce, that I went to the Department of Human Resources here in Lexington, just to see if there was any way I could get child-care assistance. You know, like a day-care center. But I was told that there wasn't anything like that. They also told me that I was making too much money to qualify for AFDC or anything else, like food stamps or Medicaid. [Working twenty hours a week at the minimum wage, Marsha earned $268 a month, or $3,216 a year. In Kentucky, to be eligible for AFDC or Medicaid, a mother of two cannot make more than $197 a month, or $2,364 a year.]

I struggled along for two more months, working just twenty hours a week at K-Mart, but finally faced up to the fact that I couldn't make it on my own. So I quit my job and went back to the Department of Human Resources and applied for welfare. I didn't want to, but it was the only way I could get help. I gave them my ex-husband's

Social Security number so that they could try to track him down, but I don't know that they even tried.

I received my first benefits in December 1984, about six weeks after I applied: an AFDC check for $197, $190 worth of food stamps, and the Medicaid card. In order to pay the rent, though, I had to sell some of my food stamps, which meant we were going hungry by the end of each month. I was always worried about getting caught, but there was nothing else I could do.

Then in the spring of 1985 I found out about two separate programs for people like me. One was the Pell Grant, which provides school-tuition money for two years. I enrolled at Lexington Community College in January of 1986 and am given $975 for each semester, which covers the tuition of about $660 as well as all course books, etc. I'm working on an associate's degree as a medical secretary, and expect to be finished by the end of 1987.

The other program was a new, city-funded, single-parent program offering low-cost housing plus a child-care center in an old apartment building with fifteen units the city was renovating. Each two-bedroom apartment is only $35 a month to rent. As soon as I read about it in the paper, I called the mayor's office to find out how to apply. I was in fact the first one to get accepted. This really gave me a boost in spirits! The apartments were supposed to be ready to move into by August of last year, but August came and went. There was one delay after another due to construction work. It was not until January 15, that I got the word we could move in and, believe me, the very next day the kids and I were moved! Being there has really helped, what with the day-care center for the kids and all. My little boy stays there while I'm at school, and he gets a hot breakfast, snack, and hot lunch. My daughter goes there after school for about forty-five minutes until I pick them up, so she gets a snack each afternoon, too. She also receives a hot lunch at school.

We still have a tough time, though. For instance, I can't remember when I last bought a new piece of clothing for any of us, except for personal items like undergarments. I buy our clothes at second-hand shops or at garage sales. The AFDC check still doesn't stretch far enough, after paying for utilities, transportation costs to and from the college, and all those personal and household items that you can't purchase with food stamps. I do get an allotment of $39 per month for utilities through the single-parent program of the city, but the total utilities usually run close to $100 each month.

I'm not complaining, mind you. I'm just explaining that it isn't as easy as you might think at first. I'm really grateful that I have been able to go to school so that I can get a decent-paying job.

After graduation, I'll have three months before I have to move out of the housing unit. You can't stay there after you get a fairly good job. But that's OK. It will make room for somebody else who needs it more than I will by then. I'll just be glad when I am finally on my own again and can get off welfare.

(C.B.G.—1987)

Marsha's ex-husband and the many like him who, in or out of wedlock, have abandoned children are receiving a lot of attention today. Federal law since 1975 has required mothers to cooperate in seeking to locate fathers, but enforcement has been loose, and the tougher laws since 1984 are only just beginning to be felt. Some states are now working hard to find the strayed fathers and wrest child support from them, and a safe prediction would be that Congress will strengthen their efforts. Indeed, doing that is a primary plank in the reform platform of Senator Patrick Moynihan and his advisers. We agree that parents, males as well as females, should take care of their offspring, and if need be, pressure should be applied. But tightening up the process for securing their support will not be a basic reform. Too many of the fathers, especially where the mothers are long-term recipients, have themselves too little to give.

It is true that divorce and separation are common impetuses driving people to welfare; if there were fewer divorces, there would probably be fewer families on welfare. Like all other support institutions, the social-welfare system can only respond to what already exists in society; trying to cure the response (here, welfare) instead of the illness (the breakup of families) won't get us any further towards a stronger, stabler social structure. As more people get divorced, turn to hard drugs, or are unable to find affordable, decent housing, dependence on welfare is not going to lessen without some strong counterforce intervening.

Some analysts today talk as though there were specific instruments that could resolve the problems, techniques like tracking down fathers or teaching basic skills through computerized programs. This is all to the good; let's keep doing these things. But they won't create jobs where there's no need for them, won't change the fact that the present economy doesn't have jobs in it for all of us.

In practical terms, the "welfare question" comes down to what to do with an Alice Grady, resident of a racial ghetto, unemployed mother of school-age children, and pregnant again while on welfare.

Her main problem is that she doesn't have enough money. All of us can talk ourselves into mental (as well as spiritual) exhaustion as to the why of that, but we still will not have changed the fact that unless Alice has more money, the prospects for her children are very dim. And those children's "costs" to society—of several kinds—are predictably going to be high. So the real question is, how can she get more money?

By working? With her qualifications, she will not get work, beyond a wage that would not pay for her to leave welfare for another eighteen years—and that's assuming she doesn't have another child after this one.

By cutting her off welfare—say when her baby is three, or six months, or whatever? Not only Vincent Matthews (of chapter 2) but some well-placed contemporary social scientists would urge this, in the belief that though job possibilities don't appear to be there, she might work something out if forced to sink or swim. Such a plan would clearly offend the accepted values of American society. I would add that American society should be equally offended by the current practice, which gives Alice inadequate assistance and no realistic chance of getting out of the system's tangles. (Indeed, that assistance, when adjusted for inflation, has fallen about a third since 1970.)

Without a full-employment economy, there can be no practicable and morally acceptable solution for Alice Grady except to give her more money. Lots more. Enough for her family's food, housing, clothing, and health needs. Society may and should couple that with strict requirements—of schooling or of basic-skills or job training for herself and her children—but only if society is willing to pay for them.

What happens if the parent says no to the requirements? That's a very perplexing question. It forces one to ask when society's interest in the children's well-being supersedes that of the parent. Recent bills in Congress do not face the question honestly. They impose the requirement, but don't confront the "what if?" Hard as it is to apply, I think that the old principle of "the best interests of the child" should control. To say that implies a reluctant readiness in dire cases to take the child into custody, though of course the commonly dismal state of foster and institutional care would then have to be vastly improved.

Assuming that work-force participation is not high enough to absorb all who would work if they could, and unemployment is therefore above 4 percent, the hard choice is this: Do we pay now what it costs to give a poor family enough to have a decent, dignified life, or do we pay later to deal with the family's later problems and social costs, and its next generation, and perhaps the next?

Can training draw the Alice Gradys from welfare into self-sustaining work? That is the premise of most contemporary welfare-reform proposals. In some states, plans are already in operation. One of the most highly regarded is in Massachusetts. Here follows the account of one person, a long-term welfare recipient now enrolled in this program. Her story should convey the reality of the problems workfare is challenged to overcome. It also shows the personal strengths that somehow survive and the hopes that don't quite die out, and it reminds us once more that all programs end up dealing not with welfare "types" but with individuals who, if they did not need skilled guidance and assistance, might not be on welfare to begin with. In short, reforms of the system will not mean much, unless administered in a caring spirit, with knowledge of contemporary society.

"If I Make It to School Every Day"

Large pictures of a tiger and a leopard, hanging on Gladys Dix's*
dingy living-room wall, hint at her fierce determination to end
thirteen years as a Boston welfare recipient. She may attain
that goal because of her enrollment in the Employment and
Training program, sponsored by the Massachusetts Department of Public Welfare and known informally as ET.

Offering four to six months of training in such skills as data-
processing, welding, clerical skills, and business-machine repair, ET received $50 million in 1987 (including $10 million
in federal funds), and reports that it has helped forty thousand
welfare recipients obtain jobs during the past four years—more
than 75 percent of them full-time. ET officials claim that the
program saved more than $100 million in 1986 through reduced
welfare benefits and increased revenues from Social Security
contributions and income and sales taxes.

Unlike programs of some other states, ET is voluntary and
offers four options to those welfare recipients who sign on.
Those who are "work-ready" may choose to be placed in jobs,
and about 45 percent do so. Or they may enroll in ET's adult
education and training, and another 40 percent choose this
option. Some, especially older welfare recipients, choose "support work" to prepare them to find jobs in the private sector.
Those who are not sure what they want to do, may opt for
career planning.

Despite ET's liberal features, critics complain that average
wages earned by women after they leave the program are not
enough to allow female heads-of-households, the program's
mainstays, to become financially independent breadwinners.
Making workfare beneficiaries work for dirt-cheap wages or on
jobs that do not prepare them for higher-paying employment,
it is contended, does not begin to address the massive structural
problems that have spawned the nation's underclass. Moreover,
critics charge that ET's success, such as it is, has occurred
mainly because Massachusetts is an atypical state, with unemployment at only around 3 percent.

Nevertheless, Gladys is impressed that the average starting

salary for full-time ET placements is more than $6.50 per hour, or $13,000 per year. That's more than twice the maximum yearly welfare grant of $6,200 for the average family of three, and 40 percent above the applicable federal poverty level of $9,300. These factors, along with Gladys's urgent need for self-validation, undergird the following account of her training.

Don't use my real name. I want to remain anonymous, but I'm not ashamed of my three children born out of wedlock and my being a welfare recipient for thirteen years. I'm not ashamed because I'm in a state employment-training program that's going to take me off of welfare and make life better for me and my kids.

I had my oldest daughter when I was thirteen, my son a year later, and my youngest daughter at eighteen. Then I said, "No more!" and had a tubal ligation the next day. My mother put the idea in my head, but it was my decision. That was ten years ago.

My kids have three different fathers, who I have not seen since I was pregnant. So the children don't know them at all. I have not received one dime from any of these guys, not even a box of Pampers when my babies were born at Boston City Hospital.

I met the first father when I was a troubled child growing up in Omaha. My mother worked two jobs because she felt that we couldn't make it on what the welfare was giving. I was going to school and running track—the hurdles, hundred-yard dash, and the four-forty. When I came home, I had to assume the responsibilities of an older child, and I got tired of it and ran away. I wanted to have time to play and run.

Instead, I slept in the streets. I slept in abandoned buildings. Or I would go to sleep at my stepmother's house on Sunday and wake up on Tuesday. Then my mother sent me down to relatives in Birmingham because I had missed a court date for commitment to an Omaha juvenile-detention home. But I also ran away down South and ended up getting raped.

My sister and I had run away in order to return to Omaha. She took me up to her boyfriend's house, because he had promised that he was going to give us our plane fare. While she was in a room with him, his two brothers raped me and threatened to throw me off the building. When my folks found me, I was sitting on some stairs with my clothes half torn off. Later, the brothers were brought to trial and deported because they were West Indians. For a long time after that I thought that men were good for nothing but usage.

I became involved with the last father because he promised to marry me and help me get off welfare. He was twenty-four and I was eighteen. When he found out I was pregnant, he left town. I'm bitter about him because he tried to deny my daughter. But there's no way that he can deny her. She looks just like him.

My son's father denied him and moved to another state. And my oldest daughter's father lives in Omaha. I don't have the money to sue them, but I've given the welfare people all of the information that I possibly can, so that they can find and prosecute them.

I tried to return to school when my mother moved me from Omaha to Boston, but I was pregnant and the girls in the school didn't like me. They always picked on me, so I dropped out in the tenth grade, even though I was a straight-A student. I never stopped studying, though. I used to sit in a little neighborhood grocery store and do my work. The owner, who was very intelligent, would correct it for me. That was about six months before my first daughter was born.

Today my kids are thirteen, twelve, and nine. The principal thinks my oldest daughter is smart enough to handle a double promotion from the sixth grade if she works hard for it. She'll be doing 126 hours of community service as well as advancing her grades. My son goes to a school for advanced students. He became interested in poetry and now, in the fifth grade, he studies French, Spanish, Polish, and a word-processor. My youngest kid is a little bit slow, but everybody in the school loves her. They tell me I have well-mannered kids.

Even though I'm a student myself at a place about three and a half miles from here, I take time to help them with their books. They teach me what they know and I try to teach them what I know and we compare report cards. Right now they have the best report cards, but I'm working at it and my grades have been no lower than B-plus.

Until recently, I had to work odd jobs to pay my bills. I couldn't tell the welfare because they would have cut me off. I don't feel that working for $25 a day should be enough to get you cut off. That's only $125 a week, which is below minimum wage [by $9].

I've been paying $500 a month rent for five rooms. Cold air seeps up from the basement, the roof is falling in, and the bathroom floor is sinking. If I complain too much, the landlord might evict me. The welfare sends me $684, which means that after I pay my rent, I only have $184 left to budget every month. My gas bill runs me up to $40 a month. The light bill is about $80. If I miss paying either one for two months, I have to pay at least $30 penalty.

Meanwhile, the welfare expects you to buy clothes for the kids out of the $125 a year they allot for each one, but you can't find a good pair of gym shoes for under $25. Blue jeans—I don't mean designer jeans—are costing between $25 and $30. I have to do my shopping at a thrift shop, where I can get nice sweaters for the kids for $3. Most of my own clothes are hand-me-downs from my mother, or I might find something at the thrift shop costing only a dollar, if I have a dollar left.

I don't understand why I have to pay a dollar a day for my daughter's lunch. That's $20 a month. I get $179 in food stamps, but they run out in two weeks because my kids are at the age where they eat excessively. I try to budget by buying more pork than beef. Sometimes the kids don't eat it. So I try dry beans, which they get sick of eating four times a week. They tell me they're not hungry, and I end up getting the things they like to eat, like soups, pork and beans, hot dogs, and lots of chicken. When I run out of food, I turn to places like the one where I take classes. They send me to a food bank or they try to get me a voucher so I can get food to last until the end of the month.

If I make it to school every day, the welfare sends me an extra $63 a month and three dollars a day for transportation. They don't help you when you run out of food. All they want you to do is just go, whether you eat or not. But some of the teachers at the school will help you if you ask them.

I started classes in April [1987], my first time back in school in thirteen years. Even though the employment-training program is about two years old, I didn't enroll back then because I didn't really know about it. Besides, at that time I was mainly trying to work odd jobs.

I finally decided that I had to get off of welfare because I wasn't making it. All I was doing was killing myself. When I found out about the employment-training program, I went up to see my social worker, and she sent me to my employment-training worker. I told her I wanted to work with computers. She said, "Fine! I have the program for you."

I attend school five days a week. How long I stay depends on my classes. Right now I'm taking up word-processing, math, English, spelling, and language arts. I was supposed to finish at the end of December 1987, but I didn't because I had a mild stroke in September. My whole left arm and leg were paralyzed, but I'm getting more and more use of them.

I suffer from headaches because of tension and stress and I have to take high-blood-pressure medicine, even though my pressure isn't high, to keep the veins in my head open so that they won't get tense and close again. The doctor told me that I might not be so lucky the next time.

My kids are trying to get me to stop smoking, but I need something. Once I worried so much that my hair fell out. I used to drink a lot of beer and occasionally gin, but now I don't because of my stomach ulcer. I used to smoke a lot of marijuana, but I stopped that years ago. It was like a pacifier, something to keep me going and help me to forget. I tried to blank out my problems because I felt nobody understood and nobody cared.

I once visited a psychiatrist three times because I dreamed I was dying. I still have those dreams, but I stopped seeing him because I figured I can handle my problems. I attend the Holiness Church from eleven to four on Sunday and from seven to nine on Wednesday evenings. The church has helped me spiritually but not materially because I've never asked for any help. I'm a very proud person and the only time I will ask for help is when it comes to feeding my kids.

I never considered committing suicide because my kids are enough to keep me going. When I feel really down and angry, I'll cry and then I'll look at them and they'll give me a big hug and say, "Momma, we love you!" They understand.

I'm almost at the end of my courses now. I just have to bring up my typing speed, which dropped because of my stroke. I feel I can raise it because I'm determined to get off welfare. My computer teacher tells me that just finishing the program and going to work really has no future. She says I should continue my schooling in data-processing because she feels I'm very good at it and I can eventually make $40,000 a year as a systems manager. I feel that if she has that much confidence in me, I should have it in myself. So I'm going to go for it. As soon as I finish this school, I'm going to enroll at a community college to study systems administration.

I figure I'll be off welfare in about three years, then they can have it. I don't want to be rich. I just want to live comfortably. I just want to be where I don't have to worry whether I'm going to be able to meet next month's rent or shop at the grocery store or buy shoes for my kids. I know I can make it. If I hadn't gotten pregnant at an early age, I probably would have made it by now. I could go to work wearing a shirt and tie and be up there. I'm going to be up there! I'm not going to let it die!

(A.P.—1987)

With a full-employment economy, the country could go back to the original concept of AFDC, appropriately modified to reflect how family life has changed. It would thus offer temporary relief for the family unit, in the interest of the children, with duration linked firmly to the children's age—stopping when they reach three or four. Mothers are working in far greater numbers than they did in 1935 when the forerunner of AFDC was enacted, and are choosing to return to work when their children are quite young. Expanded child-care facilities and flex-time will have to become commonplace. But parents are a sufficient constituency to see to that, pressing legislatures and employers. There can be but minimal confidence, however, in government initiatives aimed at "helping" people who haven't been consulted. The poor are not being consulted in contemporary drives for reform. Governments should probably go slow in instituting reforms, such as prescribing the forms of child care, which like other social or educational services should be allowed to evolve as people's conditions and outlooks change.

On the other hand, one thing federal and state governments can promptly do is extend adequate tax relief to parents choosing to obtain qualified care for their young children. So far as I know, there is no general reason to prefer the neighborhood nursery school over the retired lady in the next block. The essential is that a parent have an income or an entitlement sufficient to afford whichever suits best.

For Congressmen, administrators, and social scientists to talk as they do today is hypocrisy. They talk of "moral hazards" the poor must be protected from through discipline administered by the "system." They talk of balancing incentives to work against those slothful disincentives to work which they presume dominate the poor's culturally induced attitudes. And they often talk to each other about these assumed facts through mathematical equations. They persuade themselves that they can manage the lives of the poor so as to produce self-reliance where before there was dependence. They are, in short, the direct descendants of all the welfare reformers of Anglo-American history since the eighteenth century.

The view that there is a "culture of poverty" that traps an underclass has been adopted by contemporary spokespersons running the political gamut from the socialist Michael Harrington to the free-marketer Charles Murray. This book holds that poverty is essentially determined by lack of money, a view that also has its defenders. A recent article has the following pertinent summary:

> One-third of the persistently poor [those who have been poor for eight or more years by 1978] are elderly or live in households headed by an elderly man or woman. Two-fifths of the persistently poor live in households headed by a disabled man or disabled woman. The persistently poor are not concentrated in large northern cities: two-thirds of them live in the South; only one-fifth live in large urban areas; and the proportion of the persistently poor living in large cities is considerably smaller than the proportion who live in small towns or rural areas.[2]

Bertram M. Beck, one of America's most experienced social-work administrators, has put the matter well:

2. Mary Corcoran, Greg J. Duncan, Gerald Gurin, and Patricia Gurin, "Myth and Reality: The Causes and Persistence of Poverty," *Journal of Policy Analysis and Management*, vol. 4, no. 4 (1985), p. 526.

It is a sign of our moral bankruptcy that welfare reform has come to mean simply getting people off welfare and into work. True reform would be marked by charity and justice. It would recognize the causes of poverty embedded in our social and economic systems, as well as in the person of the poor. It would seek to provide good jobs for the vast majority who are more than willing to work and an effective program of social rehabilitation for those who lack the spirit and the will to function in a manner acceptable to themselves and society.[3]

The proposal made in the last chapter could, it goes without saying, be improved in lots of ways. The only virtue claimed for it is that it is serious. Workfare as a condition of welfare assistance is not serious. Only in an economy that needs workers can people work, and this economy does not need all of us, despite what some of our most appealing interviewees have said. The kind of jobs they suspect are out there, if they exist at all, do not pay back more than welfare, in terms of either money or self-esteem.

Mandatory work in return for subsistence—which is the essential meaning of workfare—both cheapens the work experience and robs income assistance, when needed, of its dignity as a just entitlement of citizenship or other lawful status. It has a second ugly, and expensive, flaw. It adds to administrative burdens and costs, and therefore to discretionary rule. Discretion—that is, the need to judge who is deserving—is the curse of means-tested programs, the ticket to endless regulations and numberless regulators. Workfare would be a bottomless pit of both.

Even were a sound jobs plan in place, it could not eliminate the need for welfare for some: the poor mother of an infant, the disabled worker, the woman adjusting to a divorce. But though welfare has to be, it cannot end poverty. The social insurances that protect the old (and indirectly protect their children, who otherwise might have to take on that burden) and jobs for the younger can end it. But not welfare. For those not, for whatever reason, ready to work, the need is for money.

---

3. Letter to the editor, *New York Times*, August 6, 1987.

Give them money. Enough of it. Give them training, too, and help with their children. Do all that can be done to increase their readiness to work, if work is possible at all. In the meantime, give them, and especially those who are rearing children, enough money. Give some of it, if more convenient, through food stamps or free school lunches. Or help with the heating bills. Just as there are Medicaid cards and food stamps, there could be fuel cards. Cash would probably be more sensible, though, just as it might be more sensible than food stamps. There could be housing cards, too, if the housing supply were there; unlike food and fuel, it is not. But whatever the form it takes, give money. And improve the schools. Build up the supply of jobs. Extend the adequacy of the social insurances, so that fewer of us will need welfare at all.

Welfare should be seen only for what it can be: entitlement for public assistance. It should come from the federal government; welfare ought to be thoroughly nationalized. Establishment of a uniform minimum for AFDC throughout the states, and extension into all states of AFDC-U (eligibility for families with an unemployed father), both long overdue, would be steps forward, but still not enough. The Nixonian family-assistance plan was on the right track. The Reaganite schemes—such as those already begun in New Jersey and no doubt, by the time this book is published, followed in other states—of passing responsibility for requirements and benefits down to state and local administrations are wrong.

In the previous chapter I advocated a much enlarged role for the states in jobs and training programs. They are better able to help develop opportunities and talents. But welfare, including Medicaid, should be provided strictly and solely according to legal norms—*entitlements*—and not according to anyone's opinion of other people's worthiness or deservingness. And it should be federally administered, like Social Security and Medicare: a statutory entitlement, routinely issued, derived from one's place in the national economy. It should be as routinely issued—and as routinely reviewable by federal officials—as all other entitlements should be.

Doing so would make it possible for Medicare and Medicaid

to be merged, as they should have been all along. The health of the poor, especially that of poor children, is as much a national concern as is that of the aged (who, as a matter of fact, receive a sizable share of Medicaid money: about two-thirds of Medicaid *patients* are children and adults on welfare but two-thirds or more of Medicaid *costs* are for the aged, blind, and disabled qualifying under SSI). In a merged program, medical coverage would be available to those entitled to Social Security or to income support; and like all national entitlement programs, they should be federal throughout. National health insurance will be politically attainable only in gradual steps; merging Medicare and Medicaid could be a first long stride.

ADMINISTRATION'S NATURAL TENDENCIES

The soup kitchen is an enduring staple of American society. *Webster's*, which defines the term as "an establishment dispensing minimum dietary essentials (as soup and bread) to the needy," says it has been in use since at least 1851. In virtually every city there are places where people in need of food can get it, free of charge. Most of the kitchens are operated by religious or other private organizations.

There are at least three kitchens in Rochester, New York, a metropolitan area of close to a million people whose industrial economy is dominated by the Eastman Kodak Company. Two kitchens, one run by the Catholic Worker organization and the other by Saints Peter and Paul Roman Catholic Church, serve at noon. The Open Door Mission, a nondenominational rescue mission operated by the Reverend Kenneth S. Fox, a minister of the Independent Assemblies of God, provides an evening meal, along with a religious service and "crisis housing" for men who need it.

A common public conception is that it is only homeless men, many of them addicted to alcohol, who populate soup kitchens. Some who visit the centers in Rochester fit that category, but the kitchens' operators say the true population of the hungry is much more diverse. There are more families, more children, and more teenagers than in the past. Marty Larch left a bookkeeper's job at Merrill Lynch to work full time at the Catholic Worker kitchen because he felt a call to help people. He said that many members of society still pair *soup kitchen* with *hobo*, but that such a characterization is incorrect. "Actually," he asserts, "we serve people who are not much different from suburbanites, in that most of them have once experienced a regular lifestyle. But they had a streak of bad breaks that they haven't bounced back from." Larch and his fellow workers serve from 60 to 120 meals a day.

"Their Dignity Somehow Is Broken"

A couple of miles away, on the other side of Rochester's downtown business district, St. Peter's kitchen serves a densely populated residential area that houses many low-income families. Brother Walter deCremieux, a member of the Congregation of the Sacred Hearts of Jesus and Mary, directs the kitchen in the basement of a vacant building that once housed a parish school. He estimated, in mid-1986, that more than 60,000 meals would be served there by the end of the year. As at many kitchens, the number of guests follows a pattern dictated by the arrival of welfare checks and food stamps. On the first of a typical month, when checks arrive, St. Peter's feeds 106 people. Later in the month the number more than triples, then declines quickly when the next check comes.

Unlike some providers of food, St. Peter's does not require that its guests pray, listen to sermons, or do anything else other than arrive sober and remain peaceful while they eat. The kitchen's credo is posted prominently on a wall of its spotless dining hall. It says, in part:

St. Peter's kitchen invites all God's children to table fellowship, without regard to race, religion, economic or social condition, or any other factor. It will meet the need of feeding the hungry. But it will also, we hope, meet the need of bringing together in table fellowship people of every condition. There will be no charge to eat from Peter's kitchen, but there will be no poverty test, either. All are welcome and eagerly invited.

On a recent weekday morning, eight volunteers chatted pleasantly as they worked to get the food on the table by noon. It was a relatively simple meal: cream of chicken soup, bologna sandwiches, tomato slices, pickles, and juice. Each yellow-topped table held a large plastic bin of doughnuts and bowls of mustard and mayonnaise. As they leave, guests are encouraged to take loaves of bread, muffins, or buns that, like much of the rest of the food, were donated by local supermarkets and other food-industry groups.

At precisely noon, the doors opened for the first seating of sixty-four people. Many were children, and the noise level immediately rose. Close to three-quarters of the guests were black. Only a few of them seemed to fit any of the stereotypes of hobo, bag lady, or drifter. Several whole families came in to eat. Many guests knew others at their tables, and the conversation was animated and friendly. It was, in fact, a fellowship. Almost all the guests thanked the kitchen staff as they left, or at least nodded their heads in appreciation.

In a calm moment, Brother Walter described the kitchen's operations.

The kitchen has become sort of an oasis for a lot of the people who live in the neighborhood. Many of them are on welfare assistance or food stamps. Some of them are retired, some of them are on Social Security, some of them are not. We place no conditions on anyone who wishes to come down here.

We are not financed by any federal, state, or city government. Our finances and everything else are strictly private donations or they result from appeal letters or fund-raising events or just word-of-mouth. I sent three letters off to two corporations and one college in the city, and I received a check for $700 from one corporation toward the purchase of our van. The other corporation sent me a letter referring me to a class that gives courses in how to write letters asking for money!

I was really angry about that. Because within the radius of the community we serve, on the fringes of that company's parking lot, are the people who come to the kitchen to eat. It bothered me very much. But what can one do? What can one say? It's very sad.

Anything that's not donated in food items, I supplement with the income that I get from church funds and gifts to buy the basics like hamburger and stew meat and hot dogs and bologna for sandwiches, and cheese and things of this sort. I'm not even qualified to get the government cheese, butter, and milk [from the federal surplus commodity program]. I'm sure that there's bureaucratic red tape and forms to fill out. What people do is, those who don't need it go and get it and give it to me. So I get it second-hand.

We try to make our guests feel welcome and comfortable here. We don't just feed them soup. That soup-kitchen connotation is wrong. I don't believe in it. I think it's degrading to human dignity to call it a soup kitchen. I call it just St. Peter's kitchen.

It's extremely depressing to see the state of some of the people who come down here: the physical state; what they're wearing. But there's another spirit that they carry with them, knowing that they can come down here and get a hug and be affirmed and be spiritually nourished, as well as physically nourished, by what we do. A lot of the people who come down here are hurting. And they resist coming down here, but they know they have no other choice. They really don't have anything at home. So knowing that, I try to extend that warmth and feeling of welcome when they come, as do all the rest of the volunteers who work here.

There's a spirit of brokenness a lot of them have. It's, "The whole world is against me; I have no job." One guy said, "Why don't you get me a job? You know people." I *don't* know people. I don't know where to send anyone for a job. And of course, a lot of the guests simply do not wish to start at the bottom. There's a lot of jobs available in the city. Some of them are out of this area, like in the shopping malls, which would require their being able to get on a bus to get to the jobs.

But their dignity somehow is broken—not all of them, but a lot of them. They feel there's no reason to continue; nothing to get up for in the morning. So when they do get up, they may go to the corner, ramble in the bushes and vacant lots, and sit on broken furniture outdoors and maybe drink Irish Rose wine and play craps in the street and get inebriated and then get into fights.

A lot of the people whom I confront and try to help and try to encourage, one day they'll be up here and next day they're down here [he holds his hand first high, then low]. But I accept that, because I know that I have my own brokenness. I have my own imperfections and weaknesses that I have to deal with. So who am I to pass judgment on them?

Later, Jenny Crawford,* a frequent guest at the kitchen, spoke of her experience. Her yellow-gray hair was long and straight, and her cheeks were sunken. Her eyes were bright and sharp, but they ranged about the room as she talked.

I've been coming here about seven years. I come here because I like it here. I come here because of the Lord, and I like the Lord, and I think a lot of the Lord. I don't swear. I don't steal, or anything like that. I'll be sixty-four in November. I got a boy forty-one years old, and he's right here. This is my home, in Rochester. My kids was born here.

I'm on SSI. They give me $407, and by the time I buy groceries it don't last long. I have to come here. I get food stamps, too, but they only give me $10 worth. I was wondering if I could get more because of my age. They wanted me to go to a hearing to try to get me more, but I don't know if I could pass or not.

I don't like the welfare department at all. The welfare department, they took my kids away from me when they were little.

[Jenny was asked why this had happened. Tears gathered in her eyes and her voice broke.]

I don't know. They didn't want me to have them.

I've got a lot of friends here. My friends come here, too, and they all like me. Everybody does. There's an old man here, he knows that every time I get cigarettes I give them to him. I don't get meals anywhere else. This is the only place I come.

Jenny's son, Bob,* wore a plaid flannel shirt and blue jeans. His corn-yellow hair stuck out in several directions from his head, and he, like his mother, glanced from place to place as he talked. Sometimes, when his mother was speaking, he talked, too, but he seemed to be conversing with no one in particular. And sometimes when Bob was talking, his mother did the same thing.

I'm just a young man. I'm forty-one years old. I'm a security guard. I've guarded the president of the United States. When he came here to make a speech in Rochester, I was down there with about seven hundred other guards.

I got my own apartment [Bob and his mother live in separate households], but I see a lot of people on the street, boy, eatin' out of garbage cans and whatnot, and I think it's ridiculous.

I get money, but by the time my rent's paid and everything, I'm broke. I don't get that much. I get $491 a month, from SSI, disability. My disability is that I can't read and write. But I'm smart in a lot of other ways. I'm well trained. The reason I can't read and write is that I got what you call a mind block. I have to do everything on a certain level. I can only do certain things for an hour and then I get tired, and everything goes mixed up. My mind goes tired, and I forget what I'm doing.

I work off and on as a guard. But not steady. Here, there, wherever they need one. I go to amusement parks, churches, wherever they need a guard for the day. Or if they're shorthanded. I get paid by the job. Not steady; just whenever they need me. I come here to eat. I've got to stretch my food, because by the time I buy my groceries and pay the rent, I don't have much. And that's the truth. I come here every day through the week except Sunday. On Sunday this is not open.

[Bob was asked what he thought the future would hold.]

I don't know. I have no idea what's in store. I'd just like it to get better. I just want to enjoy life and have things get better. Too many bad things are happening, and I wish it would improve.

I think if the government really wanted to do something, they would give people a half a chance that want to work. Give them a chance. Don't just, when you go for an application, say, "Well, we ain't got nothing," and things like that, slam the door right in your face before you're even heard. They should sit down and listen to each one, give them a chance, meet him halfway. I've been interviewed by a lot of people for jobs, and I have that feeling. I've seen jobs in the paper, and I've went all that distance, and I get there and they say, "Well, the jobs are full" or, "It's already taken." And that makes you feel about that high off the ground [holds his hands close to the floor].

They think I've got a lack of experience. Well, I've worked in a canning factory. I drove a tow motor. I used to run a machine in a box factory. I can unload a truck. I can paint. I can move furniture. I can mow lawns. I can do just about everything. There ain't *nothing* I can't do. All they got to do is furnish the stuff, and I'm glad to do it. I've dug ditches. I've laid blocks. I've wheeled cement. I've carried roofing. I've helped put on roofing. When I used to work in Buffalo, I used to work two jobs. Worked in a nursery all day and worked in a canning factory all night.

And I used to draw wages twice what a normal person would. I used to draw two checks a month while other people were drawing one. And now, I miss all that money. I used to make darn good money. I used to eat good. I used to dress right to the minute. You wouldn't even know me if I was dressed up. I used to buy $45 shirts, $75 shoes, $85 pants. Real expensive suit coats. Real expensive dress hats. And I'd buy a real high-class cigar. I'd walk around and you'd think I owned you. Ask my mom; she knows. She's seen pictures of me with outfits on. I had a deerskin coat and white hat when I went out to see her.

[Did Bob blame anyone for his present situation?]

No, I've just had a lot of bad luck in the past. And I've got to straighten myself out. It's just bad luck. I think everybody's had a little bit of that in their life.

(F.P.—1986)

Are there even any small cities today without at least one soup kitchen? What kind of a country has the United States allowed itself to become, where soup kitchens are part of normality? With them and with the proliferation of shelters for the homeless, are the destitute being ghettoized into a modern poorhouse system, certifying them as strange, as aliens, as radically apart from "us"?

Oppressive administration has been an enduring problem in America's treatment of the poor—of every country's treatment, it can likely be said. This is primarily a result of means-testing, and sound policy should get as far away from this as it can. When it can't get all the way away—and it cannot; some is inevitable—assistance should be converted from discretionary grants into entitlements that one qualifies for legally.

"I Try to Stretch the Truth Quite a Bit"

John LaFleur* is a down-on-his-luck fifty-five-year-old man in the semirural Midwest. No one should have this man's afflictions; no one—least of all a citizen of the United States—should have the trials he has had with the "system."

The only way I got Medicaid is that I went through my congressman's office. My nephew, Bill Walters,* works for the congressman in his district office up here. I had to go through him to get Medicaid and SSI. He said the reason I was having trouble getting it was there was a conflict between two different formulas. Whatever it was, it took me about two years to get Medicaid, going through all those forms and everything, and about six months to get SSI.

The doctors who had to sign the SSI forms for me said I was totally disabled. Couldn't do nothin'. But according to the people at Social Security, there must have been something I could do. And the doctors said, "No, there's nothing he can do. He's got congestive heart failure and hypertension and emphysema and a bad leg and you name it."

My social worker, Peg Grove,* tried to help me in every way that she could. She tried to get me Medicaid and backed me up all the way, but there was some medical board downstate that said I wasn't disabled. They said that without seeing me. They never did see me. They were just looking at a piece of paper.

But by that time, I had help from the congressman's office. Bill told the people who were helping me—my sister and her daughter— what to put on the forms: that my illness was affecting my mind. Bill told them to put on there, "Defective mind, mentally."

When I heard that, I said to Bill, "*You're* nuts." But he said, "Ask your doctor." And the doctor says, "Yes, in order to get SSI you have to lie right through your teeth. Because they'll say there must be some sort of work you can do, and you have to tell them you can't do nothin'."

When I was up at my sister's, in bed, Social Services said I could only stay there for thirty days. Her house is just over the line in Roscoe County, and my Social Services is Lake County. They said I could stay at my sister's only thirty days, and then I'd have to move back to Lake County for at least one day. Then I could go back there for another thirty days. Otherwise I'd have to sign up with Roscoe County. And that didn't make no damn sense to me, because the doctor said, "He has to stay there, and he can't be home alone, and somebody has to take care of him." Like I was an invalid, you know. I couldn't do nothin'. So they let me stay there.

I've had the best damn doctors that I've ever seen in my life. They're wonderful doctors. And the hospital in general, I wouldn't knock it in any way. Beautiful. It's the dummies over there in the government that're the problem. Social Services and Social Security.

Now they tell me, when I signed up for my food stamps yesterday, my caseworker asked me if I had a checking account, and I said, "Certainly I do. My check goes from Social Security to the bank." She said, "Well, you're not allowed to have a checking account."

I said, "In other words, you want me to go to the post office and buy money orders and pay all my bills that way. It would cost whatever the money orders cost. This way, I just automatically do it." She said, "Well, I'm sorry. Those are the rules." I said, "You know what you can do with your rules, don't you?"

But I've still got a checking account. [He chuckles. It's clear he's cajoled his social worker into ignoring his breach of rules.]

I'm getting the SSI from the federal government, and all I'm getting out of Social Services now is their Medicaid and food stamps. But if I was still getting general assistance from them, if I made $5, I'd have to report it. If I didn't report it and they found out about it, they'd cut me off for up to ninety days. My caseworker, she once told me that if I can make anything and get away with not reporting it, to keep quiet. She said, "I know that *I* couldn't live on that much a month, plus the food stamps." She said, "No way." Because I'm a diabetic, too, and I'm supposed to have special food. She said, "You walk into a store with maybe $150," which I've got to live on for food for a month, "and there's no way you can do it, with a special diet."

I try to stretch the truth quite a bit. If I can get away with it, I'll lie every way I can. If somebody said my name is Sally, my name is

Sally, just to get rid of them pot-lickers. You have to. If I could make $1,000 a week and not say anything about it, I would.

And now they're talking about cutting my food stamps off. They claim I'm making more on SSI than I was on general assistance. I went over to Social Services yesterday to get my food stamps, which were running about $80 a month, which ain't very much for food, and she said, "It'll be cut almost in half, or lower, because you're getting $363.80 a month in SSI to live on."

I said, "Yeah, but that covers my rent, which is $130 a month, plus my gas and my lights, and now the doctor says I got to have a phone, just in case, you know." They do send me a Medicaid card every month so I don't have to worry about my medication. But she said that after two years, they'll be putting in Medicare, and I won't have Medicaid anymore. And Medicare, I understand, only covers about 75 percent or something like that, and I'll have to pay the rest.

I don't know how I'm going to be able to do that. And I called Social Security yesterday also, and I asked them, "If I had a part-time job, how much can I make before it affects my SSI?" They said $65 a month. Well, that doesn't even buy smokes!

(F.P.—1986)

"It's a System That Tries to Keep You on Welfare"

A handful of constants emerge time after time in the interviews. They are seen and heard and accepted as obvious by those who frequent the many-layered world of welfare. One is that the whole system is supersaturated with catch-22s. Even many admninistrators, supervisors, and policy-makers believe this. Someone in need of assistance finds that complying with one program's regulations makes you ineligible for another, or creates some condition that leaves you worse off than before. Attempts at self-sufficiency can even be punished, not rewarded.

The painful examples just from our interviews are legion. John LaFleur, convalescing at his sister's house with a leg abscess, received family care and saved himself and the county money, but was told he would lose his benefits if he did not return to his home county once a month—even though his sister's house stands just a few yards across the county line. Luis Rodriguez, the devoted family man in the south Bronx, had to abandon his wife temporarily (or at least, have her claim that he had) to maintain their benefits. And Grace Fredericks, the homeless woman living with her family in a Westchester motel, has no means of transportation so she or her husband can look for work, even though the county spends $150 a day on taxi fare to carry her kids to school—all the way to New York City. Finally there is the example of the miner. He knows that if he fights for payments due him under the black-lung program, he will lose equal benefits he receives for another disability. There's not only wasted effort in doing this but real danger: having lost one set of benefits, he knows that the capricious black-lung program might in the future cut him off from those second hard-won benefits, leaving him with nothing at all.

Another constant about the welfare system is that it takes extra energy and tenacity just to gain a reasonable measure of what it promises. People who wait passively for the system to deliver, or whose resolution is blinded by bitterness or rage, often lose out, go hungry, or sink even further from self-sufficiency, down through the yawning rips in the so-called safety net. Those who make it are fighters, the ones the administrators refer to with admiration as the "survivors," and to be one, you have to be a pusher, too, like John LaFleur. He cajoled his social worker into bending the rules—LaFleur is good at cajoling—and he did not hesitate to telephone friends and relatives who know prominent politicians and to enlist their support. He, like several of those who were interviewed, talked about establishing a close relationship with a caseworker, one who, in LaFleur's case, advised him to lie if necessary to get the benefits to which he was entitled. Often, the interviewees said, you *have* to lie.

It does not take much investigation to conclude, as many of those I've interviewed have, that a system so contrary to reason encourages people to keep quiet and stay in it, even when they have the desire and the ability to escape. As Sam, one of the patients, explained, "If you go out and start working and get ill again and then have to quit work, it's so hard to get back in the system. It almost makes you scared to want to go out and work." Sam is an optimist. Many others would not say "almost."

Anita Buckley* is another survivor. Hers is not a typical story of the American welfare system, although she has been a "client" for much of her life, but she is a valuable and experienced interpreter of it. She is also a premier example of the sort of person who succeeds. It is important to remember that Anita Buckley is rare. For every one like her, there are thousands who do not know how to address a letter to a congressional representative or how to deal with a judgmental caseworker. And it is important to remember, too, that even in her success, Buckley is far from declaring her independence of the system.

Her mother died when Anita was a year old, and her father placed her in various homes, "to be raised," as she put it, "as best they could." She was married in 1968 at sixteen, got pregnant quickly, and found her family faced with the enormous difficulty of surviving in a southern rural county on $53 a week. Food stamps and the WIC program didn't exist then, and Buckley had to learn how to cope with the welfare system while working as a paraprofessional in a maternal-health agency, finding babysitters, getting pregnant again, serving as a foster parent (Buckley says she had dues to pay from her own unsettled childhood), and going to school (both she and her husband knew education would be the only way out of their dilemma).

Buckley has not extricated herself yet, but she is trying, by working as a waitress, making plans to continue her education, and participating actively in organizations such as the League of Women Voters. She also counsels and assists other women in similar situations. She knows from her own experience, for example, that signing up for an assistance program is not just a matter of strolling down the street and endorsing a few papers.

There are no workers who are going to come out and sign you up for WIC. Sometimes it's really hard for somebody, first, to take their pride in their hands and go apply for WIC, and second, to let their pride go enough that they would ask a neighbor or a friend to take them to apply for free food. They're going to have to admit that they can't feed their kid. That's a big deal, for one adult to say to another adult, "I can't feed my child, and I need your help getting me in to sign up."

You have to have friends or family who can drive you to the welfare office, and there are parts of this county where that may be sixty miles. And there's the limitation of having to go in and talk to an agency person. Anybody who's ever been on AFDC knows that a hell of a lot depends on what worker you get.

[What bothers her the most, she said, is the way programs such as AFDC work against family solidarity.] You're destroying the whole fabric of the family life right there when you say, "OK, if your husband leaves, we'll help you. We'll give you AFDC, we'll give you food stamps, and we'll give you a medical card. But if we find out he's sneaking back or he's home, no help for you" [her state does not offer AFDC-U].

The husband can't find a job. The woman has children to care for and probably can't find a job. Or together, working at minimum-wage jobs, they still can't make ends meet. So they can split up and do better. So what happens? Why do you think there are so many female-headed households in the United States?

You walk through the front door of the welfare office. You see all these other people in the same kind of situation you're in, they're there for food stamps, or a medical card, or AFDC. You walk up to the front desk. It's not a private front desk. You state your name and what you're there to apply for. Food stamps, medical care, or whatever.

And you are going to be overheard by the other people who are sitting there. When you get back to a worker, you sit there until that worker has time to see you. You sit in her little cubicle and hear every word that's being said at the next cubicle. It's not private at all.

If you go in for food stamps, they have legally thirty days to work that case. You know how hungry you can get in thirty days? How hungry a *family* can get? You have to have proof of income, or proof of *no* income. If you're applying for AFDC, you've got to have statements from your landlord, from close neighbors—who have a telephone, so the worker can call and verify—saying that the father is not present in the home. You need many other documents.

Place yourself in a position of being someone who may or may not have transportation, who may or may not have a babysitter, who may or may not have a Social Security card, who may not even know her landlord's name because it's rented through some kind of corporation, whose nearest neighbors are people who don't have a phone. If you're uneducated, you know what this is going to sound like to you? It's going to sound like they could be speaking Spanish with you and you're an English-speaking person.

You're revealing the most private parts of your life to a worker, with another person at another desk overhearing you. The end of all this is that it's a system that tries to keep you on welfare. Why, for example, can't people trying to leave the system keep their medical benefits for six months, to ease the transition? And why can't the AFDC mother keep her food stamps for six months to help her get started?

Maybe she loses that job. She gets fired. Maybe the babysitter didn't show up two days in a row. Maybe her old car conked out, or whatever. She loses that job. It's going to take her three months to get back through the process, have that last check's income disregarded, get back on food stamps, and get back to where she started from. She goes right back to square one. And it's going to take at least three months to even get back to square one.

So she decides, "Hell, this didn't work. I worked my tail off, and I didn't make it. I'm back where I started, and I'm going to stay here." And then what happens? The kids get to be eighteen years old. All those kids have ever known is, "Momma tried, and every time Momma tried, she got kicked down, so what's the use of *me* trying? What's the use of me trying to get a high-school education? What's the use of me trying to get a job? Because Momma couldn't make it, so how'm *I* going to make it?" It breeds hopelessness.

(F.P.—1987)

Anita Buckley thinks the future is dismal, both for her and for others trapped in the American social-welfare system. And that is not an unusual attitude. Even the survivors, the people who have learned to work with the system and sometimes make it work for them, even they are pessimistic about the years to come. They don't expect the system itself to deliver them from their situations. At best, they said, the system might buy them some time, put some food in their bellies, enable them to get some medical care. But it was clear that they felt any permanent change could come only from their own energies. And these people do not have much energy to spare.

Social-welfare policies will always be, and probably should be, debated within partisan politics. But that doesn't have to mean being locked into one way of acting; political parties and candidates can outgrow their pasts. "Nigger politics" is no longer acceptable in the South, although but a generation ago it still had life to it. A nation *can* grow up. America has matured spectacularly since World War II, in one way (if only one way). It now understands the idea of "consent of the governed." Blacks, Hispanics, Indians, even white women were in the past hardly part of those from whose consent the "just powers" of government arose. The great achievement of our times has been the democratizing of our political and social life. It would be a profound betrayal of that progress were a new concept to take root, of some "underclass" not fully and actually part of us—not surprisingly, heavily composed of racial minorities, of whom it is now unacceptable to speak in racial terms.

We have to look forward, therefore, to a time perhaps not far off, when *welfare bums*, or euphemisms for the same, will be beyond the tolerated limits of political debate, in a society become mature enough to seek serious solutions to the problems it has caused or allowed to grow.

CHAPTER FIVE

A   Just   Entitlement:

THAT   CHILDREN
MAY   GROW   IN
GOOD   NURTURE

THE IMPORTANCE to any nation of the good growth
of its children, and the natural dependence of children on the
adults who surround them, hardly needs to be elaborated on.
Marian Wright Edelman, in her recent fine book, puts it well:

> Children are utterly dependent on adult society to meet their
> most basic needs so they can survive and grow into self-sufficient
> adults—caring parents, competent workers with a fair oppor-
> tunity for success and fulfillment, responsible citizens in a de-
> mocracy. They need our help to be born healthy and at normal
> birth weight, which means that every mother must receive early
> and continuous prenatal health care and nutrition. They need
> adult society to meet their needs for food, shelter, and clothing.
> They need to grow up in an environment that is both secure
> and stimulating. And they need our help to get the education
> they require to prepare to compete in the world of work, to make
> sound decisions about when to become parents, to feel valued
> and valuable, and to feel that there is a fair chance to succeed.[1]

If these points seem obvious and universally acceptable, then
the status of a great many American children must be a matter

---

1. *Families in Peril* (Harvard University Press, 1987), p. 30.

of common concern and shame. The conditions suggested by the following well-known data should inspire a great sense of public urgency:

- One-fifth of all children live below the poverty line.
- Two-fifths of all the poor are children.
- One-third of all children are poor sometime during their childhood.

And the danger signs stretch a distance further: high infant-mortality rates, low birth weights, poor school performance. In one key index after another, the children of the poor are down on their luck—even before they are born. If the public does want something to be done about this, what should that be? The followup questions are no different from those that have to be asked in other areas:

- What is the goal?
- To what extent is its achievement a responsibility of the public?
- Should the public, if responsible at all, directly intervene on behalf of the children or try to enable parents to care for their children better?

The goal would seem uncontroversial. The children of the poor should have the same quality of care deemed necessary for the children of the nonpoor. That is, and should be, an evolving standard. All frills aside, there is a shared sense within the nonpoor public that certain kinds of prenatal, neonatal, and infant health care are basic. Poor children need the same. They need likewise the opportunity to attend schools that are as well supported and as well staffed as any others. They also deserve to be treated with respect, and with expectations that they can succeed.

"She Looks at It Differently Than What I Do"

Among the chief beneficiaries of social-welfare programs in the United States are, as one might expect, old people, disabled people, and those who need medical help but can't afford it. But there is another large group of Americans—the children of poor homes—who depend on a variety of social programs for their basic health when they are infants, for one or two of their daily meals when they are students, even for their clothes and sneakers and the roofs over their heads. Assistance flows through an array of programs, ranging from Aid to Families with Dependent Children to Social Security survivors' benefits to Project Head Start to WIC and other efforts designed to make sure that young Americans don't begin life with nutritional deficits.

Parents of all economic stations try to insulate their offspring against the harsher and more discouraging aspects of life. Consequently, children who society defines as poor may not really understand that fact until they have reached the high-school years, particularly if most everyone else in their lives exists at the same economic level. This is strikingly evident in Appalachia, the long, gently curving scroll of mountains, ridges, valleys, and poverty that stretches from near Birmingham, Alabama, eastward and north into New York State. In eastern Kentucky, the region's heart, impoverishment is virtually the norm.

A half-dozen Appalachian children, aged ten through twelve, were interviewed about their experiences with government assistance programs, with school, and with their lives in general. All of them receive some help. They know most immediately the federal food programs, especially school lunch and food stamps. Some are well aware too of Medicaid and certain privately run programs.

Most of them didn't feel their status as recipients of welfare had singled them out for discrimination. But most added, when questioned further or when their mothers were asked to join the conversation, that there were instances in which they had been made to feel uncomfortable, either by their peers or by school officials.

The official policy is to make books, food, and materials available free to children whose parents can't afford them, and to keep the process anonymous, according to one school superintendent in eastern Kentucky. But it was clear from comments of the children themselves that it's easy to determine who's enrolled in the free-lunch program. It was equally clear that, in this part of the state, to stigmatize the recipients of welfare would be to stigmatize the majority. On the whole, the children tended not to describe themselves as poor or as rich but most commonly as "somewhere in between."

Linda: We live at a farm. We live close to our grandma, because she gets sick. She's got high blood pressure, and we have to keep close to her sometimes. My mom and dad's divorced, and she's married again. We live with her and our stepdad. We're doing OK. We get along with what we've got. We like it over there in the holler. You can get out and do anything you want, and no one to bother you or anything. So far I like it pretty much.

I do music and art, and sometimes I sit around and I just draw and put things together that way.

[And what to do you, Ericka? Ericka giggles.]

Linda: She giggles. I watch television a lot. I live on my TV and radio. I don't watch it in the morning, because I go to school from six, when we get on the school bus, till three. Then from three o'clock on, until about nine, I watch TV.

Ericka: Television's OK, but I don't watch as much as she does. I listen to the radio quite a bit. I listen to FM 104. It's a little bit of country, and sometimes you'll get a little bit of rock and roll, but not much. Soft rock. I don't like rock and roll very much. I love country.

Linda: I get my news *mostly* from the newspaper. But really most of it from school. We watch the news on TV, and science; every other room has a TV set in it. And we watch educational TV. We watch the MacNeil-Lehrer Report in Mr. Fawcett's room—he's my seventh-grade teacher—because he's the one that likes that; they tape it and run it during the day, when we're there.

I try to keep up with things that are fashionable. I'm particular about what I wear and the way I look. A lot of people, they'll use real dark eye shadow. I like it sort of medium—not too light, not too dark, but just in between. And with my glasses, I have to do it just right.

Ericka: She doesn't like to wear her glasses.

Linda: I got them through the school. You can sign a piece of paper that you need them, and they test your eyes then. And then they'll take you down there to [the county seat, several miles away], and it doesn't hardly cost you anything. They do all that through school.

[Linda explained that her family had a "medical card."]

Ericka's got some kind of disease [a skin rash] on her legs, and she just has got rid of it, some time back. But there's some still in her hair, and we used the medical card to get that, and one little bitty tube of medicine is about $70. The medical card covers that. You can use it in the hospitals or any time you need it.

We get food stamps. And sometimes when they have the cheese line [the distribution of surplus agricultural commodities, including cheese, flour, and honey], we go down and get it. And sometimes dry milk. We get free lunch at school, and breakfast. I would say the number of people at school who get the free lunch is in the hundreds. We've got twenty-three kids in my class who eat lunch and breakfast, and only five of them pay.

Ericka: There's thirty in our room, and there's about seven that has to pay.

[Are the people around here who don't have much money discriminated against?]

Ericka: No.

Linda: Not very much. We've got two eighth grades in our school, and one eighth grade acts real big. They dress real fancylike. And in our class, they just dress the way they want, and we don't say nothing about them. Whether people look good or they don't, we're all still friends. One eighth grade, the one that acts so big, has the higher grades. If they have pretty low grades, they go to the other eighth grade.

We've got two fourth grades and two sixth grades, and the people in those rooms that's rich, they just buy radios for about $100 each, and if one bangs hers up, puts a mark on it, they're just as likely to go get another radio. Thinks it's swell. They just waste their money.

Jane Schmidt,* their mother: Linda wanted to be on the drill team this year. She tried out every day up until the last day. She was real good. She practiced. Practiced day and night. And she went all the way to the last day, and the last day they would not pick her. I think it's really unfair, because she was good. But it was because we didn't have the money to buy the uniforms and all.

Linda: On some things, you have to be real good at it, and you have to smile and you have to have confidence in yourself, and I didn't.

Jane Schmidt: But it was because we didn't have the money. She looks at it differently than what I do. She's not as experienced with this as I am.

[If you could change the world, what would you do to make it better?]

Ericka: I would let people have a cure so that people would not get cancer.

Linda: I would let everybody who needs things like food stamps and cheese be able to get it, and not have a hard life.

Jane Schmidt: Tell him what you want to be.

Linda: A nurse. I'm going to college. I'm going to study to be a nurse. I think it would be fun, actually.

Linda and Ericka's parents see the world through less-trusting eyes; they offered examples of discrimination where their children did not. Like parents everywhere, they want their sons and daughters to inherit a better world than they did. In Appalachia, this often means (and did mean, for most of these children and their parents) a world in which there is promise of indoor plumbing, a job, enough economic security to allow one to finish high school, and a food budget that is not so closely tied to the receipt of food stamps and welfare checks that the monthly menu starts with such delicacies as chicken and hamburgers and ends with beans and cornbread.

The children live in Kentucky's fifth congressional district, which was described, in a 1986 report on education and economic development from the Mountain Association for Community Economic Development, as being "to the state what the state is to the nation—lagging behind on most measures of educational attainment and success. . . . The district has the highest dropout rate, the lowest holding power, and the lowest standardized test scores in Kentucky." Census figures from the beginning of the current decade showed the median family income in the children's home county to be about half that of Kentucky as a whole. Two-thirds of the county's children were classified as "economically deprived."

And yet, the children who were interviewed looked bright and healthy. A visitor from the lowlands who had spent time here twenty-five years before did not see the tired, sloping shoulders, the listless arms and eyes that he had seen previously. The children were poor, but they were hopeful.

(F.P.—1987)

Administration is the arms and legs of any policy. Services for children seem particularly dependent on how adequately and how sensitively they are carried out. Most large cities and some smaller ones have volunteer groups, comparable to New York's Citizens Committee for Children, which devote themselves to the indispensable task of monitoring administration. The problems are legion: adoption and foster-care placements and supervision; incarceration of "delinquents"; the trials of alleged delinquents; schooling and other services for pregnant school-age girls; day-care funding—the list could stretch on and on. The children of the poor, even more than the adult poor, are involved with government and its administrators to a degree that middle-class people can hardly be aware of. They are surrounded by government. To a considerable extent they are shaped by government's treatment of them. That treatment is generally wretched, as even superficial observation shows. Listening to the opinions of those who devotedly work within or monitor the institutions meant to care for these children only makes that conclusion more inescapable and more despairing.

The record thus gives added weight to the second question at the start of this chapter: What is the extent of public responsibility? But there can be no clear answer to this. In fact, there should not be one. The question reflects one of those tensions within a political order between the individual and the collectivity that need to be resolved from time to time without prescribed formulas.

The real issue, then, is not whether society should and will play an active child-rearing role—because it will—but how it acts, with what intent. Not all children, unfortunately, live with their parents; all do live with society, and are shaped by it. That was ancient wisdom and is still true. The political theory of the West began in the city-states of classical Greece, which were concerned almost above everything with the proper upbringing of their youth, or at least those who were well-born. Indeed, one modernizing shift since those days has been the assertion of the family's rights over the children, as against the state's. That has not gone all the way, by far. The state still insists on certain years of school attendance and is jealous of its prerogative of putting older children into uniform to fight its wars.

State and local governments have throughout American history taken a large part in children's rearing; since President William Howard Taft in 1912 signed legislation creating the U.S. Children's Bureau, the federal government has, too, though irregularly. Its role has been small compared to that of the states.

In earlier times we might have said that all governmental influences were small, compared to that of the churches. Today instead, neither government nor church has more influence on children and adolescents than Hollywood, television, the music industry, and the magazines that reinforce them. Certainly those state and federal programs aimed at discouraging or preventing teenage pregnancies seem outmatched, to the point of futility, by the entertainment industry's depiction of sexual intercourse as a routine part of boy-girl relationships.

The hardest question is our third: Should the public responsibility emphasize direct intervention in the child's rearing; or should its emphasize strengthening the parents? The latter can only mean, at bottom, first strengthening their finances.

Even rich children, of course, sometimes need counsel or help from people from outside their own families. And all children, rich or poor, need help *now*. Their needs don't wait on their parents' better fortunes. But if it is *prevention* of child-hood problems that is sought, then *fortunes* should be taken literally: nothing is more important than parental income. The better care of children begins with the financial well-being of their parents. As with the care of the poor and the aged, so with children: in an economy based on the exchange of money, more money in hand is the essential condition of any serious improvement of social-welfare practice.

That point is key. The conditions of poor children have wors-ened in recent years, despite sizable governmental expenditures and programs, because the status of their parents has sunk. Think back, for instance, on the long struggle, which shook Congresses for a couple of decades at least, to enact federal aid to education, resulting in the Elementary and Secondary Ed-ucation Act of 1965. That aid is by now too organic a part of the American educational structure to be tampered with. But who would want to contend that since 1965 schools serving low-income neighborhoods, except possibly in the rural South, have much improved?

There has been a lot of debate recently about the failure of public-school education. Schools undoubtedly can always do better. But it is the homes and streets that drag down the schools, not the other way around. What makes a good school doesn't change: good teachers and good teaching conditions. But schools cannot work miracles. Give them children from impoverished households where hopes are extinguished, lo-cated among other households much the same, and isolated from those who can live well and have infectious hopes. Give a school children from neighborhoods where sales of drugs are open and commonplace because our government has neither the competence to eradicate them nor the political courage to decriminalize them, and thus to remove the blood-sucking prof-its. Give a school hardly any children but these, and now and again that school will succeed, will touch a child with the capacity to learn, to do, and to hope. But not very often. In 1987 a score or so of famous social scientists and lawyers pro-claimed "a new consensus on family and welfare" and con-cluded that "at the heart of the poverty problems in 1987 is, then, the problem of behavioral dependency"—meaning conventionally immoral conduct.[2] I would say, rather, that at the heart of the problem is too little cash. For with the social order in the United States as it is, only cash can give the poor and their children the chance to become self-reliant.

"We Believe They Deserve a Future"

The architects of the Johnson administration's Great Society believed that if disadvantaged children are to benefit from what schools have to offer, they need a head start in order to catch up with the more fortunate. Thus the program of that name. As Robert Cooke, chairman of a White House panel, wrote in a report that later became the blueprint for Head Start:

> There is considerable evidence that the early years of childhood are a most critical point in the poverty cycle. During these years, the creation of learning patterns, emotional development and the formation of individual expectations and aspirations take place at a very rapid rate. For the child of poverty, there are clearly observable deficiencies [preparing] for a pattern of failure, and thus, a pattern of poverty throughout the child's entire life.

The Head Start program is based on the premise that all children share certain needs, and that children of low-income families will benefit from a comprehensive program outside their homes to help them meet those needs. The goal is to bring about a greater degree of "social competence" in these children. Social competence refers to the child's everyday effectiveness in dealing with both present environment and later responsibilities in school and life. It takes into account the interrelatedness of intellectual development with physical and mental health. While local communities are allowed latitude in designing programs, national objectives and performance standards are set.

---

2. The working Seminar on the Family and American Welfare Policy, chaired by Michael Novak, *A Community of Self-Reliances* (American Enterprise Institute, 1987), p. 99.

Full-year programs are primarily for children from age three to the time the child enters the school system, but may include some younger children. A minimum of 10 percent of the total enrollment in each state must be made available for handicapped children. At least 90 percent of the enrollment must come from families receiving AFDC or whose income is below the poverty line. Support comes in annual federal appropriations administered by state and local agencies, with no matching requirements.

In no state has Head Start been more important than in Mississippi, which typically has received a somewhat disproportionate share of the total federal outlay. One multicounty program is called Friends of the Children of Mississippi (FCM). In 1986 it served 4,959 children at sixty-two centers in fifteen counties. Thelma Moore, a veteran local worker, described FCM's Tepper Head Start Center, which she administers in Humphreys County, in the Delta region, where 44 percent of the residents live below the poverty line.

Our program operates nine months out of the year and is open to all children. About 16 percent of our enrollment around the state is white; we have a few among the 201 kids at the center I administer. We're open from 7:30 AM to 3:30 PM, but the children are there from 8:00 until 2:00.

Right away, we deal with their self-image. Some children never get praised at home. They always get scorned and pushed back into a corner. So we try to build a positive self-image in the children, by praising them and making them feel good about themselves.

We teach them skills that make them ready for learning. So they learn their alphabets and how to print their names and their basic colors. Because we feel the transfer from Head Start to public school is one of the greatest breaks our kids will encounter before they go into young adulthood, we meet with school principals, superintendents, and special-education teachers to familiarize them with the children's needs before they leave us.

But before they do, they learn good eating habits. We teach them to tell their mothers that "potato chips are good, but I need to have fruit and juices and stuff, not candy and junk foods." Many children entering Head Start have not received good, nutritious meals at home. In the program, we serve them a minimum of one hot meal and a snack each day, in order to meet at least one-third of their daily nutritional needs.

We have kids coming to the center who know they're not clean. One little boy, who has several brothers, told me: "Mrs. Moore, I have on the shorts this morning. I beat my brothers to them." In other words, since there're not enough shorts to go around, whoever gets to them first wears them. We ask parents to visit us any day they want to and spend the day with the kids. Many parents serve in our program either as volunteers or paid teacher's aides, special-service personnel, and as cooks, storytellers, and play supervisors.

We also try to involve parents in workshops on early-childhood-development training so that they can work with their children at home. If you get parents where they can see their children in a learning setting, they become interested in what we're trying to do. This makes the children want to learn more and more. Sometimes we send work home with the kids, because we found out that helps promote parental participation. In fact, the members of the policy council for our center all have children in the program.

We also try to help parents become self-sufficient by offering them training suitable to their skills or the needs in the community. It can be training that will qualify them for a job. We've had cash-register training, dental-technician training, basic adult education. Head Start itself is the third-largest source of jobs in Humphreys County and was the first major source of employment and decent wages for blacks independent of the state and plantation owners. The program has motivated a lot of parents who had only completed eighth or ninth grade to get their high-school diplomas. Some have become so motivated they started new careers.

We still have community meetings once a month that involve the entire community. Everyone is invited. In that way, we stay constantly in touch with everyone's concerns. We don't ever want to lose sight of the community. Those are the people we serve.

Kids from our program have gone on to college and beyond. But I worry about the eight thousand kids who had to remain on our waiting lists around the state last year, because we were funded to serve only 4,939 (though we did take in twenty extra). Besides that eight thousand, we had to turn away many others, because they didn't meet Head Start poverty guidelines. They're called high-income children, when they live in families of five with incomes of only $12,000 a year. I feel the federal government should change those guidelines, because even if we had all the aid possible from our communities we would still need a lot of federal help for those people. Our communities just don't have enough resources.

We in Head Start try to educate the general public about the needs of children and encourage preventive investment in them before they get sick, drop out of school, or get in trouble. We believe they deserve a future, an education, good health, and jobs. We also believe society will pay more tomorrow if we neglect their overall development today.

(A.P.—1986)

Among poverty analysts, there is some debate as to the best time in people's lives to catch hold and give effective assistance. Lay people have the same concern. "If we could only reach the people," they'll say, or "We must above all keep the teenagers in school." The social scientists who produced the Novak report apparently think the key lies in imposing self-discipline on welfare mothers and errant fathers. Another theory popular today is that the one defect of the poor that our social services know how to remedy is basic skills, of literacy and numeracy; therefore that should be a priority. I pointed earlier to a sort of handhold theory, stressing the importance of a youth policy.

The debate is ultimately sterile, however, because it amounts, once again, to an attempt to understand the problems in terms of *them* as different from *us*. The only answer that can rise above momentary responses to the latest research "findings," or to those "truths" induced by budget decisions, is that society ought to meet all people at the crucial periods of their life cycles: care for children; opportunity and growth in values for youth; responsible self-reliance for adults; and dignity for the old.

The issue lurking behind all this discussion of how the cage of poverty can be shattered is the one the nation has come to call the underclass. Returning to the third question above—

Should primary emphasis be on enabling parents to care for their children better?—if one accepts the true meaning of an underclass, there would be no realistic chance of those parents *ever* taking good care of their children. For if the notion of underclass means anything, it is that a discrete group of people have fallen so far (regardless of cause or fault) and become so morally depraved as to be beyond the reach of economic up-swings or civilizing influences. They are lost.

"That Kid Is Not the Problem That Really Distresses Me"

East Elementary School is located in a rundown four-square-mile area that was once called the black bottom of a large Midwestern city. The area has some of the city's worst poverty, highest unemployment, and highest crime rates. Most of its families receive some form of public assistance and are headed by females. These facts are part of a hidden curriculum, for they are among the ABCs that the children learn, almost by osmosis, long before they enroll at East Elementary.

Built in the early 1960s to serve a thousand or so students from a nearby housing project, the school must somehow counteract the drenching psychological impact on children awash in a flood tide of human deprivation. The area it serves has been abandoned by successive waves of European immigrants and abandoned, finally, even by the black middle class. Dope peddling, prostitution, violence, and other forms of personal decay abound. There is little chance for the area's residents to help each other because they are all suffocating. There is little leadership among them for Girl and Boy Scout troops, for YMCA groups, for the PTA, or for any broader social activism.

Somehow the school, were it truly to succeed in educating the youth of this neighborhood, would need to rescue the teen-age girls from males cruising the area looking for young prostitutes. It would need to save the young boys who daily see full-grown men sitting around unemployed and unengaged in anything worthwhile. Somehow the school would have to inspire its more than seven hundred students to believe that academics could eventually help them to succeed in life.

Clearly, it has a nearly impossible mission, for there is little long-range planning by most of the residents in the neighborhood, little chance of a college education for its children, and little prospect of a comfortable "good life." Most likely the children will remain poor, standing against the wall of extinction, unable to project themselves into a future because their present is so precarious.

The school's principal, Frank Anderson, is thoroughly familiar with the neighborhood, having walked its streets for nine of his thirty-five years as a teacher and administrator in the city's school system. Often he has been a sort of caseworker, responding to pleas from mothers asking him to help protect them from estranged husbands or boyfriends coming around to harass them. Or he will press charges against parents guilty of child neglect. Or he will sponsor workshops several times a year to teach young mothers and fathers a few parenting skills.

Some of our saddest experiences are with the grandmothers. You have these young mothers—babies having babies—and they can't cope. So the grandmothers always become involved as those central figures who, though they are getting old and don't have any energy, serve as the backbones of their families. They usually cry for a great deal of help from the schools. It's a never-ending struggle.

If you're born and reared with few options, life is likely to be difficult. In any case, that's the expectation of many, if not most, of my students. Many of them are burdened with low self-esteem. About 80 percent of them don't have fathers at home and their mothers, most of whom are on public welfare, are often too young to deal with child-rearing problems.

The kids come from an area that has one of the greatest drug-traffic and crime rates in the city. We don't see any drug trafficking here at school, but many of the kids are runners and lookouts for adult drug pushers.

Given our students' debilitating street environment, the staff here has to bombard them constantly with the idea that they are as good as anyone else. We try to build up their self-confidence, knowing that many of them have come to school not ready for the academic discipline that we require. Many of them can't read because they haven't had that kind of experience at home, unlike middle-class black and white kids who come from print-oriented families.

But we don't use our kids' limited exposure as an excuse not to teach them. After all, that's what we're getting paid for. We believe that if they don't make it here in eight years, we're not doing our job. We know that the only way a lot of these kids are going to make it is through what we can do for them in school. They're certainly not going to make it in the streets. There's nothing there for them. So we have to give our kids successes. If we don't, well shame on us.

We try to create a very warm, positive school atmosphere with positive, friendly, supportive teachers. We have a number of recognition programs for our students, programs like our essay-writing contests which stimulate self-expression and an interest in reading, or our marching band which is one of the best. If they don't have a feeling of success—forget it! They're not going to make it!

But one of our greatest problems is getting parents to help us. Just before the 1986 summer break, we had our band awards program. We have sixty-five members in the band. But only about 120 parents, friends, and children showed up.

We're a unique school, offering kindergarten through eighth-grade instruction, unlike the typical K-through-five or six-through-eight school here. Because we have our kids for eight years without a break in continuity, we probably service their psychological needs much better than most area schools.

Thus, for example, when our kids come to school tardy, we often call up their mothers to find out why. Once they get here, we take care of them. We spend a great deal of money feeding them breakfast and lunch. If their clothes are soiled, we take them off and wash them. We have to protect them right away because peer pressure affects the learning process. If they don't feel good about themselves, if they are wearing dirty clothes and smell bad, if their hair is not combed, their peers are going to make fun of them.

You take care of that problem as quietly and expeditiously as you can and get the child back in the mainstream of school life. Those are some of the nonacademic kinds of things you have to do in this setting if you want to give success to students.

Academically, in three of the last four years, more of our seventh-grade kids than those in the citywide population mastered 75 percent to 100 percent of the basic reading and math skills measured by the educational assessment test. Similarly, during the same period, they scored above the national norm on the California Test of Achievement, which also measures math and reading skills.

Our test scores during the last five years document the fact that our kids are teachable because we have high expectations. We demand that they succeed. We believe in high motivation and active participation. In our all-day kindergarten, we read. We don't play! I don't say that play isn't important for social development, but we make it more academically oriented because we realize that we have to get these little children ready. We have to push them hard. Our science program, our computer program, our field trips—everything we do supports the objective of giving these kids some basic tools before they leave here.

We have twelve computer terminals on which we teach them some very simple programming. They really enjoy the computer, which they pick up very quickly. Working with it is a good, positive experience for them. They learn a language. They learn a discipline. The computer motivates them to read and calculate. It's a very good instructional tool, one they know they're going to be able to use in our society. They'll see it again and again, as long as they live.

When our students get depressed and want to chuck it all, I tell them: "You gotta have hope! You gotta have hope! You gotta keep on trying!" Some of the kids don't believe me. They look at me and say politely: "Yes! Yeah! Sure! No way am I ever going to make it." They can't see themselves breaking the bind that they're in. They don't see a way out through education. They say they're not going to get a job because there are no jobs for blacks. I say, "Yes there are." They say, "Look at the number of blacks that are in there." I say, "Yes, that's true, but there are *some* in there. You got to keep on going. You can't give up hope. If you do, you're dead."

Generally, I don't believe in student retention. I believe that most of the time if you retain a student, you program that student for failure. When a child feels that he's unsuccessful, he's not even going to try. Rather than fail kids, I believe that it's up to us as professionals to teach them. All the research points out that you can identify high-school dropouts by the third grade. That's another indication that failure is a very important aspect affecting a child's feeling about success. Research also shows that children develop in spurts, depending on the child. If you hold them back a grade, you're self-destructing. If you keep them on, generally they'll catch up. If a child fails, a teacher fails.

Fighting is our major discipline problem. The kids sometimes strike out at each other and curse each other. Occasionally, I may have a big, muscular, fourteen- or fifteen-year-old boy who is so hostile you can hardly approach him. He's just mad at everybody and everything. If you even attempt to roll your eyes at him, he's going to knock your head right off. It's no use getting angry with him because he's just looking for a fight anyway.

We have a federally funded, work-study program whereby one period a day we pay students to tutor other students. So here's this big, unruly boy assigned to three or four kindergarten or first-grade students. Ask him to maybe show flash cards. Now if you know little five- and six-year-olds, the first thing you know that they do is they get close to you and lean on you. Little children always touch you.

So they'll get close to this boy and after a while they'll get to know his name. They lean on him and that kind of physical contact does something to him. It just opens him up and he assumes that adult, protective, father figure. Later, he'll come to you complaining: "The children won't sit still." Or, "The kids won't listen to me." Or, "I hate to raise my voice all the time." He eventually realizes that these were the same kinds of things that he was doing himself, and he sees the importance of attention in the learning process.

But that kid is not the problem that really distresses me. I think that what's happening in public education today is the biggest crime in the world. The politicians know what it costs to keep a man in prison. I can't understand why they won't spend the money on education to keep him out of prison.

Our federal monies were up to an annual $300,000 at one time. This year [1985–86] we were cut back 20 percent. Washington is really doing it to us. The cuts have reduced our teacher's aides, supplies, equipment, field trips, and—this is very important—staff in-service training. In this school alone, they've taken out typing, shop, art, and other things that might motivate a child. We don't have a balanced curriculum because we have no money for one. We receive very little funding for these programs from the city and state, because they have no money.

I recall that after World War II there was a great hue and cry against spending money for educational benefits under the GI Bill of Rights. But look at what came out of it! Look at all the opportunities it created! Look at the strength it gave to the country! It demonstrated the massive potential of education. It offered equal access to education regardless of whether recipients hailed from the rich suburbs or the poor inner cities.

I believe there are no differences in children, only differences in the experiences they have. You can't worry about where they come from and who they are. You just have to do the best you can. If you can't do that in a school setting, where in heaven's name are kids from low-income families going to get what they need for success? There are few role models in the neighborhood. There are no federal programs that are going to help them. Their parents receive enough welfare to live on and that's it. What else is there? If we educators can't do it—forget it!

(A.P.—1986)

Charles Murray has said that "what set the black ghetto in the 1970s apart from historical precedents, including black ghettos in earlier years, was that the barrier separating the ghetto youth from the larger society had become nearly an airtight seal."[3] By any count, that is an overstatement, but for many youths there does seem to be neither the cultural conditioning, incentive, nor opportunity to become a self-reliant person and a contributing member of society. The trend of much recent discussion has been to ascribe the cause of this to the youths themselves. Usually, though not always, they are seen as victims of bad policies or neglect that have turned them into "lost" souls, dangerous social misfits.

The United States is getting into an ugly, even vicious mood. We are making an underclass a fact by expecting there to be such, by setting up all the conditions for self-fulfilling prophecies. The ugly side of the United States always has been its

---

3. *Losing Ground* (Basic Books, 1984), p. 191.

historic conviction that it is beset by some great threat. Jealous of our own good fortune, we have lived with the belief that its continuation depends on holding back some enemy. Indians, backwoodsmen, immigrants (the Irish, then eastern and southern Europeans, then Hispanics), anarchists, communists, the North (as seen from the South), blacks (as seen in yesterday's South and often enough in the North, too), "the Huns" (Germans), "the Japs," Russia—one after another and often more than one at a time, these threats have kept us in a tizzy through our couple of centuries. Are we not now in danger of creating another such "threat," transferring old but now unacceptable racial antagonisms to a group we call the underclass, and putting it thereby beyond claims on our respect?

Social contract is another frequently used term. Its historical origin was with a group of philosophers of widely divergent views—from Hobbes to Rousseau—who agreed on at least this one thing: that a political order rests on the consent of individuals, and that consent can be withdrawn if the political order no longer satisfies the needs of at least a significant number of its members. These social-contract philosophers, who included Jefferson and other Americans, emphatically did not teach that individuals had to be worthy of society, had to be accepted by it. To them, it was society that had to be accepted, had to merit consent. The social contract was an agreement of *all* to establish public justice and to recognize each other's rights. And from that kind of thinking came the idea of individual rights, enshrined in American constitutionalism.

Does the social-contract view of politics require no responsibility of the individual to society? Actually, the old writers tended to be quite firm that it did. Civic virtue occupied a big place in their thought (even that of Hobbes—if you allow him to define his own terms). But the spirit loosed was a liberating one, radiating outward into a common belief in men and their essential capacity for responsible freedom. This became the New World gospel—the "good news"—the faith shared by common men and women and first-rate minds, an Emerson or Walt Whitman alike. It is impossible to reconcile "underclass" theory with their optimism. Whitman could even look up from the gloom of his *Democratic Vistas* to say:

> The great word Solidarity has arisen. Of all dangers to a nation, as things exist in our day, there can be no greater one than having certain portions of the people set off from the rest by a line drawn—they not privileged as others, but degraded, humiliated, made of no account.[4]

It is impossible to reconcile the fearful view of a threatening underclass with that vision. Impossible, too, to reconcile it with the political work and values of a Franklin D. Roosevelt, or of the Republican Progressives of the early twentieth century. Theirs was a politics of purpose, of a determined search for fairness. That is the vision and the sense of obligation the United States needs to recapture.

---

4. Quoted from *The Portable Walt Whitman* (Viking, 1945), pp. 414–15.

AFTERWORD

THE SOCIAL-WELFARE practices of the United States are hardly a rational system, but in these pages we have tried to picture them as at least (and at most) a mass of connected parts.

The common characteristics among their different facets are income transfers or service provisions, in both cases supported by the public treasuries. By looking at the whole (or as much of it as my associates and I could take in), I have indicated my strong doubt of the usefulness, beyond technical analyses, of policy studies or enactments that focus on single parts. I simply do not believe there is such a thing as sound welfare reform that does not stimulate the job market, both urban and rural; or sound reform of health services for the aged that does not relate that subject to all other demands on the health industry, especially those resulting from private insurance schemes and poor people's health services (Medicaid). Policy must be formed within a firmly grasped sense of context.

We inevitably fall short whenever we consider social welfare as an isolable problem. In truth, whatever problems it presents are reflections of the economy as a whole. They also reflect what kind of society, what kind of political order, the nation is—or wants. They reflect whether ours is a society which

219

consciously believes that among its people there is a "common interest" (and a number around the globe have no such shared conviction); and if so, what that common interest is. I think the common interest of the United States lies in there being realistic opportunities for all citizens to contribute to the realization of a society at peace with itself—because all have enough—and with other societies.

Economies are combinations of production and distribution, in infinite varieties of mix. Social-welfare policies begin when we recognize that not all citizens are or should be equally productive—consider, as we have, the ill, the aged, the young. A good society will take care that the former two groups can live in dignity, comfort, and with needed medical service; and it will have a special care that all its children thrive through fair opportunities for nurture and education.

But there is another large class of the non-productive: those made so, or kept so, by the economy itself. A good society will do what it can—and it can do much—to compensate for its own faults by opening itself to the participation of all. That means full employment.

The 1980s have witnessed an erosion of the ability of the lower 30 to 40 percent of our people to gain a decent life from work. It is not only the unemployed who are shut out. There are *at least* two million persons who work full time for less than enough to reach the poverty level. About a fourth of all American families in the late 1980s have incomes below half the median national income. The Tax Reform Act of 1986 has, it is claimed, removed six million poor from the federal income tax rolls, but increases in Social Security and excise taxes have kept the tax burden on the poorest of us constant or even rising; in late 1987, the Congressional Budget Office estimated that our bottom tenth of taxpayers would pay 20 percent more of their income on taxes in 1988 than they had a decade earlier. Since the early 1970s, the income prospects of younger workers have shrunk steadily, dimming the likelihood that they will progress farther, or even as far, as earlier modern generations.[1]

---

1. See Frank Levy, *Dollars and Dreams: The Changing American Income Distribution* (Russell Sage, 1987).

Jerry Douglas, the Northwest lumberman, is right to worry about the future for his children. It is not a pretty picture.

There is much truth to Peter L. Berger's statement, that "The modern democratic state, by its very nature, is a gigantic mechanism handing out entitlements."[2] Is that wrong? Only if the entitlements lack a purpose that accords with the national, or common, interest—or if, even though they are well directed, they are too scant to achieve their purpose. This book has argued the case for entitlements that serve the purpose of building a productive citizenry and are adequate to need. That applies both to the poor on welfare and the working or unemployed poor. A fashionable phrase calls for "reform of welfare through work." Were there a similar call to reform bad housing or malnutrition or inferior schools through work, it would rightly make much sense to few, being a nonspecific remedy. Is welfare any different? Is it not also an aspect of poverty, one that will endure as long as people are poor? Work is, I have argued, the only practical way out of poverty. But the work needed is not of the sort that is custom-designed for those who are, in the opinion of most employers, now unemployable. It must be work that produces what society wants, and will pay for through taxes if not prices. A tight labor market is the only practicable solution to poverty.

As we have emphasized, a key element in maintaining a healthy labor market must be unions, whether traditional or newer forms of workplace organization. People ought to represent their own concerns and interests. Isn't that what democracy is all about? The shame of the AFL-CIO is that it does so little in behalf of organizing low income workers; the shame of the federal government, deepened but not created by the Reagan administration, is that it has made union organizing and collective bargaining even harder. The National Labor Relations Act has become a system of barriers. Recognizing that a free labor movement is essential for democracy, Americans criticize the Russians for not having one—and then undermine our own.

Employment is not enough. Decent wages are necessary too.

---

2. *The Capitalist Revolution* (Basic Books, 1986), p. 88.

Only strong worker organizations can defend that principle. Only they can effectively insist that the assumed lockstep between unemployment, low wages, and low inflation be broken, by adjustments of other economic forces driving up the price levels. Only they can effectively champion the common-sense proposition that productivity increases and demand increases must move together, and that the latter requires full employment at decent wages.

The country does not have a union movement today strong enough to serve these ends. Nor is the one we do have itself a model of social integrity, though as long as the spirit of democratic unionism burns bright enough to create groups like the Association for Union Democracy or Teamsters for a Democratic Union there is hope.

It cannot be, at this time, a credible hope, however. Reinvigorating the established labor movement seems as realistic as believing that low-income workers will organize themselves in new and suitable patterns. But who can say? The civil rights movement of the 1960s was hardly predictable. The cause of adequacy in employment and wages needs a strong constituency. State governments could provide it. Those whom the shoe pinches know best what works. The present welfare and poverty "reform" movements consist of a few politicians, administrators, and social scientists. That won't suffice. The missing element is the crucial one: the people affected. Otherwise, we stay in the age-old American practice, of "us" deciding what is best, and what can be spared from our wealth, for "them." True reform awaits self-representation. It is less an issue of economics than of political values.

A strong element of this book has been, therefore, the necessity of building a constituency for stable and adequate social-welfare policies. I have raised two leading possibilities: state governments and worker organizations. Do we want policies that don't change with every new administration or Congress? Policies adequate to the needs? Policies that draw us closer together rather than lead to squabbles over who gets the larger share? Policies that refuse to accept the ugly, un-American idea of an "underclass"?

If we believe in democracy, then democracy is the only path toward affirming those questions. And if we believe in democracy, we then know that its goals can be attained only when a constituency is strong enough to win them.

INDEX

225

LESLIE W. DUNBAR, a longtime activist in the civil-rights movement, lives in Durham, North Carolina. He is a former director of the Field Foundation as well as of the Southern Regional Council. He is also the editor of the book *Minority Report*.

CHARLES V. HAMILTON is Wallace S. Sayre Professor of Political Science at Columbia University and coauthor, with Stokely Carmichael, of *Black Power*.

ANTHONY BORDEN has contributed to the *Nation, Dissent, In These Times*, and *American Lawyer*, among other national publications.

CALVIN GEORGE is executive director of the National Committee for Full Employment, in Washington, D.C.

CHAROLETT GOODWIN is a national peace activist in Washington, D.C.

ALEX POINSETT has written for a number of national magazines.

FRED POWLEDGE, former *New York Times* correspondent, is the author of ten books, concentrating on civil rights and environmental issues.

WALLACE TERRY, former head of the *New York Times* Vietnam Bureau, is professor of journalism at Howard University and the author of *Bloods*.